Praise for *Are You the Pet for Me?*

"Mary Jane Checchi gives excellent advice to families on all aspects of helping children choose and care for pets. Pets are more than great companions—they are also wonderful teachers, and caring for them helps children learn about responsibility, respect, love, and other important values that will last a lifetime. Checchi's wise counsel will be welcomed by parents and children everywhere."

Senator Edward M. Kennedy

"Finally! A book that really gets to the heart of the 'animals-and-kids' matter. *Are You the Pet for Me?* is a must-have for parents who are considering adding an animal to the family. Mary Jane Checchi has done her homework, and offers superlative advice on which pets suit what families—and what families would be better served by having no pets at all. With the preponderance of evidence linking animal abuse to human abuse, the role of the family pet is no small consideration. I highly recommend this book."

Susan Chernak McElroy,
Author of the *New York Times* bestseller
Animals as Teachers and Healers

"This book will be a godsend to parents who don't know what pet to get for their child, or whether to get one at all. The author's clean, clear prose, and her obvious understanding of both animals and children, will help them make the right choice."

Marguerite Kelly
Author of the nationally syndicated column,
The Family Almanac
Coauthor of the bestselling *The Mother's Almanac*
Author of *The Mother's Almanac II*

"There should be a law that everyone considering pet ownership must read this book. The messages shared will strengthen the human/animal bond, increasing the pet owner's enjoyment. At the same time, and perhaps more importantly, these wonderful creatures that share our homes and lives will be saved the suffering and abandonment brought about by ignorance."

Clayton MacKay, DVM
Former President, American Animal Hospital
Association (AAHA)

"It is said that a pet is the only relative that you can choose. This book will help you make that choice. It is essential reading for anyone who is even considering buying a pet for themselves, their children and their home."

Stephen L. Glasser, OD, FAAO
Volunteer, Friends of Homeless Animals

"Mary Jane Checchi's *Are You the Pet For Me?* treats lovingly, logically, and thoroughly all the joys and responsibilities a family will experience when they elect to bring a pet into their lives. After reading it, I came away with a deeper appreciation for what wholesome value God's creatures can bring to each other."

Marv Levy
Former Buffalo Bills Head Coach

"For parents who do their homework *before* bringing home a pet, this book will be a godsend. It is a realistic look at pet ownership and the time and commitment it takes to do it right, and takes the pressure of success or failure off the child's shoulders."

Jacque Shultz
Director of Special Projects, ASPCA

"With a bracing mix of knowledge, sanity, and compassion, Mary Jane Checchi joins a long line of friends of animals. She writes as a peacemaker. Her words—if heeded—are sure to decrease the violence done to our pets while increasing the joy of companionship."

Colman McCarthy
Former *Washington Post* syndicated columnist
Author of *All of One Peace*

ARE YOU THE PET FOR ME?

Choosing the Right Pet for Your Family

Mary Jane Checchi

St. Martin's Paperbacks

To my parents, Vince and Mary Checchi
To my husband and son, John C. and John V. Culver
Thanks for everything

Contents

Preface   ix

Acknowledgments   xiii

Introduction   1

PART ONE:
FAMILIES, CHILDREN, AND PETS

1. What Companion Animals Give to Children
   and Parents   5

2. How to Choose a Pet for Your Child   18

3. Making It Work No Matter What Pet You Get   32

4. Dilemmas: Should Every Child Have a Pet?
   How Old Should My Child Be? How Do We
   Say No?   39

PART TWO:
CHILDREN, DOGS, AND CATS

5. Dogs   49

6. Cats   79

PART THREE:
CHILDREN AND SMALL, FURRY PETS

7. Small, Furry Pets: Overview   107

8. Fancy Mice   120

9. Fancy Rats   132

10. Gerbils   145

11. Guinea Pigs (Cavies)   156
12. Hamsters   169
13. Rabbits   180
14. A Footnote About Ferrets   195

PART FOUR:
CHILDREN, WINGS, AND FINS

15. Birds   203
16. Fish   226

PART FIVE:
UNUSUAL, WILD, AND EXOTIC PETS

17. Unusual and Exotic Pets   253
18. Wildlife as Pets   274

PART SIX:
PETS FOR CHILDREN WITH
SPECIAL NEEDS

19. Service and Therapy Pets   279

PART SEVEN:
CHILDREN, PETS, AND SAFETY

20. Protecting Children and Pets   287

Preface

As a child, I had the privilege of growing up in a house filled with pets. My parents were animal lovers, a quality they inherited from their parents. My dad's father raised sentry dogs for the military. My mother's father, a Methodist minister, felt his mission was to tend to all God's creatures, including animals. So the battle in our household was not over whether we children could have "a" pet, it was whether we could have "another" one.

Most of the animals we shared our home with were rescued from the street or acquired from neighbors or friends who were giving them away. But every dog or cat who joined our family came into our house only after Mom and Dad had agreed to the addition.

A critical lesson I learned about adding a four-legged family member to our home occurred when I was 13 or 14. Each summer, I was shipped off to camp in the beautiful Ozark Mountains. In addition to the normal camp activities, I participated in the basic "I'm a typical teenager" activities. That year, my mother had warned me not to come home if I had once again bleached my hair white with peroxide. During this camp session, I not only bleached my hair, but also acquired a new friend. My cabinmates and I found an abandoned litter of puppies in the woods, and

I decided to keep one. On the train trip home at the close of camp, I assured my friends that the puppy would be welcome in our home because my parents loved animals and wouldn't mind "just one more."

I couldn't have been more wrong. The day after my arrival home, I found myself at the hairdresser and the puppy found himself at the local humane society. After many tears and slammed doors, I finally realized that my mother's decision to surrender the puppy to the humane society was best for everyone: the puppy, who needed more attention than we could give him; my mom and me, who were already too busy with school, church, and sports activities; and our adult dog, who was not happy to be joined by an active young puppy. As my mother pointed out, neither the current dog-in-residence nor anyone else had been considered or consulted about the new addition.

As one who has spent the past two decades advocating for animals, I am aware of the consequences when the decision to acquire a pet (or two) is **not** a carefully considered family decision. Every day, animal shelters collectively see thousands upon thousands of adult and "teenage" animals who "just didn't work out." Indeed, unrealistic expectations on the part of pet owners—about everything from how large an animal will grow to common behavior problems like the cat scratching the furniture or the dog jumping on houseguests—are the top reason people relinquish their animals.

That is why I am thrilled that Mary Jane Checchi has written this book. It is a wonderful resource for parents who are being pressured by their children to buy or adopt a furred, finned, or feathered creature. Mary Jane takes parents through the costs of acquiring a pet as well as the financial resources needed to keep that animal in good health. She addresses the time involved in walking a dog, grooming a cat and cleaning a cage, tank or litter box. She reminds the reader about who is ultimately responsible for ensuring that these tasks are accomplished. Throughout this book, parents will find answers to questions about which animal is best for their family, at what age a child can be expected to contribute to the care of that animal, and how to say "no" to a child when either the timing, the animal, or both, are wrong for your household.

The Humane Society of the United States firmly believes that "Pets Are Family, Too!" Though not all animals need to share your child's bed or have a place at the dining room table, they must be given regular care, exercise, and plenty of love. Children can provide some of these daily essentials and will be amply rewarded with licks, purrs, grunts, chirps, and squeaks, but adults must be willing partners in this relationship. Mary Jane Checchi has written this book to help parents who often struggle with responding to their child's plea of "Can I have a . . . dog, cat, hamster, parakeet, turtle, snake?" Something tells me that Mary Jane and Mom are somehow related.

> Martha C. Armstrong
> Vice President for Companion Animals
> and Equine Protection
> The Humane Society of the United States

Acknowledgments

Many people helped me with their encouragement, guidance, and expertise. A list of all their names would go on for many pages. But I particularly want to mention and thank Ann Church and Martha Armstrong of the Humane Society of the United States; Martha Handman of the Paw Print Post and Collie Rescue League; Dr. Clayton MacKay of the Ontario Veterinary College; Jim Monsma and Donna Marsden of the Washington, D.C. Humane Society; Susan Wiener, Heather Bancroft, and Adelaide Soares of the Montgomery County, MD, Humane Society; Dr. Julie Giles, Dr. Jennifer Scarlett, Dr. Bruce Herwald, Beth Xanten, and Karen Sparks of the Dupont Circle Veterinary Clinic, Washington, D.C.; Dr. Michael Riegger, Northwest Animal Clinic, Albuquerque; Dr. Connie Orcutt, Angell Memorial Animal Hospital, Boston; Carter Luke of the Massachusetts SPCA and American Humane Education Society; Debbie Ducommon, founder, The Rat Fan Club; Susan Wong of the House Rabbit Society; Caroline Seitz, "The Reptile Lady"; Jacque Lynn Schultz, ASPCA; Pam Grant of STAR Ferret Rescue.

I also want to thank Ellen and Tom Werts, Gina Sangster Hayman, Sharon Alperovitz, Bonnie Willette, Melissa Ludtke, Barbara Ranagan, Abby Saffold, Judith Hollinger, my sister Dina Davis and brother Vince Checchi, and my agent Nina Graybill for their moral support and invaluable advice.

My gratitude, also, to a long line of four legged friends who made me laugh, taught me a lot, and in one way or another helped me write this book.

Introduction

"Mom! I want a dog!"

Sooner or later, this is a plea that most parents will hear. Maybe you have already heard it or a variation thereof.

"Dad! Matthew's gerbils had gerbils. Can I have one? *Please?*"

"Hannah's got an iguana! It is *soooooo cool!* Can we get one?"

"Stevie's brother got a boa constrictor! Can I—?"

The refrain that accompanies these pleas in almost every case is the same: "I can take care of it myself. I promise!"

Although most children have a natural affinity for animals, it is in fact the rare child of any age who takes full responsibility for a pet. Teenagers leave home for college or a job, and guess who is in charge of the pet that is left behind? Often, well-intentioned but uninformed parents find themselves

- stuck with the care of a pet they don't like or don't have time for
- nagging and fighting with their child about the pet's care or behavior
- delivering an unwanted pet to the local animal shelter,

leaving their child with a residue of guilt, anger, and
the wrong lessons about responsibility
- disposing, amidst a child's tears, of a pet that has met
an untimely death due to lack of proper care

Of all the purchases that you make as parents, few have
more impact on your child and family than a pet. A dog
can live for ten to fifteen years; a cat, for fifteen to twenty;
a bird, for thirty years or more. The cost of purchasing and
maintaining a pet can easily run to thousands of dollars,
and pets need daily care.

Should every child have a pet? Should your child have
one? What kind? What do pets do for kids, anyway? How
old should your child be before he or she has a companion
animal? If pets and kids go together like peanut butter and
jelly, why are millions of healthy family pets dumped at
animal shelters every year?

Because every child, every family, and every pet is
unique, there are no one-size-fits-all answers to these questions. Instead, I suggest some criteria you can use to evaluate your family's pet resources and provide basic
information about pets to help you select the companion
animal that fits your family.

PART ONE

Families, Children, and Pets

ONE

What Companion Animals Give to Children and Parents

What Companion Animals Give to Children

A CHANCE TO NURTURE. *It was December 26. Jane crouched behind the television set, unplugging and plugging in cables and cords. Unsure of herself, she was struggling to install Nintendo '64, a Christmas gift to her seven-year-old son, Michael.*

Full of energy, Michael bounced into the room and picked up the remote control. "Mom! Can I turn the TV on now?"

"No! Michael! You might electrocute me!" Electronics were not Jane's strongest suit, and she was nervous to begin with.

"You'll be all right, Mom."

"Michael, I could get hurt. People die from electrocution."

"I don't think so, Mom."

"Michael, if you electrocute me, you won't have a mother."

Before this point could be discussed, Michael's cocker spaniel, Pink, slipped behind the TV to investigate.

"You don't have to worry now, Mom," said Michael

reassuringly. "Pink's back there, so I won't turn on the TV. I wouldn't want to electro-shoot him."

Michael is a bright and happy child who is close to both his parents. He assumes that they will be there to care for him no matter what. With Pink, Michael can reverse the roles: He becomes the caretaker and parent, a role he is proud of.

Eleven-year-old Jenny, who lives with her family in an apartment in Manhattan, was explicit about her relationship with her new kitten.

"I'm its mother," she said. Then, turning to her dad, Jenny asked the kitten, "Would you like to meet your grandfather?"

Pets give children the chance to feel needed and to take care of another living thing. Because most pet caretaking is optional for children—Michael's mother provides most of Pink's care—it is not a threatening or overwhelming challenge.

In our society, which emphasizes the development of independence and self-sufficiency, parents find that pets provide their children with the opportunity to learn the satisfaction of caring for another. Parents of boys find an extra bonus here. Caring for a pet is seen as gender neutral by adults and children. It is a nurturing behavior open to boys as well as girls, while other nurturing roles—whether helping to care for a baby or playing with a doll—are less available to boys.

COMPANIONSHIP AND LOVE. *I had just met Michael and told him of my interest in pets when he announced, "Pink is my best friend."*

When I talk with children about why they like pets or want one, they frequently use the word *friend.* When parents and other kids are busy, a pet is always available to play or entertain. As Michael said, "Pink is happy to see me every day when I come home from school."

A pet doesn't care if you come home with torn clothes or a bad report card. A pet listens to your complaints, boasts, and fantasies. Teenagers report that they pour out their feelings of frustration and anger to their pets; some psychologists feel that this outlet may make it less likely that a teenager will act out such feelings in destructive ways. A study on self-esteem in early adolescents, described by Janet Haggerty Davis in *Anthrozoos*, revealed that "when [young teens] listed things that made them feel satisfied and good about themselves, pets were ranked below parents and friends but above other social referents such as teachers."

COMFORT. Pets can be a source of physical as well as emotional comfort. Samantha, a first grader, explained to me that patting her rabbit was "the best feeling in the world because he's so soft." Many children agree, for they often describe how much they like to cuddle their pets. Pets literally are touchable in ways that people in our society often are not. What we know instinctively about this good feeling has been confirmed by medical studies that show that touching a beloved pet—whether it's a bird, dog, hamster, or cat—lowers blood pressure, reduces stress, and has an overall calming effect. As Davis summarized, "Research has revealed that young owners see pets as special friends who display consistency, constancy, empathy, gentleness, and warmth."

SECURITY. *Nick recently had turned ten, but that was no protection against nightmares, especially if he had seen a scary movie or read a scary book. The gerbil colony that he, his brother, mother, and father jointly cared for in the family room was thriving and growing, so Nick asked if a pair of gerbils could live in his bedroom, in their own tank. When his parents agreed, he was thrilled.*

"I can sleep better now," he confided to his mother, and this turned out to be true. "I'm not afraid with the gerbils here." Each gerbil weighs about four ounces, less than an apple.

At the same time that children feel they can take care

of and protect their pet, they also say that their pet makes them feel more safe and secure. How can this be, especially when the pet is very small or even confined in a cage? In his article "Pet Ownership and Human Well-Being," B. Burt Gerstman suggests that our human response is "a remnant of man's evolutionary origins," harking back to a time when safety meant the ability to detect and escape predators. Because animals have more acute senses than people— of sight, smell, or hearing, as well as "motion detectors" in some species—if they sleep undisturbed near us, their presence signals safety on a primitive, subconscious level.

Pets help children feel secure in other ways. From a child's point of view, they do not give advice, ask if your homework is done, or remind you to clean up your room. (They don't even notice that it's dirty.) Because friends can be fickle, and even the most patient and tolerant parents make demands, a pet is a welcome source of unquestioning acceptance. Companion animals have more consistent behavior, compared to humans. How reassuring in a world that, from a child's point of view, is often confusing and sometimes frightening.

ROUTINE. *It is nearly 6:30 A.M., and I am awakened by the sound of a small motor that seems to be located above my left ear. I do not need to open my eyes to know that the sound originates with Buster, our tabby cat. His magically precise body clock rouses me just in time to turn off my alarm clock seconds before it rings.*

Buster and his sister, Ribbon, accompany me first to the bathroom, where I dress, and then with great dignity escort me to the kitchen where the first order of business is their breakfast.

Cats and other pets may insist on being fed at certain times. Dogs walked on a regular schedule set their body clocks accordingly, making "accidents" in the house less likely. Confined pets of all kinds—birds, rabbits, mice, hamsters, fish—do better with a consistent schedule for feeding, play, and exercise. These routines are reassuring to children, who also benefit from consistency.

Attending to pets can help a family or children organize routines of their own. Nick's family cleans the gerbil tanks on Sunday evening. Jenny or her mother cleans the litter box every morning. In our home, I walk the dogs in the morning and at noon, my son John walks them after school, and my husband walks them at night. These walks are a relaxing beginning and end to the day and punctuation in between.

ENTERTAINMENT. Pets are fun. They bring us laughter, smiles, and the gift of wonder. Some children are fascinated watching the silent world of fish in a tank; these pets provide a peaceful, quiet interlude. For some, pets are a stimulus for exercise, especially if the pet is a dog that likes to romp outdoors. For others, pets challenge their ingenuity: Six-year-old Reilly spent hours constructing mazes out of blocks and then watching his hermit crab navigate each maze.

CREATIVITY AND LEARNING. Pets can stimulate, or at least assist, creativity and learning in all kinds of ways. When we were kids, my sister and I dressed up our dogs and used them as characters in plays written and directed by us. Pets everywhere, from turtles to gerbils, have been known to serve as audiences for dramatic productions, not to mention early ventures into dance and music. My sister wrote short stories about her dog, Blackie. I learned to love reading because I could read books about animals. Who can guess how many rabbits, birds, dogs, cats, turtles, and even fish have populated makeshift schoolrooms ruled by ten-year-old teachers?

Pets are interesting to children, an invitation to learn while having fun. Scan the children's shelves in your local bookstore or library and note how frequently animals are featured in both fiction and nonfiction. Children who live with a pet learn about its characteristics and care. The experience of owning a pet can stimulate a child's interest in

other companion animals, wildlife, the environment, and
veterinary medicine. A household pet can also be a bridge
to the wider world of nature, an important part of childhood.

SOCIAL INTERACTION. *Each weekday morning at 8:25,
Sunny, Dandy, and I leave the house to accompany John
to the school bus stop on the corner. Sunny is a seventy-
five-pound mixed breed, and Dandy is a collie of equal size
and splendor. As soon as we arrive, Nick and Greg head
straight for the dogs. John joins them. They pat the dogs,
follow them, make up stories and jokes about them, and
giggle. Sometimes one of the dogs ends up wearing a back-
pack. Margaret, younger and shyer, watches, reaching out
occasionally to pat a dog. Christian doesn't choose to play
with the other boys. Once in a while he asks me a question
about the dogs, but he has never spoken to me about anything else.*

Children who have pets share a kindred feeling for others who have pets or like animals. Pets are an invitation to
talk and something to talk about. They help kids interact
with each other and with grown-ups. If a child is walking
a dog, both children and adults find it easier to approach
and begin a conversation. For children with confined pets
such as birds, fish, and small mammals, hobby clubs and
pet shows offer a way to meet other children who share a
common interest.

What Children Learn

RESPONSIBILITY. A comment that parents frequently
make is that "pets teach responsibility." Of course, pets
themselves don't teach responsibility, but they can help parents do so. Dr. Haim Ginott, a leading authority on child
development and guidance, wrote in *Between Parent &
Child*, ". . . responsibility cannot be imposed. It can only
grow from within." Love for a pet, its reciprocal affection

and loyalty, and its obvious dependence (it can't get its own food, clean its own cage, open the door to go out) can strongly motivate a child.

No matter how strong a child's love for a pet, it cannot motivate her to be any more mature, capable, or knowledgeable than she actually is. No parent expects a six-year-old to train a seventy-pound boxer single-handedly. Intuitively, we know that this task is beyond a six-year-old's capability and that we would be setting the child up for failure if we gave her this responsibility. Yet, if the pet is small in size—bird, guinea pig, kitten, goldfish—parents sometimes make the mistake of assuming that the responsibility is also small enough for a child.

The amount and type of responsibility that your child can handle depends on several factors: her age, level of physical coordination (particularly important with small, frail pets), possibly her size and strength (as in the case of a large dog), her temperament (patient or not, gentle or rough, active or quiet), mental and emotional development (ability to understand and carry out instructions, exercise self-control), and the information and time available to her.

Evaluate your child's capabilities and, within these bounds, encourage him or her to be responsible for at least one pet-care chore. Helping to care for a pet is satisfying and can add to self-confidence. It is also an effective way to create a bond with a pet and promote understanding and interest. Here are some suggestions for maximizing the success of this venture:

- Together with your child, read about how to care for your family's pet.
- Help your child choose the task for which she will be responsible, keeping in mind her abilities and limits. Steer her away from choices you feel are unrealistic.
- Define the task very clearly. Be specific about when, where, and how. Help your child perform the task several times until you are sure she understands it and

can do it alone. If she is too young for this, be there to help.

- Write a schedule to help your child keep track of her job, and post copies where she will see them—on the refrigerator, on her closet door, next to the litter box or gerbil tank. It may help to use a calendar and attach a pencil so that your child can check off the task as it is finished each day.
- Make certain that you have on hand everything needed to get the job done.
- Review your child's assignment from time to time and make adjustments to reflect changes in her abilities or schedule.
- Encourage, praise, and reward a job well and consistently done.

Supervise and be available to help or pinch-hit. Be prepared to do the pet-related chores that your child can't do. Don't expect your child to be solely responsible for the care of a pet; this is an adult-size responsibility. As Ginott wrote, "When a child promises to take care of a pet, he is merely showing good intentions, not proof of ability."

VALUES. *You've had an exhausting day at work. You arrive home late, and it starts to rain. You know that if you don't walk the dog before going to bed, he'll be uncomfortable and have an accident in the house, which will annoy you in the morning, even though you know it's not his fault.* When you get out your umbrella, your kids learn that responsibility isn't optional and often isn't fun or convenient. Consciously or unconsciously, they have learned something. Ginott put it this way: "Values cannot be taught directly. They are absorbed."

Roger Caras, author, naturalist, conservationist, and former president of the ASPCA, wrote in *The Roger Caras Pet Book*, "But what are the values of pet ownership in a home with children? My answers do not imply that these values are available only from pets, but I know from long experience that pets do help children grow up. In a home with pets, children can learn to be gentle. They can learn to care for creatures more helpless than themselves. . . . There are all kinds of love in this world: some you learn from parents, some from siblings, some from grandparents, some from teddy bears, some from friends, and some from pets. . . . There are lots of ways of instilling a reverence for life in children. Pet ownership is one way.''

Your children learn from watching you. They will quickly figure out how you feel about the animal you've brought into your home and draw their own conclusions, some of which might surprise you. If you let the rabbit's cage become filthy, you are sending a message that its habitat and health aren't important, and you may also be sending a message that keeping one's room clean isn't too important, either. If you kick the cat because you are in a bad mood and she's climbed up the living room curtains again, your children will deduce that it's okay for them to do the same—and maybe physical violence will work on that obnoxious kid in the playground as well.

Children learn how to hold, touch, and play with pets by being coached (usually by you), by imitating, and sometimes by reading. By learning about your pet and its needs, you convey respect for this animal and a sense of wonder and delight. By treating it well, you can teach your child to cherish and nurture it.

What Companion Animals Give to Parents

Pets can help parents to fill some fundamental needs in children's development:

- the need to feel loved
- the need to feel safe
- the need to feel competent
- the need to learn
- the need to give

Pets frequently play an important role in parents' lives. I have heard countless stories about the pet adopted "for my child" that Mom or Dad ended up not only caring for but greatly loving. Animals are companions and fun for grown-ups, too.

Caring about an animal offers a special joy with many dimensions: emotional, intellectual, and even spiritual. Writes Chris Davis in "Celebrating the Bird/Human Bond": "A friend and I were talking about how animals had profoundly affected our lives and how birds, especially, possessed a particular magical quality that changed everyone around them. Working professionally with avian behavior for more than 20 years, I have had similar conversations with many of my clients. Repeatedly, they comment on how surprised they were by the impact that their birds had upon them. They were astounded to find themselves sharing their lives with creatures infinitely more intelligent and interactive than they ever thought they would be."

Caring for animals can bring people in touch with enduring values that we treasure as adults and try to pass on to our children. "To educate our people, and especially our children, to humane attitudes and actions toward living things is to preserve and strengthen our national heritage and the moral values we champion in the world," said John F. Kennedy. Throughout the centuries, influential religious, political, literary, and scientific figures from many cultures have taught the moral value of respect and kindness toward animals. Among those who have written movingly about this are St. Francis of Assisi, Leonardo da Vinci, Francis Bacon, Abraham Lincoln, Victor Hugo, Thomas Paine, Samuel Taylor Coleridge, George Bernard Shaw, Ralph Waldo Emerson, Henry Wadsworth Longfellow, the Dalai Lama, Cardinal Henry Newman, Feodor Dostoevski, Thomas Merton, Isaac Bashevis Singer, Mohandas K. Gandhi.

These people give voice to the conviction that our full humanity includes a positive relationship with animals. In the words of Albert Schweitzer, "Until he extends the circle of his compassion to all living things, man will not himself find peace." For most of us, the circle of compassion begins with kindness toward our pets.

Owning an animal is not just a responsibility; it is an opportunity to experience a special bond. Tina Albrecht, a thirty-nine-year-old woman who suffers from a debilitating disease, wrote in "A Feathered Blessing," "Every day when I concentrate on taking care of my companion, I can forget about some of my pain. I have learned to respect all animals. I realize how fortunate I have been to know one of God's creatures. I appreciate and treasure the gifts of love and friendship my cockatiel gives to me."

A few years ago two British authors studied and confirmed the many benefits that companion animals confer on people. But they cautioned in the Medical and Health Annual of the Encyclopaedia Britannica: "If the wrong animal is selected, it will probably suffer, while its human owner will derive little or no benefit." Read on, do your homework, make the right choice, and you and your family will be on the road to many hours of happiness and new experiences.

Resources

NATIONAL ORGANIZATIONS

American Humane Association
63 Inverness Drive East
Englewood, CO 80112
(303) 792-9900

American Humane Education Society
Massachusetts Society for the Prevention of Cruelty to Animals (MSPCA)
350 South Huntington Avenue
Boston, MA 02130
(617) 522-7400

American Society for the Prevention of Cruelty to Animals (ASPCA)
424 East 92nd Street
New York, NY 10128-6804
(212) 876-7700

Delta Society (human/animal bond)
321 Burnett Avenue South
Renton, WA 98055
(206) 226-7357
                    and
300 Park Avenue
Second floor
New York, NY 10022-7499
(212) 310-2802

Doris Day Animal League
227 Massachusetts Avenue NE
Suite 100
Washington, DC 20002-6084
(202) 546-1761

Friends of Animals, Inc.
777 Post Road
Darien, CT 06820
(203) 656-1522

Fund For Animals
200 West 57th Street
New York, NY 10019
(212) 246-2096

Humane Society of the United States
2100 L Street NW
Washington, DC 20037
(202) 452-1100

Local humane societies, SPCAs, rescue leagues, and animal shelters also provide information and advice about pets and pet care.

BOOKS FOR ADULTS

Beck, Alan and Aaron Katcher. *Between Pets and People: The Importance of Animal Companionship*. West Lafayette, IN: Purdue University Press, 1996.

Canfield, Jack, Mark Victor Hansen, Marty Becker D.V.M. and Carol Kline. *Chicken Soup for the Pet Lover's Soul: Stories About Pets as Teachers, Healers, Heroes and Friends*. Deerfield Beach, FL: Health Communications, 1998.

Caras, Roger A. *A Perfect Harmony*. New York: Simon & Schuster, 1996.

Leon, Jane E., and Lisa D. Horowitz. *Becoming Best Friends: Building a Loving Relationship Between Your Pet and Your Child*. New York: Berkley Books, 1993.

McElroy, Susan Chernak. *Animals as Teachers & Healers: True Stories & Reflections*. Troutdale, OR: NewSage Press, 1996.

NONFICTION FOR CHILDREN

Capuzzo, Mike. *Wild Things: The Wacky and Wonderful Truth About the Animal Kingdom*. New York: Ballantine, 1995.

Comfort, David. *The First Pet History*. New York: Simon & Schuster, 1994.

Few, Roger. *Macmillan Animal Encyclopedia for Children*. New York: Macmillan, 1991.

Newkirk, Ingrid. *Kids Can Save the Animals! 101 Easy Things To Do*. New York: Warner Books, 1991.

FICTION FOR CHILDREN
Herriot, James. *James Herriot's Treasury for Children*. New York: St. Martin's Press, 1992.

Sewell, Anna. *Black Beauty: The Autobiography of a Horse*. New York: Grosset & Dunlap, 1945.

TWO

How to Choose a Pet for Your Child

Before You Begin

In this book you will read about some delightful animals that you probably never considered as pet options for your family. To the uninitiated, fish may be boring and rats scary. But children are enthralled when they discover that fish play and sleep, learn to respond to people who feed them, and communicate by movement and even by changing color. Pet rats have pretty coats, are clean, intelligent, playful, and affectionate, and they are loved by children who own them.

As you begin your journey toward a decision, try to keep an open mind. Don't let stereotypes, old wives' tales, or your own history limit your options. You may have grown up with a dog or cat that you loved dearly, but this may not be the right pet for your family at this time.

If you live in an apartment and worry that you won't have time to walk a dog, then a guinea pig or an aquarium full of beautiful fish may be a better choice. Don't think of these pets as a consolation prize or substitute for a larger animal, and don't get one unless you really want it for its own sake. So-called low-maintenance pets really don't seem that way unless they are wanted and enjoyed.

If you begin this journey with the idea that all pets are equal in their potential to fascinate a child and enrich his or her life, but that some are better matched to your family and your child at a given time, you will have a great trip and your destination will be worth the effort. Who knows what can happen along the way? If you are not hemmed in by stereotypes or your own memories, you may fall in love—most unexpectedly—with a budgie or a bunny and be able to transmit your own wonder and enthusiasm to your child.

Where to Begin

Many of us grew up with pets. I did. A sable-and-white collie pup named Mac came into our household when I was eleven, ostensibly a dog for my father. How vividly I remember walking into the kitchen after school one day and nearly tripping over a chubby ball of fur. I immediately appropriated Mac for my own and thus began a twelve-year friendship.

Many of us, those who grew up with pets and those who didn't, believe that finding the right pet is almost instinctive. We want to proceed on memory or gut feeling to repeat or create for our own children the special experience of loving and being loved by a pet. But your search for the right pet must begin in the present, not in the past.

Much has changed. In 1956, when Mac joined our family, we lived in a close-in suburb of Washington, D.C. Our house was surrounded by a two-acre yard, unfenced, which was surrounded by many more acres of undeveloped woods, which in turn bordered on parkland. No dog I knew, including Mac, was walked on a leash. Poop scoops were unheard of. Dogs, cats, and children roamed freely. My parents still live in that house, but the yard is now fenced, as are the others in the neighborhood. The woods have been cut down to make way for a housing development, and the park improved with playgrounds, bike paths, and ''leash your pet'' signs. New roads have been built and others widened to accommodate ever-increasing traffic. Neither a child nor a dog can go far before meeting a heavily traveled road, fence, or some other barrier.

Governments at all levels have gotten involved with pet ownership, and for good reason. Most jurisdictions now have leash laws, and most require owners to clean up after their pets. Other regulations limit the number and even the type of pets permitted in certain areas or neighborhoods. Some areas have mandatory spay and neuter ordinances. Such changes, which impose additional demands on pet owners' time and pocketbooks, indicate that the past no longer serves as a reliable guide to pet ownership.

As for proceeding on emotion, some pet owners impulsively choose a pet because it is cute, because they couldn't resist, or because they fell in love with an adorable animal. Granted, it feels good to make a decision from the heart. Unfortunately, relying on emotion alone can lead to dismal results. About ten million dogs, cats, rabbits, reptiles, and other pets are euthanized every year in America, not because of age or illness, but because they are not wanted. Most people who surrender their pet to a shelter have had the animal for less than a year; more than a third are surrendered within a few months of being acquired. Said Dr. Mo Salman of Colorado State University, author of a recent study in *Best Friends* magazine, ''Most of the problems are really not with the animals, but rather with pet owners who may not be knowledgeable enough about or prepared for the realities of owning a pet.'' Pet decisions that are well thought out shouldn't end in a trip to the animal shelter.

A wise decision will take into account your feelings and wishes and those of your children, but it also will be based on realistic expectations of your children's ability to help you care for a pet, careful planning, an understanding of what it takes to care for a pet, and a matching of your family's lifestyle and resources to a pet's needs.

Commitment

"Isn't she beautiful?" cooed Linda. *"She's iridescent. She's like a jewel."*

I looked at the tank, and then at Linda, and then again at the tank.

"Umm, yes," I said. Iguanas—indeed, reptiles of all kinds—were not my cup of tea, at least not yet. Madonna was definitely a green iguana, no doubt about it, all two feet of her, and I was signing on to care for her for the next ten days.

"Why," I asked, *"did you get an iguana for Hannah?"*

"Simple," said Linda, in her matter-of-fact way. *"Hannah's allergic to just about every type of animal fur. She saw an iguana in school. Then her best friend got one. We did some reading. We even found an iguana page on the Internet."*

Then came the clincher.

"I've always liked reptiles. Ever since I was a child, I was fascinated by them."

Linda, as well as her ten-year-old daughter Hannah, was committed to caring for Madonna, who at twelve months of age had already outlived most iguanas sold in the United States. Linda's enthusiasm and interest reinforced Hannah's, and Linda was happy to share the feeding and cleaning chores.

Not everyone in the family has to like or want the pet with equal fervor. But if Dad truly detests the rabbit his daughter has her eye on, or if Mom becomes hysterical at the thought of a guinea pig her son desperately wants, the chances of that pet being surrendered to an animal shelter go up. Even if the pet survives, a new source of tension has been added to the family, and this is not what pet ownership is about.

Roberta, proud owner of a year-old Portuguese water

dog, described to me how she and her children "worked on" her husband for three years before they convinced him to agree to adding a dog to their family. "He had not grown up with pets," she explained, "so he just didn't get it. We gave him books, took him to dog shows, and introduced him to every dog in the neighborhood. After a while he was comfortable with the idea. Now he's crazy about our dog."

It's easy to be committed if you choose a pet that you, as well as your children, will enjoy, not one that you are afraid of or don't want to handle. Commitment means that *you* have the time and money as well as the willingness to take on the responsibility of pet ownership. This is a daily commitment as well as a commitment over the pet's lifetime, which for some animals may be longer than yours!

Realistic Expectations

Wrapped in a soft wool coat, a woman with glossy black hair sat on a metal chair in the waiting area of the county animal shelter. She held a ten-month-old gray-and-white kitten that she stroked as she wept into its fur. The kitten purred and gazed at her.

"I'm sorry, I'm sorry," the woman whispered over and over again and then surrendered the kitten to the shelter employee who was waiting.

"Why?" the employee asked her. "Why are you giving her up?"

The woman explained. "I got her for my daughter, who wanted a kitten desperately. She swore to me that she would take care of her. But I've been nagging her for months now, and she always forgets to clean the litter box or to feed the kitty. I warned her that if she was not responsible for Buttons, she couldn't keep her. I have to follow through with what I said, or I'll be teaching my daughter the wrong lesson. Now she's not even speaking to me."

The woman's daughter was nine years old, a reasonably

responsible child for her age. Her distraught mother was not trying to be cruel but to teach her child responsibility. Because the mother's original expectations were unrealistic, what could have been a wonderful experience ended in sadness for mother, daughter, and kitten (whose fate it was to be euthanized, as is the case with most animals given up to shelters). The daughter felt guilty and too angry at her mother to seek comfort for the pain and sorrow she felt over losing her kitten.

Your child may be ten, twelve, or fourteen years old, mature and responsible, and a real animal lover. Even so, you are not being fair to him or to yourself if you expect him to be the sole or primary pet caretaker, no matter how sincerely he promises he will be. The simple fact is that kids are kids: When they are young enough to be at home most of the time, they are too young to take care of a pet; when they are old enough to assume this responsibility, they are developing interests and friendships outside the home and probably won't be around enough to follow through.

Parents are the primary caretakers of family pets. Even though more mothers are working outside the home than ever before, they usually tend to the family's pet. According to a survey by the American Animal Hospital Association, in 66 percent of households with pets, an adult female takes care of the family pet, and a male head of household does so in 19 percent of families. A son or daughter (age not specified) takes primary care of the pet in 7 percent of families (and "others" do so in the other 8 percent). In a survey of the age of caregivers, it was reported that only 5 percent of all caregivers were less than twenty years of age; unfortunately, there are no figures available to show how many of these were young children. It is likely that in your family, too, Mom or Dad will become the primary pet caretaker.

Think back for a moment. What do you *really* remember about the beloved dog, cat, or bird you grew up with? Who fed it every day? Took it to the vet? Bought its food? Gave it medicine? Who cleaned the cage or the litter box? Chances are, when you were a kid, your "job" was to play with your pet. This is a realistic expectation. Pets of all kinds need attention, and this includes birds, bunnies, and gerbils as well as dogs and cats.

I remember many wonderful moments with my dog Mac and other family pets. Hide-and-seek was a big favorite. The first real "chore" I was assigned was to take Mac to obedience training, and that turned out to be great fun. Yet it was my parents who paid for the classes and my mother who located an obedience school, handled the paperwork, and drove us back and forth every Saturday morning for three months. As I got older, I groomed Mac more often, and in summer I washed him with a hose (which he loudly protested). When I entered junior high and then high school, I spent more hours away from home. After-school athletics, service clubs, and the class play claimed my afternoons during the week. On the weekends there were parties and football games. I left home for college and then graduate school. I missed my dog terribly, and I know he missed me. Luckily, my parents were "dog people" and took good care of him.

Kids today are even busier than we were thirty or forty years ago. Think about your own children. What do you see in their future in addition to school and homework? Summer camp? Jobs during the summer, after school, or on weekends? Are they active in sports or interested in other activities? Will they be likely to leave home for college or a job? Even the most responsible child won't always be around to care for a pet.

I am not suggesting that children cannot or should not help to care for a pet; they definitely should. But your expectations should be realistic, based on your children's ages, abilities, and temperaments. Will you need to remind them? Yes. Often. Your role will always be to backstop and supervise.

Plan Ahead

Robert had grown up on a farm, and he loved animals. He doted on his wife and three-year-old son, and he liked to bring home surprises—flowers, a toy, a book. One day, the surprise was a frisky golden retriever puppy. Robert's wife, Cathy, liked dogs but had never owned one. She explained later that she "just wasn't ready" for a dog, and neither was their son, Matt. The puppy grew faster than Matt and soon was stronger and heavier. The playful, energetic dog knocked the boy over more than once. Robert, who could handle the dog and enjoyed it most, worked long hours and frequently traveled on business. Cathy resented caring for the dog by herself, and Matt was too young to help. After a year, it became clear that the best solution was to find the retriever a good home, which Cathy was able to do after putting in many hours of effort.

If you buy a pet on impulse, you may live to regret it, but your pet may not. It costs money to care for a pet, and many animals need special food and equipment (sometimes expensive) to survive. An iguana, for example, can be bought for as little as $25, but the equipment needed to keep it alive typically costs about ten times that much. This fascinating reptile is very popular these days; sadly, most of them die within a few months of purchase for lack of proper care, although their normal life span is fifteen to twenty years.

In addition to costs, pet owners report that they spend, on average, one to two hours *per day* taking care of and playing with a pet. You need to plan *before* you get a pet, not after, how you are going to handle this extra work, since much of it will fall on your shoulders.

What You Need to Know About a Pet *Before* You Get One

To be able to plan ahead and decide whether you are up to making a commitment, you need to know what it takes to take care of a pet. Later chapters give you the basic information you need about different types of pets:

- initial investment and continuing cost to feed and care for it
- how big it gets
- amount of time required to feed, exercise, and groom the pet, clean cages or aquariums
- how long you can expect it to live
- amount of indoor space and outdoor exercise needed
- equipment needed
- whether it sheds or smells
- temperamental or physical characteristics that may make a pet unsuitable for a particular age group or child (because it will bite or scratch, is too frail to be easily handled, or requires special expertise)
- personality traits that may help you match a pet to your child (noisy or quiet, calm or excitable, trainable or not, affectionate or not, solitary or social, diurnal or nocturnal)
- ages at which children can safely interact with this pet without parental supervision
- how much help you can realistically expect from children of different ages in caring for it
- legal restrictions

If you want to learn more about the feeding, care, and training of certain types of pets, a list of books and organizations is provided at the end of each chapter. Excellent magazines devoted to nearly every type of pet are available through subscription and in libraries and bookstores. In addition, browse the Internet for good pet Web sites and talk with your local vet, neighbors, and friends who have pets. Animal shelter and rescue league personnel are usually eager to share their experience and have no profit motive to try to sell you on a particular pet. There are rescue leagues not only for cats and dogs but also for rabbits, birds, and other pets. Reputable breeders are knowledgeable and honorable; they want to find the right home for the animals they breed, not just sell you one.

Including children in this learning stage can be fun, useful, and a yardstick for measuring their interest and commitment. Videos and books about pets written for children can be found in public libraries, bookstores, and some pet supply stores. Hobby clubs exist for every type of pet: fish, reptiles and amphibians, birds, rabbits, fancy mice and rats, guinea pigs, hamsters, gerbils, cats, and dogs. If you are lucky, you will find one in your area. Some have junior memberships, and almost all sponsor shows or expos that you and your children might enjoy visiting.

Your Family's Pet Resources

Pet resources are the resources available to your family that you can choose to devote to a pet. Once you evaluate them, you can match your resources to the needs of pets you like and determine what type or types of pet—if any—your family can best handle. Ask your children to help you survey your pet resources. Here are some items to consider:

- **Time.** How much time do family members have available on weekday mornings, afternoons, evenings, and on weekends, and how much of it are you willing to devote to pet care? Be realistic. If you live in an apartment and want a dog, who is going to get up in the morning, and how early, to walk it—and still get to school or work on time?
- **Money.** How much money can you afford and are will-

ing to spend on veterinary care, food, equipment, and other costs that may arise (such as boarding, grooming, training)? Think in terms of optimal, not minimal care.

- **Ability.** Who is able and willing (by virtue of age and availability) to take on various pet care tasks? Young children, for example, can't walk a dog alone or clean a fish tank, but they may be able to help keep a birdcage clean or feed gerbils.
- **Place and Space.** Do you have a fenced-in yard? Is there a park nearby where a dog can be exercised? Where will the kitty litter box go? Will your home feel crowded if you add a large or active pet? If you are interested in a pet that requires an enclosure (small mammals, fish, birds), do you have the space for a large enough aquarium, tank or cage? If you live in a condominium or rental unit, are there restrictions on pet ownership?
- **Health.** Are any members of your family allergic to feathers or animals with fur (allergies that may extend to rabbits and other small mammals, as well as dogs and cats)? Are any family members allergic to substances that might be used as animal bedding, such as cage litter, shavings, hay? If you even suspect such allergies, or if anyone in your family has asthma, consult an allergist before choosing a pet. Do members of your extended family or others who visit frequently, such as a nanny, babysitter, or housekeeper, have allergies that you need to take into account? Are members of your family seniors, infants or immuno-compromised and thus susceptible to diseases that may be transmitted to humans by animals?
- **Travel.** Who will care for the pet during family vacations? If you plan to take your pet with you on vacation, how will you do that? If one or both parents expect a lot of business travel, who is in charge of pet care during these absences? Is there a nanny or au pair in the home, and is she able and willing to care for the pet?
- **Housekeeping.** Does the thought of dog or cat hair

on furniture or pawprints in the foyer upset you?
What about the smell that some animals, including
those in cages, give off?

- **Special Issues.** Do you expect to be moving a lot?
Can the pet go with you? Will you be moving over-
seas? Who will take care of your pet for you or give
it a new home? Do any of your children fear particular animals, such as dogs, cats, or birds?

- **Sensitivities.** Giovanni, a gorgeous macaw parrot, has
a squawk that sounds to me like a woman being mur-
dered, or at least hung by her thumbs. No matter how
often I have heard it, my feet leave the ground when
that parrot squawks. Living with this bird would give
me a nervous breakdown, but his owner doesn't bat
an eyelash. Snakes dine on frozen or live rodents. If
this makes you feel squeamish, you may want to
think it through very carefully before you agree to
get that snake your son is begging for. Do members
of your family have special sensitivities about what
some animals do?

Include Your Children in Decision-Making

As a parent you have no doubt already discovered that it's
a good idea to ask kids for their input before you make
plans that assume their cooperation. A pet will be in your
home, as part of your family, for years. You can make this
decision unilaterally, with the best of intentions, and inform
your kids, taking a chance that it will work, or you can
include them in the decision-making.

Including your child in all steps of the pet selection process—learning about pets, identifying the family's pet
resources, making the final decision—will help to ensure
that you end up with a *wanted* pet that fits your family.
Chances are that your children will enjoy and be proud to
play a role in the process. That pride and interest can translate into commitment to the pet's well-being.

Including your child does not mean that a pet cannot be a gift; it does mean that it is not a surprise or an impulse buy. First, go through the steps outlined in this chapter with your child. If you want to surprise your child for her birthday, Christmas, or Hanukkah, give her a symbolic gift and then go on to choose the pet together. The gift could be a dog bowl and leash, a cat toy and book about cats, a rabbit cage and stuffed rabbit.

Just a minute! you may be thinking. My daughter has been begging for a parakeet for months. I *know* what she wants. So why not surprise her with one on her birthday? First, each bird, just like each dog, cat, or rabbit, has an individual personality. If this will be your daughter's bird, let her share in choosing one that appeals to her.

Second, children change their minds. *A lot.* George's two children besieged him with pleas for a parrot, and finally, he surprised them with one. They were pleased—at first. Now it is up to George and his wife to take care of the bird because, as he says, "The kids never really got into it." In another family, the children begged for a hamster or bunny. By the time Mom caved in and bought one as a surprise, the children had lost interest but hadn't bothered to inform Mom.

Your Pet, Your Family, Your Decision

Fresh from watching Arnold Schwarzenegger with a pet ferret in the movie Kindergarten Cop, *Justin begged his parents for permission to buy a ferret. He would use his own money, he assured them, and take care of the ferret himself. His parents finally relented, buying a young, healthy male from Pam and Tom Grant. Unlike most breeders, the Grants promise a full refund if the pet is returned within thirty days. On the thirtieth day, Justin's father appeared with the ferret.*

"After the first couple of days," he explained, "Justin completely lost interest. I had to remind him every day to

feed, much less play with, the ferret. The animal seemed to be depressed, just sitting in the cage all the time. This isn't a pet my wife or I want, so I'm bringing it back.''

The pet you choose will belong to your family, and the commitment will be yours, so make certain that the decision belongs to your family as well. Don't let a fad, a stereotype, or a neighbor make the decision for you. Justin's foray into the ferret world turned out all right for the ferret, the child, and the parents. But during the Teenage Mutant Ninja Turtle craze, thousands of turtles were bought and then surrendered to humane societies, while others were "freed" to starve or freeze to death in lakes and ponds.

In the "olden days," as my son refers to my childhood, a series of male collies played a beautiful female, "Lassie," in movies and a television series. Thanks to Lassie, collies became one of the most popular dog breeds in America. Movies such as *101 Dalmatians* have sparked national trends in dog ownership. Children and adults may become enamored of a particular type of pet because of its portrayal in a movie, book, or TV show but may not understand how much work is involved, or the true temperament of the animal or breed. If you and your children do your pet homework together, you'll avoid the temptation of the latest, perhaps ill-advised, trend.

This is a pet for your family, not anyone else's, so your decision should be tailor-made. A pet that fits well into your neighbor's family may not fit well into yours. They may have the same size house and yard, even the same size family that you have, but their temperaments, lifestyle, preferences, and schedules are bound to be different.

Decision

After you and your child have done your homework and made a decision, you can follow some of my suggestions for adopting or buying a pet. Your family will be able to give a good home to a companion animal and have a wonderful time.

THREE

Making It Work No Matter What Pet You Get

Before You Bring a New Pet Home

There are important things to take care of *before* you bring a new pet home.

Buy, read, and keep for reference at least one good book that tells you how to care for your pet. Taking care of another species doesn't come naturally; it has to be learned. Make life easy for you and your pet: Call on published experts for the basics and double-check the advice you receive. One iguana owner followed the advice of the pet shop where she bought her pet and fed it only lettuce. As a result, the iguana suffered so badly from calcium deficiency that its bones began to break spontaneously. A good book would have recommended a varied diet, ultraviolet light, and vitamin and calcium supplements. The book you buy should thoroughly describe what your pet needs for its:

- healthy diet
- housing and bedding
- equipment
- grooming
- exercise and handling or training

- health care, safety, and first aid
- special care for the very young or very old

Books are available for every type of pet and can be found in bookstores and pet shops. Some pet care books are written specifically for children. If you find one of these and it is appropriate for your child's age, get this for him or her but also get a more detailed book for yourself. I have suggested several books at the end of each pet chapter. Breeders, trainers, veterinarians, pet owners, and shelter and rescue personnel may also have recommendations.

When choosing books, bear in mind that children are interested in *why*. *Why* is it important for a rabbit to eat timothy? *Why* do some rabbits dislike being picked up? A child who finds answers to questions like these is learning about a piece of nature and even learning how to see the world from a different perspective. Children are proud of newfound knowledge and will use it: "Picking up my rabbit scares her, so instead I will pat her to show her I love her." Caretaking tasks are easier to remember because they have meaning: "If I forget the timothy, my rabbit could get sick."

If the book you buy is good enough, it will guide you through a pet lifetime and help you and your child prevent and solve problems. Research into animal health and behavior has increased substantially in recent years; much of the information and advice available today is dramatically better than twenty or even ten years ago. Myths and misconceptions about pets persist, but an up-to-date pet book will dispel them.

Videos, magazines, and the Internet can supplement your books. Browse for Web sites, but compare and evaluate the information you find because sites vary in quality.

Purchase all the equipment that you will need to take care of your pet and a supply of food. Find out what you need by reading, then talking to your veterinarian, breeder, pet shop employees, or the animal shelter or rescue league workers who helped you find your pet. Include your child in the "research" and the shopping, so that he will better understand the purpose of the equipment you buy. Allowing your child to help select equipment—whether it's a kitty feeding bowl or a chewable gerbil house—will encourage him or her to feel responsible for the animal's well-being.

Decide where your pet will live or sleep, and set up the necessary housing or bedding. Do you remember how carefully you searched for the right apartment or house for your family? You knew that where you lived mattered to you a great deal, not only in terms of cost and physical comfort but also in terms of social contact, convenience, access to recreation, and even health and safety (like most parents, we worried about traffic, crime, and even water hazards when house-hunting with a five-year-old). Where your pet lives is important to its mental and physical health—perhaps even more so than in the case of humans, because your pet has no place else to go. This becomes particularly critical for confined animals such as rabbits, hamsters, gerbils, birds, and fish.

Inadequate housing, or the right house in the wrong place, can literally be death to a pet. A birdcage placed too close to an air-conditioning vent or a drafty window can lead to serious health problems for your bird. Other problems result when you put the cage in an out-of-the-way room, because birds are intelligent and alert animals that need stimulation.

After you have learned about your pet's housing needs, review the space in your home and give some thought to your family's lifestyle. What location will give your pet the conditions it needs? Discuss the options with your child and let him have a say in the decision. Be willing to say no if he wants the birdcage, fish aquarium or gerbil tank in a location that you feel is impractical or unsafe.

Get a vet for your pet. Ten years ago, when I was pregnant, I was advised to pick out a pediatrician before our baby was born. The idea hadn't occurred to me (I'd never been pregnant before), but once I heard it, it immediately made good sense. What was I going to do once we left the hospital—start thumbing through the Yellow Pages at midnight if our baby woke up with a fever?

The story is not very different when you have a new pet. According to the American Animal Hospital Association (AAHA), "It's important to choose a veterinary hospital before you need one." You can find an accredited veterinary hospital in your area by calling AAHA at (800) 252-2242 and by asking for recommendations from animal shelter and rescue league personnel, breeders, trainers, and other pet owners. Birds, small mammals, fish, and exotic pets require specialized care; because fewer vets are trained in these specialties, they are harder to find.

Once you find a veterinary hospital, AAHA advises that you take some time to check it out. "Ask for a tour . . . and use your eyes and nose to detect cleanliness. . . . If it doesn't meet your expectations, turn around and leave." AAHA cautions that, "It's important that you and your pet are comfortable with the doctor. The veterinarian should be able to communicate with you and make you feel comfortable asking questions. Even if the doctor is highly qualified, if you don't hit it off, you may need to go elsewhere."

In choosing a veterinarian, just as in choosing a pediatrician, convenience is a factor. A long drive or a frustrating hunt for a parking space is no fun when you have a sick or injured animal with you. Weekend and evening office hours can be helpful, and you should also check the clinic's fees and payment policies ahead of time.

You may also want to look into a pet health insurance policy, or a pet health care savings program. Ask your veterinarian if he or she participates in a savings program, or check the Internet or pet magazines for information about insurance.

Discuss and assign pet care chores. After you and your child have read through your pet care book, you should have a pretty good sense of what needs to be done to care for your new pet. Sit down and discuss these chores with your child and other family members. Taking into account your child's age and schedule—and your own!—make specific job assignments that everyone thoroughly understands and agrees to, and designate one adult as the Head Honcho, Prime Caretaker, Person in Charge of Pet Well-being. Make a written list of the assignments and post one copy on the refrigerator door, another on your child's closet door (highlighting his or her assignments), and another where the pet sleeps or eats.

Begin your pet care routine the first day you bring your pet home. This will help to calm the animal and smooth its assimilation into your family's schedule. As your pet grows and its needs change, and as your children grow and their schedules change, you may need to review and revise the assignments from time to time.

Bring your pet home at a quiet time. A new home is stressful for any pet, whether it's confined to a tank or cage or has the run of the house, and a new pet is stressful for any family. There are new and different kinds of chores to be done and perhaps an animal underfoot for the first time. Both people and animals need time to adjust.

To ease the adjustment, bring your pet home at a quiet time in your household. The beginning of a weekend, especially a long weekend, or an at-home vacation is ideal. Try not to bring a new pet home during times of change such as the start of the school year, before a move, during a pregnancy, or just after a divorce or the adoption or birth of a child. Your life will already be stressful enough. Holidays are not a good time because your household will probably be anything but calm. Already nervous in a new environment, pets can become even more anxious during holiday bustle, and this is not an easy time for excited children and busy parents to maintain a consistent pet care routine. Wait until your household returns to normal before introducing a pet.

Things to Do *After* You Bring Your Pet Home

Teach, listen to, and talk to your child about this pet.
Your child's sweet temperament and love of animals do not
translate automatically into knowing how to pick up a rabbit (*not* by the ears) or pat a dog. What is obvious to you
may not be obvious to a child. When it comes to pet care
and handling, it's best to err on the side of explaining rather
than assuming.

Give the pet the best care. Parents often say that they
want a pet because "it will be a good experience for my
child." Owning a pet doesn't automatically lead to a good
experience, any more than owning a piano automatically
turns your child into a good musician. The quality of your
child's experience can only be as good as the quality of
life you give the pet. A pet needs pretty much what children
need—appropriate, consistent care, including:

- safe, comfortable housing
- nutritious food and clean water
- preventive medical care and medical attention for illness or injury
- exercise
- mental stimulation
- limits
- attention
- understanding
- respect
- love

A pet whose needs are not met, who has been neglected
or abused, will be unresponsive at best, fearful and hostile
at worst. Your child will not be able to form a bond with
this pet, or enjoy or learn from it.

A well-cared-for pet is responsive and often affectionate;
wants to cuddle and play; can provide love, companionship,

comfort, and entertainment; and can be an inspiration for creativity and learning and a social bridge to other children. Your care of a pet will help to bring routine and order to your child's schedule and help to instill an appreciation of the meaning and rewards of taking responsibility for the care of another living thing.

FOUR

Dilemmas

Should Every Child Have a Pet?

Not every child wants a pet. Not every parent wants one, either. These are two good reasons not to get one. A third is inability to care for the pet throughout its lifetime. Obviously, many children have happy childhoods and grow to be fine adults without ever living with a companion animal.

Every child is different. Before you enter into pet ownership, think about your child's disposition, interests, and strengths. Perhaps she likes to read about animals or draw them but wouldn't really like to live with one. With the help of this book, review your family's preferences and resources before you decide on any pet.

How Old Should My Child Be?

The real question is, "Old enough for what?" Old enough to enjoy a pet? To form a bond and become attached to it? Play with it without supervision? Help care for it? The answers to these questions are highly individualized, depending on the child, the family, and the type of pet. Here are some guideposts, which you can supplement with an evaluation of your child's emotional, physical, and mental development.

INFANTS. Researchers have found that infants from six to twelve months old respond with a smile when the family dog or cat appears. Slightly older babies, in the eight- to twelve-month range, either follow or try to follow the pet. At least some babies seem to "enjoy" having a pet around to watch or chase.

A one-year-old likes to grab, grasp, and hold onto things, whether it's a stuffed animal or a live one. They are too young to follow directions or cautions about handling an animal. It is not safe to leave infants alone with pets.

AGES ONE TO THREE. Toddlers can walk and find this is a great development. They are very active. They love to dash around, throw things, explore, be busy. They rarely pay attention to a verbal command to cease and desist. They tend to treat living things—parents, siblings, pets—as objects that can be stepped on, hit, or kicked with impunity. Dr. Michael Fox of the Humane Society of the United States, author of several books about companion animals, put it this way: "Most children under the age of three tend to treat animals like stuffed toys."

Toddlers can form an attachment to family pets. But with their high energy level, these youngsters tend to poke, prod, and otherwise hurt, frighten, or annoy animals, and they may end up getting scratched or bitten. Small or fragile pets such as birds, gerbils, guinea pigs, rats, hamsters, and mice that cannot escape a toddler's reach can be injured and even killed.

This is not an easy age for children and pets to coexist. The added stress on parents of keeping the two separated or under close supervision can be significant. Many animal shelters will not adopt out kittens or puppies to families with toddlers. Instead, they encourage families either to wait until the children are older, or consider adopting a more mature cat or dog.

AGES THREE TO FIVE. Most three-year-olds are not yet in control of the impulse to chase, grab, tease, and occasionally scream at animals. (The more nervous the animal becomes as a result, the more exciting the game.) They don't seem to realize that animals feel pain. On the bright side, many see their pets as a "special friend," protector, and playmate.

As children reach four and five, they gain more control over their impulses and behavior. Many learn to follow simple directions about not grabbing, dropping, or hurting companion animals. Children at this age are usually less wild and frenetic and so less threatening to pets. However, they should not be left alone with animals—a supervisory challenge that can be burdensome to parents.

AGES SIX TO NINE. Children this age may need to be reminded to be gentle. They can learn how to pat, handle, and hold pets, but someone needs to show them—this is not innate knowledge. They may begin to show empathy for their pets and concern for their well-being. They prize the loyalty and love that pets can give, and they often confide in them. They begin to understand "pet language"— such as what it means when a cat purrs—if you will explain it to them. They can help with simple pet care chores.

AGES NINE TO ELEVEN. By this age, children can understand that their pets feel pain and fear. They enjoy the companionship of a pet, confide in it, and look to it for comfort. Their understanding of animal behavior grows, if you will supply the information. Many enjoy taking care of their pet and are proud to be responsible for some pet care chores. Some children this age can train pets. Parents need to help with and supervise pet care and training.

AGES TEN TO THIRTEEN. Children this age can feel empathy for their pets and often feel that their pets empathize back. They love their pets and feel love in return—they experience a two-way relationship and two-way communication and may believe that their pets show understanding through body language. Some children in this age group become very attached to their pet, are anxious to learn about it and about other animals, and are able to take on more responsibility for its care. Parents still need to supervise.

TEENAGERS. Some teenagers become more closely attached to pets than before, while others move away, just as they distance themselves from family members. Some teens report that they confide in and find comfort in pets. Some become very interested in ethical issues about pets, wildlife, and the environment. While teenagers have the mental and physical capacity to care for and train pets, they often simply are "not there" either physically or emotionally for parents to rely on. Parents of teens—as well as every other age group—are usually the primary pet caregivers. Pets often remain at home when teens leave home for college, marriage, or jobs, leaving parents solely responsible for their care.

                    *   *   *

Every child is unique, and every family is different. Your child's age is only one of the factors to consider when you decide whether your family is ready for a pet.

How Do We Say No?

On Sunday morning, Malik and Susan found a handwritten letter from their two children on the kitchen table, begging for any kind of furry pet: dog, cat, hamster, guinea pig, rabbit. Susan looked at her husband sadly.

"What do we do?" she asked. She and her husband both suffer from allergies to fur bearing animals.

"What do I say?" Shelley asked plaintively one summer evening after her two sons had asked, yet again, for a dog. Shelley is a single mother who works long hours, juggling

a business she runs at home with taking care of the boys.

"I don't have time for a dog," she said. "I don't particularly want one, and the boys aren't old enough to walk a dog without me."

"I'm under constant pressure—underline the word constant," moaned Della. "A dog, a rabbit, a bird, whatever. How can I take that on with a new baby and three other kids under ten?"

There are times when no pet is the right pet for a family. For some families, because of financial constraints, health issues, work schedules, restrictions in a lease, or other reasons, there may never be a right time. For other families, the "right time" is in the future.

The best way to respond to children who ask (beg, plead) for a pet is to say no and give an honest, clear explanation. Malik and Susan need to explain the illness they would suffer if a pet were in their home, and that it would be cruel to keep a pet isolated in the garage or basement.

Shelley can explain to the boys that she does not have time to help them take care of a dog. She can tell them that caring for a dog is not just their responsibility, but a family responsibility because a dog is a family member.

Della can explain that this is such a busy time for the family, especially for her, that it would not be fair to the pet, the baby, the parents, *or* the other children to add a companion animal now. If she and her husband are prepared to follow through, she can say that when the baby is older, the family will choose a pet.

It is difficult for some parents to refuse a child's request for a pet. But both your child and the pet will suffer if you get a pet and then have to give it up after your child has become attached to it. Even worse, the wrong pet or the wrong time could result in your child getting hurt or the pet dying for lack of proper attention. If your child asked for a machete or a Waterford vase to play with, you would say no. Getting an animal that can injure your child or be injured by it makes less sense. Waiting for the right time, and finding the right kind of pet, is a safer, happier solution.

If your children won't accept no for an answer, a psychologist suggests that, "If children are pushing really hard for a pet, and just can't seem to back off of it, it may be that they are pushing for something else. Sometimes the real message isn't about the dog, but about something else that is going on." Parents need to listen, pay attention, and ask a few questions. It could be that your child is lonely, or feeling left out because of a new sibling, or under unusual social or academic stress. Parents can help a child discuss the problem.

Saying no to acquiring a family pet, either temporarily or permanently, does not have to be the end of your child's opportunities to interact with animals. Depending on your child's interests, age, where your family lives, and the amount of money and time you can afford, there are alternatives.

WILD BIRD FEEDER. Whether you live in a house or an apartment, a wild bird feeder is feasible and fun. Start with a good book that will advise you about types of feeders, placement, species of birds in your region, and the foods they like. Keep in mind that feeding should be done consistently, not on a haphazard basis.

VOLUNTEERING AT A SHELTER OR RESCUE LEAGUE. Some animal welfare organizations welcome and train young volunteers. Check with a local shelter, SPCA, humane society, or rescue league to find out if they have a program and the age of children they accept. Programs vary, but they typically include training children to work in the shelter after school, on weekends, and during vacations. Kids help care for animals by cleaning cages, feeding, grooming, walking, and playing with them. In some communities, young volunteers help to collect much-needed supplies such as old towels and blankets. It is rewarding for children to see their efforts put to immediate, good use.

PET-SITTING AND PET WALKING. If your child is old enough, enterprising, and responsible, he can start his own business as a pet-sitter and walker. Kids advertise these services by distributing flyers in their neighborhoods.

Sitters usually charge by the day in return for coming into a vacationing neighbor's home to feed, water, and care for pets. Chores vary with the type of pet and include such tasks as cleaning litter boxes or cages. The number of visits per day or per week depends on the owner's preference.

Dog walkers exercise dogs either during the day while owners are away at work, or several times a day if owners are on vacation. This is not a responsibility to be undertaken lightly. Even a well-trained dog can get into a fight or flee under certain circumstances. Your child should be mature and experienced with dogs and limit her clients to dogs that are well behaved.

Whether your child wants to pet-sit or walk, satisfy yourself, either by talking to the pet owner or making a home visit or both, that your child will not injure or be injured by the pet, and that she fully understands and can carry out the responsibility entrusted to her.

HELPING NEIGHBORS. When I was a kid, I quasi-adopted a Great Dane/boxer mix named Duke, who was given to roaming the neighborhood. The couple who owned him worked during the day. While they were gone, they kept him in a small yard, from which he regularly escaped. His owners were pleased when Duke found me, as I loved playing with him and he never left our yard to roam the streets. At dinnertime, he trotted home, tired and happy.

You may have elderly neighbors, or neighbors who work long hours, who would welcome your child's attention to their pets. Acquaint yourself with the neighbors whose pet your child is playing with and make certain that you, and they, feel comfortable with the arrangement.

SPONSORING AN ENDANGERED OR ABANDONED ANIMAL. Your child may want to contribute to a nonprofit animal welfare organization, if you or he can afford it. Some organizations focus their efforts on improving the well-being of companion animals in America through spay and neuter campaigns, or rescue, adoption, and educational programs. Others work to protect endangered species in America and around the world. These organizations send publications to their contributors that include stories, photographs, and usually a section for and about children. Some organizations invite contributors to sponsor an individual animal.

Resources

ORGANIZATIONS

Adopt A Wolf
Defenders of Wildlife
1101 Fourteenth Street, NW
Room 1400
Washington, DC 20005
www.Defenders.org

Animal Sponsorship Program
Wildlife Waystation
14831 Little Tujunga Canyon Road
Angeles National Forest, CA 91342-5999
www.waystation.org

ASPCA Animaland
PO Box 97288
Washington, DC 20077-714

Your local humane society, SPCA, rescue league, shelter, and assorted animal welfare organizations are also in need of financial assistance, and many keep contributors informed with newsletters that may interest your child.

BOOKS

Amory, Cleveland. *Ranch of Dreams: The Heartwarming Story of America's Most Unusual Animal Sanctuary*. New York: Viking, 1997.

PART TWO

Children, Dogs, and Cats

FIVE

Dogs

The picket fence was new, not yet painted. It surrounded the yard. In one corner of the yard was a ten-foot by ten-foot enclosure. A small, constant crying came from there.

Although the enclosure included a snug doghouse, Taffy would not stay inside it. She heard human voices. Her nine-week-old Labrador retriever body was soaking wet and shivering from the ice-cold rain. Taffy alternately tried to climb up the fence or force her small, chubby body between the slats. I stood beneath my umbrella, trying to pat her, and then went inside to the warm kitchen, where Beth, my hostess, was busy with dinner.

"Why?" I couldn't resist asking Beth. "Why can't the puppy come inside the house?"

"Because I'm allergic to dogs," she answered. "She has a doghouse, and the breeder said she'd be fine outside."

"You mean she'll never be allowed in the house?"

"That's the idea," said Beth.

Pushing my luck, I asked, "Why did you get a dog?"

"Because the kids wanted one," she said. "I thought it would be a good experience for them. Our neighbors have Labs, and they really like them, so we chose one, too."

Beth—school volunteer, mother of four, lawyer (tempo-

Dogs
Facts At a Glance

COST	$6,000–$12,000 over the dog's lifetime
SIZE	2–200 pounds
LONGEVITY	8–16 years
TIME REQUIREMENT	1 to 2 hours per day to exercise and feed, plus additional time each week for grooming, training
SPACE	Enough square feet for bed and/or crate plus walking around and sprawling room
EXERCISE	Must be walked/run outdoors daily
EQUIPMENT	Food and water bowls, collar, leash, ID tags, bedding, crate (optional), grooming utensils, fence (for a yard), poop scoop
ODOR	A "doggy odor" that varies in intensity with type of coat and individual dog
SHEDDING	Varies from light to heavy with season, breed, and individual dog
PHYSICAL CHARACTERISTICS AFFECTING KIDS	Some dogs are too strong and/or too large for children to control on leash; small dogs can be injured by children; any dog can bite if provoked
TEMPERAMENTAL CHARACTERISTICS AFFECTING KIDS	Sociable, need human interaction and bonding; trainable, though ease of training varies; many but not all dogs like children
PERSONALITY TRAITS	Range from noisy and excitable to quiet and calm, from easygoing and patient to high-strung, from demonstrative and affectionate to standoffish
PARENTAL SUPERVISION	Young children should not be left unsupervised with a dog or puppy
LEGAL RESTRICTIONS	Almost all jurisdictions require rabies vaccinations and licensing; most have leash laws and require poop-scooping; many landlords and condo associations prohibit dogs or restrict size and number of dogs allowed

rarily retired)—is a kind, warm, intelligent woman. Few parents can claim to be more dedicated to, or more involved in, their children's lives. With the best of intentions, she had made a series of decisions about a pet that would turn out badly.

Taffy languished alone in the outdoor pen. During the cold winter months, the children, much as they liked the puppy, spent little time outside playing with her. Desperate for affection and attention, Taffy began to jump on any child who ventured inside the enclosure. Instead of becoming gentler and calmer as she matured, she became wilder. The children, eventually overwhelmed by Taffy's weight and strength, played with her less and finally began to avoid her. What Beth had hoped would be a good experience for the children ended up being one more chore for her and a sad and lonely existence for Taffy.

ORIGINS. The domestic dog, *Canis familiaris*, is one of thirty-eight species of the family *Canidae*, which includes the wolf, fox, coyote, and jackal. The scientific consensus is that dogs are descended from wolves. Anthropologists believe that wolves were the first animals domesticated by man—allowed or invited by cave dwellers some fourteen thousand years ago to share a bone or the protection of a campfire in return for help in the hunt and, possibly, guard duty. Within about two thousand years, dogs that were distinct and different from wolves had evolved, their very nature defined by their relationship to humans.

Dogs come in every shape, color, and size, from two pounds up to two hundred pounds. The American Kennel Club officially recognizes 142 breeds, and another 300 are recognized in other parts of the world. The variety of mixed breeds is limitless. The species *Canis familiaris* has greater diversity of appearance than any other species on earth, and, as every owner knows, each dog has its own unique personality. There are fifty-three million dogs in America today, and the majority of them are owned by families with children.

NEEDS. Wolves are highly social animals, living in packs with a leader and a definite hierarchical structure. A "lone wolf" is notable because it is rare. Like their wolf ancestors, dogs are social. Your family is the pack, and a dog will bond closely with your family, according it great loyalty and probably feeling at least some degree of protectiveness toward it. You, or another member of your family, are the "leader of the pack" or "alpha dog," and this relationship works in your favor when you are training your dog. Because dogs naturally want to belong to the pack and obey their leader, families that socialize and train their dogs will have a companion that is gentle (or at least careful) with kids, loyal, and well behaved. A dog that has been banished to the yard, basement, or garage has been deprived of the opportunity to form this important attachment. This is a hardship for the dog and a loss for the family.

According to an article in *Dog Fancy* magazine, "Dogs need to learn how to behave around people. Isolating a dog in the back yard is a great way to drive it crazy. It becomes bored, destructive and makes a general nuisance out of itself to attract attention. If isolated long enough, it becomes ill-behaved and antisocial. Either integrate your dog into the family or give it to a family that will."

Of course, dogs have physical needs as well: a healthful diet, fresh water, indoor shelter, proper grooming, and veterinary care, which includes routine physical examinations and vaccinations, and protection against fleas, worms, and other parasites. All but the tiniest, frailest, and oldest dogs need substantial outdoor exercise. Exercise is a prerequisite to good health *and* good behavior. Dogs that are unable to expend physical energy are likely to become excitable, mischievous, destructive, and harder to train.

Beth's dog Taffy was not only deprived of the human companionship she desperately needed, she was never exercised the way a Labrador needs to be (which is a lot). After a year, Beth recognized that Taffy's life in exile was not a good one. Beth described the by-now large Lab as

*"depressed" and said that she was reminded of the "fail-
ure to thrive" syndrome that characterizes neglected children. Beth's solution, which was the right one, was to call
on the local Labrador Rescue League to find a new home
for Taffy, but Beth's children were heartbroken.*

CHILDREN AND DOGS. Children turn to dogs to love and
be loved, to find companionship and comfort. A dog, more
than any other pet, becomes a member of your family.
When I was a kid, my collie and I played games (hide-and-
seek was the favorite both inside and outside), slept in the
same room (fears never visited with Mac there), read books
together (with Mac serving as a furry pillow). Because of
Mac, I devoured Albert Payson Terhune's novels (about
collies, of course) and moved on to other animal fiction,
from Jack London's *Call of the Wild* to Anna Sewell's
Black Beauty.

As a teenager, when I was angry, moody, or sad (and
what teenager isn't?), I turned to Mac. I would hug him
and talk to him, sometimes weeping into his fur—an experience and a relationship that surveys show are both typical and beneficial to children and teens.

Dogs give unconditional, nonjudgmental love and ado-
ration. They help children learn to be considerate, nurturing, and empathic. A child's deepest attachment is to
parents, a relationship defined by the child's dependence,
but dogs are dependent on humans from puppyhood
through old age. In this relationship the child can be the
boss and the nurturer. Many children learn intuitively their
dog's need for consistent human affection and attention and
for a dependable schedule that includes meals, play, rest,
and exercise. This is what children need, too, which may
be why children often understand and get along well with
dogs.

COMMITMENT. Until recently, the dog was the most popular pet in America. Today, it is the second most popular
pet, after the cat, a reversal that reflects the pressures of

modern life that leave parents with barely enough time to look after themselves and their children, much less a dog.

Between two and four million dogs are euthanized in America every year. Most of these are neither sick nor old; they are just not wanted. According to one study, more than 40 percent of the dogs surrendered to shelters have been owned six months or less, and 22 percent are owned six to twelve months. In most of these cases, the owners did not understand the amount of effort, time, or expense involved in caring for a dog, and when they found out, they weren't willing to make the commitment. Before you decide to get a dog, be certain that you understand the considerable demands and responsibilities, as well as the joys, of dog ownership and that you have the *desire*, time, and money to care for this pet throughout its lifetime, which may last fifteen years or more.

What You Need to Know About Dogs *Before* You Get One

SIZE. Of all pets, the dog is most variable in size, ranging from less than five to more than 150 pounds. The size of your dog will affect your family in many ways: how much money you spend feeding and caring for it, how much space the dog takes up, how much exercise it needs, whether it is too strong for your child to control on a leash, or so small it can easily be stepped on or injured, whether it fits in your car with the rest of the family.

LONGEVITY. A dog's life span is controlled by its genes, its environment, and the care it receives. Larger breeds age more rapidly than medium and small breeds. Giant breeds, such as Saint Bernard, bullmastiff, Great Dane, and Newfoundland, and large breeds, such as Doberman, rottweiler, German shepherd, and collie, have the shortest life span—on average, ten to twelve years, or even less. Medium and small breeds on average live ten to fifteen years. Some dogs live beyond fifteen years. I recently met a dachshund mix that was twenty-one years old.

Mixed breeds tend to have fewer hereditary health problems than pure breeds and often live longer, a phenomenon known as "hybrid vigor." Because of selective breeding, pure breeds suffer from a high incidence of inherited disorders such as epilepsy, deafness, degenerative eye disease, and hip dysplasia. In addition, the "desirable" characteristics of some pure breeds, such as abnormally large size, flattened face, elongated back, or shortened limbs can, in and of themselves, cause health problems.

Size may be a legal issue for those who live in condominiums or apartments that prohibit dogs over a certain weight. Some hotels and motels allow small—but not large—dogs to stay in guests' rooms, so size matters if you want to travel with your dog.

LEGAL RESTRICTIONS. Some condominium and homeowners' associations, and many landlords, prohibit dogs or limit the number or size of dogs permitted. Check your lease or the covenants that govern your association. Be sure your dog will be "legal" before you bring it home. Your local government (usually through an agency designated "animal control"), animal shelter, or veterinarian can advise you about legal requirements of dog ownership in your jurisdiction, which almost certainly will require rabies vaccinations and licensing, prohibit dogs from running loose ("leash laws"), and require owners to clean up after their dogs ("poop scoop laws"). Some jurisdictions require owners to obtain a special breeder's license if they plan to breed their dog.

COSTS. The care of a dog, excluding extraordinary veterinary expenses, will be roughly $6,000 to $12,000 over its lifetime. There are many variables in this figure, in addition to regional price differences that can be substantial. A major variable is the size of your dog: Practically everything, from food and equipment to veterinary care, costs more for a large dog. A puppy costs more than a dog because of the need for early veterinary care and special equipment.

Food is the largest single maintenance expense. A five-pound Chihuahua costs a lot less to feed than a two-hundred-pound mastiff. (On the other hand, small dogs typically live longer than large ones.) It will cost about $1,000 a year to feed the mastiff, compared to $150 for the Chihuahua. Ask a veterinarian, breeder, or shelter or rescue league worker to recommend the proper amount and type of food your dog will need and then estimate your weekly or monthly expenditure.

Basic equipment includes:

• comprehensive book about dog care	$10–30
• food and water bowl (unbreakable)	$5–50
• leash	$5–15
• collar	$5–15
• identification tag	$5–15
• poop scoop (or a supply of plastic bags)	$20–35
• nail clipper, comb, brush, toothpaste, toothbrush	$40–75
• toys	$0–25
• crate (optional)	$50–350
• dog bed (optional)	$25–200
• traveling crate (optional)	$40–250

Routine *veterinary care*, including annual exams, vaccinations, and heartworm prevention, runs from $75 to

$150 a year, plus an indeterminate amount for flea prevention. Spaying or neutering, *a must,* is a one-time expense that costs from $75 to $250. Before you choose a dog, call the veterinary clinic you plan to use and request figures for all these routine, necessary procedures. In some areas, low-cost spay and neuter services are available.

Some first-time dog owners are shocked when they learn the cost of treating their pet for an illness or injury. While the cost of dog food is buried in the grocery bill each week, owners don't like to come face-to-face with a major expenditure for their pet. Yet few dogs go through life without an illness or injury. Veterinarians are among the best-trained and lowest-paid professionals in the country. (Did you know that it's harder to get into veterinary school than medical school?) Great advances have been made in the last ten years in animal medicine, and much more can be done for a sick or injured dog—at a lower cost—than ever before.

Discarding a dog that gets sick or hurt sends a negative and even frightening message to children. If they have become attached to the dog, they are being told that their love doesn't count, that this companion is just another "thing" to be disposed of when its care becomes inconvenient—hardly a healthy lesson for children to learn. Children, who often identify with their pets, can be frightened by the idea that getting sick creates a "burden" and that sick things can be gotten rid of. A better approach for everyone is for you to set aside, either mentally or in fact, a *veterinary emergency fund* of at least $500. If you're not prepared for this eventuality, rethink your commitment to owning a dog.

The cost of *training* varies, from free or low-cost classes sponsored by local government or community groups, to pricey private lessons at $50 an hour and more. Depending on your lifestyle and the type of dog you choose, you may have additional expenses: kennel boarding, professional grooming, dog walkers. If you have a yard but no fence, you need to build one, an investment to research and make before you bring a dog home.

The continuing cost of caring for a dog far exceeds its *acquisition* cost, although, if you try really hard, you can probably spend $10,000 on a purebred dog. I cannot think of any reason you would want to do this for a family pet. A reputable breeder can sell you a healthy dog or puppy for about $300 to $1,000. You can also find wonderful and healthy dogs and puppies that are much cheaper at a shelter or through a breed rescue league, where you will be asked to pay only a nominal amount to cover the cost of the dog's care, usually between $35 and $85, which often includes puppy vaccinations and sterilization—a great bargain. A good option is to find your dog or puppy at a shelter or rescue league and use the money you save to pay for training or a veterinary emergency fund.

EQUIPMENT. Basic equipment includes at least one comprehensive book about dog care; unbreakable bowls, usually made of heavy plastic or stainless steel (one for water, one for food), sized for your dog; at least one sturdy six-foot training and walking leash; mesh or leather collar, properly sized; identification tag; poop scoop or a supply of small plastic bags; grooming brush or combs, and nail clippers (size and type vary depending on the dog—ask a vet or groomer for advice); canine toothbrush and toothpaste; long-lasting chew toys. A fence is a must if you have a yard. Some owners also prefer to have a dog bed, crate, and traveling crate. For any of these, make certain that it is sturdy and large enough for your dog or puppy to comfortably turn around and lie down. Puppies require puppy collars and chew toys, and their owners require stain- and odor-eliminating cleaners for rugs, floors, and furniture.

SPACE. A big dog such a Labrador retriever, currently the most popular breed in America, weighs from sixty to eighty pounds and stands about twenty-four inches at the shoulder. A dog this size or larger takes up a lot of floor space.

A large dog can be happy in a small house or apartment—if it is given plenty of outdoor exercise and the human members of its family don't mind stepping over it. While a small dog takes up a lot less indoor space, it's not wise to generalize about the suitability of a small dog to a small home because any dog, even a small one, can be very energetic and active.

Barbara, a statistical analyst who works at home, explained why she and her husband decided not to get a dog, despite the pleas of their two children, ages eight and ten. "We live in a small row house in Washington, D.C. It's a great neighborhood, but there aren't any parks within easy walking distance. In the morning, our house is a zoo, with my husband getting ready to leave for work and the kids getting ready for school. I really feel that no matter how small a dog, it would be one more live body, and that would be one too many. If we move into a larger house or a place with a yard, we'll rethink the dog option."

TIME REQUIREMENT. The age, type of coat, size, and any special health or behavioral problems of your dog will affect the amount of time you spend caring for it. A puppy requires far more time than a trained adult dog, and a puppy cannot be left alone for more than a few hours.

Regardless of the size or type you get, someone in your family will have to spend at least an hour a day *exercising* it. Some dogs and some breeds need more exercise than others. An energetic sporting dog, such as a retriever or a retriever mix, needs to run or walk farther and longer than a toy breed or toy mix.

A dog and a fenced-in yard do not equal exercise. Except for those sad specimens that are left outdoors all day and have become so neurotic that they ceaselessly run back and forth inside a fence, barking at every rustling leaf (a behavior so annoying that the dog is universally hated), dogs in yards are quite sedentary.

The Santos family has a two-acre fenced yard, complete with trees, squirrels, and rabbits. Their golden retriever and their spaniel mix are happy to run in the yard, provided that a human is running with them or they are chasing a tennis ball that a human has thrown for them.

Another daily chore is to *feed* your dog, once or twice a day for adults and more often for puppies, and give it fresh, clean drinking water. You may find yourself making shopping trips to a pet supermarket if you decide not to use the dog food sold in grocery stores.

Dogs need to be kept clean, for good health as well as appearance. The number of times per week and the amount of time that you spend *grooming* your dog will depend on at least three factors: (1) how fastidious you are about dog hair in your house and on your clothes; (2) the type of coat that your dog has; and (3) where your dog exercises—does it run in mud, swim in the creek, roll in smelly things? Some types of dog coat need daily brushing, a few require professional grooming, and most require at least one or two brushings a week, or about thirty minutes to an hour of grooming per week. Dogs also need to have their ears checked, their nails clipped regularly, and their teeth brushed once a week.

Puppies and dogs need to be *trained.* In addition to house training, basic obedience training typically involves a one-hour class per week for eight to ten weeks, plus practicing at home for ten minutes twice a day during that period.

SHEDS OR SMELLS? All dogs shed, and all dogs smell, some more than others. Dog coats vary tremendously: long, short, coarse, silky, wiry, straight, curly, wavy. All dogs lose some hair year-round, and most shed seasonally once or twice a year. Alaskan malamutes are among the heavy seasonal shedders. Some dogs, such as the dalmatian, shed heavily year-round, and others, such as the basenji, don't shed much. Mixed breeds can fall anywhere along the continuum.

Your dog's "doggy" smell and breath will depend on its own chemistry, how often it is brushed or bathed, what it is fed, and how often you brush its teeth.

CHARACTERISTICS AFFECTING CHILDREN. A medium-size dog, one weighing between twenty-five and fifty pounds, is a strong animal. Obviously, larger dogs are even stronger. Many adults cannot control a dog that weighs sixty pounds, particularly if it is vigorous and independent minded. Unless your child weighs more than the dog and is physically strong, and your dog is well trained, your child will not be able to control a medium or large dog on a leash.

Small dogs, weighing from two to fifteen pounds, can easily be hurt if they are stepped on or played with roughly. Some small dogs are afraid of children. A child is, after all, bigger than a ten-pound dog, and a child's voice and movements may be perceived as threatening. A fearful dog is more likely than a secure one to bite.

Any dog, no matter what the size, can bite—a painful and frightening experience for any child (and parent). Look for a dog that is stable, friendly, and easily trained to obedience. Socialize and train your dog, supervise your children with the dog, and teach them how to treat it.

Dogs that jump on people, even in friendly greeting, can hurt a child by knocking her down or scratching her with its nails. Training can break a dog of this habit.

PERSONALITY TRAITS. Dog personalities, like people personalities, run the gamut: shy, timid, quiet, calm, outgoing, demonstrative, excitable, gregarious, independent, mellow, effusive, affectionate, standoffish, noisy, aggressive, active, sluggish. Carefully study breed traits by reading and by talking to breeders, owners, veterinarians, and rescue league and shelter workers. More important, study individual dogs or puppies. Within any breed or litter, there is a range of personalities. Several books recommended at the end of this chapter tell you how to "interview" a prospective dog or puppy. One advantage to selecting an adult dog, mixed or purebred, is that its personality is already developed and therefore a known quantity.

Don, an outgoing housepainter and father of two, talked about their new pet, a sweet but very submissive and retiring golden retriever pup. "I can't understand it," he lamented. "Before I was married I had the friendliest, the most rambunctious and energetic golden you ever saw. She was so smart! My kids would have loved her! That's the kind of dog they need, to run all day and play with them. The dog we got—I love her, but she's kind of dumb and almost afraid to roughhouse. Loud noises frighten her. You wouldn't know they were the same breed."

NEED FOR PARENTAL SUPERVISION. Children under the age of six need careful supervision when interacting with any dog. Very young children do not understand that their actions can cause pain or fear in an animal; indeed, they do not even understand that an animal can feel pain. Young children are inquisitive and impulsive, given to quick movements and lots of physical activity. As one veterinarian commented, "Virtually every movement a toddler makes toward a dog can be viewed as threatening by the dog: waving hands and arms in front of a dog's face, grabbing, pulling, flailing, whacking, poking." Because the dog can't say, "Cut it out!" or call for help, the dog might snap or bite if it feels trapped and cannot get away from the child. Indeed, half of all bites to children under four are inflicted by their own pets, and 90 percent of these bites take place at home.

Roger, who was three years old, had been warned repeatedly by his mother not to bother their sheltie, Cassie, while she was eating. This morning, however, Roger's mother was upstairs, Cassie was eating in the kitchen, and Roger saw a chance for some fun. Dragging a blanket from his bed, he threw it over Cassie and her bowl. Then he stuck his head under the blanket, too, pretending to eat from Cassie's bowl. Cassie had other ideas, and she bit Roger's cheek.

This is not an example of a "bad" child or "bad" dog. Roger is a normal and rather adorable boy. Cassie is a calm and friendly pet. Like other children his age, Roger simply doesn't have enough self-control to resist his own impulse to play or tease. He has a vivid imagination, and his "games" are unpredictable. Cassie felt trapped and threatened by Roger's "tent."

Parents must always supervise young children and dogs. Brian Kilcommons, preeminent dog trainer and author, put it this way: "The number one cause of bites between dogs and children is lack of parental supervision. Leaving a dog alone with a child is like leaving two toddlers in the same room, one with a pair of scissors. Even the best dog in the world can bite if he is surprised or hurt."

Maria, mother of thirty-month-old Anna, attests to how enormously stressful it is to "always worry where the dog is, and where Anna is, and is the dog asleep or eating, and to be constantly separating them, putting one here and the other there, or else need to be in the room myself. The more I tell Anna no, she more she wants to take Sandy's chew toys or grab his tail. She just loves getting a reaction out of that dog, or out of me."

The good news is that a dog that is loved, socialized, and well trained can tolerate a lot of childish behavior. As they mature, kids can learn, too. Kilcommons suggests that, "The basic rule to live by with children and dogs is, 'Do not allow your child to do to the dog what you would not allow done to a younger sibling.' This rule covers chasing around the house, harassing, teasing, pinching, kicking, screaming in ears, jumping on top of or otherwise hurting the dog."

It's easier to wait until your child is at least six before bringing a dog or puppy into the family. By this age, most children are able to abide by simple rules about how to treat—and how not to treat—a dog. Whatever age your child is, the quality of the relationship that he or she has with the family dog will depend largely on how well you teach your dog and your child to treat each other with respect.

Child's Age and Care of Dog

Children's mental and emotional development and physical abilities vary tremendously. You know your child's capabilities better than anyone, and you are in the best position to evaluate what tasks he or she can reasonably be expected to perform. Use your common sense to decide whether the chores that I suggest for children of different ages fit your child, and take time to teach your child how to do each chore.

Children **age three to five** can hang up the dog's leash, put away dog food, and fill a water bowl: give your child a plastic container with a small mouth, filled with cold water, and have her empty it into the dog's bowl.

Children **age five to seven** also can pour premeasured dry dog food into a bowl.

Children **age seven to ten** also can help an adult measure, pour, and mix food. They can be in charge of keeping bowls clean, either by washing them or by putting them in the dishwasher.

Children **age ten to twelve** also can poop-scoop the yard, help an adult to obedience-train, and walk an obedience-trained dog on leash.

Children **age twelve and up** also can obedience-train and groom.

Your Family's Pet Resources

Inventory your resources to see if they enable your family to keep a dog.

TIME. Which family member(s) will walk the dog, feed it, groom it, clean its teeth and ears, clip its nails, take it to obedience classes and the veterinarian, poop-scoop the yard? If you are thinking of getting a puppy, who will be home during the day to care for it? Who will get up at night when it needs to be taken outside?

COST. Can you afford the ongoing cost of food and veterinary care? A veterinary emergency? Do you foresee special expenses such as professional grooming, building a fence, or boarding the dog when you travel?

ABILITY. Are your children old enough to help with any of the chores?

PLACE AND SPACE. Do you have a fenced-in yard? How close is a park where you can exercise the dog? Will your home feel crowded with a dog in it? Are there legal restrictions on keeping a dog in your home?

HEALTH. Is anyone in your family allergic to dogs? How about regular visitors such as a nanny, housekeeper, or grandparent?

TRAVEL. Who will care for the dog when the family travels? Can you afford to board it in a kennel if necessary?

HOUSEKEEPING. Will dog hair on the furniture or pawprints in the hall upset you? What about doggy odor or drool?

SPECIAL ISSUES. Do you expect to be moving? Can the dog go with you? If you expect to move abroad, bear in mind that long-distance travel is hard on dogs, and some countries require prohibitively long quarantines.

* * *

Bardi McLennan, author of *On Good Behavior,* sums up what you need to know before you get a dog: "Responsible dog ownership begins with spay/neuter, a fence, a leash, good food, good health care, good training—and that's just the beginning!''

Where to Get a Dog or Puppy

There are three places to get a dog or puppy: rescue league, animal shelter, breeder. *Do not* buy a puppy from a pet shop. More than 70 percent of these puppies come from puppy mills, cruel commercial enterprises that breed dogs inhumanely and indiscriminately. These puppies are over-priced, stressed, and physically and temperamentally unsound, problems not remedied by the fact that they are purebred.

A **breed rescue league** is what it sounds like: an association of people who ''rescue'' dogs of a particular breed that have been, or are about to be, discarded. Typically, a league does not have an office or kennel, but operates out of private homes. These folks usually own, are dedicated to, and are very knowledgeable about their particular breed. They provide foster homes until suitable permanent homes are found for the dogs.

Rescue leagues are an excellent source for dogs and, less often, puppies. Because the dogs are kept in foster homes, they avoid the stress of shelter life. League workers are careful about matching the right dog to the right family and are an excellent source of information and advice. Leagues require spaying and neutering and charge modest fees to cover the cost of these procedures and care of the animal. They will interview you and your family before they place a dog with you. Ask a vet, breeders, or your local animal shelter for information about rescue leagues in your area, or contact Project BREED (see ''Resources'' at the end of this chapter).

An **animal rescue league** such as an SPCA is also privately operated and funded but includes dogs and puppies of all kinds, including mixed breeds, as well as cats and other types of pets. An animal rescue league may have a kennel facility and offices. Their adoption procedures are similar to those of breed rescue leagues. These rescue leagues are usually listed in the telephone directory.

Animal shelters are local facilities that may be government-owned and -operated, privately funded, or hybrid private and public. These facilities are run by trained animal care and control professionals to receive relinquished and stray animals. Because the level of funding varies from state to state and county to county, the quality of services can vary a great deal. Many shelters offer the services of adoption counselors to help match the right dog or puppy to the right family, as well as advice about dealing with behavior problems.

Increasingly, purebred dogs as well as mixed-breeds are found in shelters. In my suburb outside of Washington, D.C., pure breeds make up at least 25 percent of dogs surrendered to the local shelter.

The dog or puppy that you obtain at a shelter will be inexpensive. You may be charged $35 to $85 for the adoption, which may include vaccinations, veterinary exam, and spaying or neutering. Although living in a cage in a shelter, even for a brief period, can be stressful for a dog, many dogs and puppies obtained from shelters prove to be wonderful family pets. Shelters are listed in the local government section of your telephone directory, usually under a listing such as "animal control" "humane society," or "animal services."

Breeders sell purebred puppies, with prices that vary from about $300 to $1,000, depending on the quality of the puppy and the relative availability and popularity of the breed.

How to find a responsible breeder and avoid amateur "backyard breeders" and commercial puppy mills? One of the best sources for this information are the people who run the rescue league for the breed you are interested in. Veterinarians, trainers, breed clubs, and local kennel clubs are other sources. Organizations such as the American Kennel Club do not screen out puppy mills or amateur backyard breeders, so you will have to do some research on your own. Look for a breeder who:

- interviews *you* and wants to meet your family
- is happy to be a source of advice and information
- provides a health guarantee
- can show you at least one of the puppy's parents
- breeds only a few dogs at a time and usually only one breed
- does not breed a female more than once a year and not before she is two years old
- can answer your questions with authority and first-hand experience
- screens for genetic defects common to the breed and provides written proof of the parents' screening
- runs a clean facility
- socializes and trains the puppies
- requires you to spay or neuter dogs that are not show quality
- emphasizes temperament in breeding
- provides references and a written contract
- will not let you have a puppy that is less than eight weeks old
- will not sell you a puppy if you plan to keep it in the basement or yard

Questions That Parents Ask

When can we expect our child to become fully responsible for the care of a dog? Realistically, never. Be prepared to make a continuing investment of *your* time, money, and effort, for ten to fifteen years, to feed, exercise, groom, and ensure veterinary care. You will need to care for the dog when your child is sick, busy with school and other activities, or away from home.

How old should our child be before we get a dog? Old enough to be able to understand and follow some simple rules about how to act around and treat dogs. This varies with the child, but most children can manage by the time they are six years old. If you are thinking about getting a puppy, that is another matter. Read on.

It is true that only a puppy will become fully attached to a child or family? No.

Should we get a puppy or a dog? Puppies are especially appealing to children but far more work for parents. Be prepared to spend time and money to puppyproof your home and yard, to lose sleep, and to spend several hours a day socializing, exercising, feeding, and training a puppy. Puppies need to be taken outside every few hours until they are housetrained, and they cannot be left alone for long periods of time. Puppies homesick for their mothers and littermates may cry at night. Like infants, they explore the world with their mouths by chewing and biting, and they also go through a teething process, including chewing behavior that can be destructive to furniture, clothes, and carpets.

The ASPCA advises that if your children are under seven years old, "they are usually not developmentally suited for puppies 5 months old and under . . . Puppies have ultra sharp 'milk teeth' and toenails and often teethe on and scratch children, resulting in unintentional injury to the child. The puppy becomes something to be feared rather than loved."

An adult dog's personality is already a developed and known quantity, and this is helpful when selecting a dog. If you are considering an adult dog, look for one that is used to being around children. Not all adult dogs are well trained or socialized. But, according to Barbara Woodhouse in *Dog Training My Way*. "Are there limits as to when one can train a dog? My answer is, any age between 3 months and 8 years old, providing the dog is fit. After that the dog should not be bothered."

What kind of dog is best for a child? First, consider your child's personality and age. Does he prefer to stay indoors and read, or to romp outside? Is she athletic and strong, or cerebral and delicate? Look for a dog whose personality and activity level will complement your child's.

When it comes to the dog, give top consideration to temperament. Some dogs are more compatible than others with children. Talk to owners, breeders, and trainers to learn about breeds and mixed-breed dogs, and take time to read through more than one book about dog selection.

Within a given breed or litter, there is a range of temperaments. Look for a friendly, gentle, emotionally stable dog that likes being handled, and avoid extremes—a dog or puppy that is extremely excitable, aggressive, or timid. Mixed as well as purebred dogs make great family pets.

As to the dog's size, the ASPCA advises against small dogs (under fifteen pounds) for children under seven because "these are fine-boned, touch-sensitive creatures that do not weather rough or clumsy handling well. They break relatively easily and are quicker to bite than their larger-boned, mellower relatives."

Isn't a purebred AKC dog a safer bet around kids? Not necessarily. For the average family looking for a pet, AKC papers don't mean much. A publication of the Humane Society of the United States explains: "Many people purchase a purebred, registered dog because they think they are buying the best. They may also believe that registration papers guarantee a healthy dog of good bloodlines. But registration papers indicate *only* that the registry involved— the American Kennel Club (AKC) is the largest—maintains a record of the dog's birth and his/her parents. . . . Papers do not in any way guarantee health or quality; in fact, purebred dogs, with papers or not, may actually be more prone to health problems than mixed-breed dogs." Because many genetic problems do not appear until a dog matures, it is difficult or impossible to screen them out when selecting a puppy.

What you get with a purebred puppy is a certain amount of predictability. You have an excellent idea what your Irish setter puppy will look like as an adult and how large it will be. You also know that, as a sporting breed, setters tend to be outdoorsy, high-energy dogs. A mixed-breed puppy has less predictability, but if you are lucky enough to meet both parents, you can make some educated guesses, at least about temperament and in some cases about size as well. Two small parents are not going to produce a huge dog, nor two large parents produce a tiny one.

Even though I have owned and loved purebred dogs with excellent character, I am wary of generalizations about the superiority of purebred dogs. Dr. James Serpell, a highly respected authority on canine development and behavior, noted in his book *The Domestic Dog,* "There can be little doubt that the recent overwhelming emphasis on aesthetically 'ideal' physical conformation in most purebred dogs, has had, and will continue to have, a damaging influence on behavior and temperament."

Aren't purebred dogs smarter and easier to train? According to Barbara Woodhouse, "I am always being asked whether a pedigree dog is easier to train than a mongrel. My answer is that all dogs can be trained if the owner is made of the right stuff." My own experience as an owner of mixed as well as purebred dogs is that "mongrels" are every bit as smart and trainable as purebreds.

Won't a female dog be more gentle around children than a male? Not necessarily. A dog's temperament depends on the genes it is born with and the medical care, socializing, training, and overall treatment that it receives.

In some breeds, male dogs are larger and stronger than females, but physical strength is a separate issue from temperament. Male dogs should be neutered and female dogs spayed for improved health *and* better behavior. According to the American Animal Hospital Association, "Often female dogs will experience some personality changes during heat cycles such as becoming short-tempered or anxious." After a female is spayed, she no longer goes into heat, and these problems disappear. The American Veterinary Medical Association states that, after neutering, "Males usually become less aggressive. . . . And most neutered pets tend to be more gentle and affectionate."

How do kids learn how to take care of a dog or puppy? From you, from books and videos, and from asking questions of your veterinarian, trainer, breeder, and shelter or rescue league worker. Unlike training, which is actually school for both the owner and the pet, care can be learned from a book. There are good ones available for children as well as for adults.

What is the best book to get when it is time to train the dog? The phone book. Look up dog obedience training, or ask your vet, breeder, fellow dog owner, local humane society, or the National Association of Dog Obedience Instructors or Association of Pet Dog Trainers for a reference. It is the humans, as much as the dogs, who need to be trained. Most dogs benefit from being trained in a class with other dogs. In addition to privately owned dog obedience schools, there are training classes for dogs and owners sponsored by many urban and suburban governments. Sign up the kids—they'll have fun, learn a lot, and gain in self-confidence.

Ask a potential trainer to supply references and explain his or her experience and methods. Avoid any trainer who relies on pain or fear to ''teach'' (hitting, yelling, electric shock collars). Observe a class before you sign up and decide whether the training seems to be effective and fun. It should be both. If the trainer won't let you watch a class, go elsewhere.

Will our children benefit from witnessing the ''miracle of birth''? No. There are videos and books for kids about animal reproduction, and you are well advised to rely on these.

There are important reasons to spay and neuter dogs. Breeding is hard work, expensive, messy, and can be threatening to your dog's health. The AKC reports that the average purebred litter *loses* more than $1,200 for the owner. Children often don't ''witness'' the birth because it is likely to take place at night, in isolation. You will be stuck with the difficult job of finding homes for the puppies.

Overpopulation is the number-one canine problem in

America. Your children will learn the wrong lesson if you add to it. Spayed and neutered dogs don't breed, are easier to train, have fewer health problems, and are less likely to wander, fight, or bite.

Isn't a dog from an animal shelter going to be a problem with children? Not necessarily. My parents adopted a beautiful and beautifully behaved golden retriever that had been surrendered to a shelter when his owner, a soldier and a bachelor, was shipped off to fight in the Gulf War. This dog is wonderful with my son. Other dogs are relinquished because of divorce, job loss, or death of an owner—in other words, not because there is anything wrong with the dog.

Some dogs found in shelters and rescue leagues do have behavior problems because they have been neglected or abused. Some problems can be resolved with love, patience, socialization, training, and proper food and medical care, but some behavior can render a dog too iffy to be brought into a home with children. If you have doubts about a dog, talk them over with the shelter's adoption counselor and err on the side of your children's safety and your sanity.

Our daughter desperately wants a dog, but she is allergic to them. A friend told us that there are certain "nonallergic" breeds. How can we find out what breed our child can live with? Begin by consulting an allergist and be guided by this professional's advice concerning your daughter's health. Of the fifty-five million Americans with allergies, nearly one-third are allergic to their own pets, so you may have some options.

People who are allergic to dogs are allergic to a protein found in both a dog's saliva and its skin. Although it's difficult for a child to avoid all drool and slurpy kisses, determine if your child is mature enough to at least minimize them.

Dogs continually shed small particles of dead skin, called dander. Some of it falls out as the dog sheds its coat. There is no such thing as a dog that has no dander. There are breeds, including the poodle and bichon frise, that don't shed, as most dogs do, although they do lose dead hair.

Some owners and breeders (but not most allergists) believe that these breeds are less likely to provoke allergies, and you might want to consider one of them. See if you can find a friend who owns one who will "lend" it to you for a couple of days for a trial run. (Keep in mind that some allergies take weeks or even months to develop.)

There are other steps you can take to minimize allergic reactions. Keep the dog out of your child's bedroom. The dog should be bathed and groomed frequently, but not in the house and not by your child. Minimize or remove carpets and upholstered furniture, because they collect dander. You can purchase a high-efficiency particulate air filter (HEPA) and HEPA vacuum cleaner to remove dander from your home.

Our son, who is ten, has been asking for a dog. My wife and I are agreed that we are willing to help him take care of it, and we want to surprise him at Christmas. We've been told that some breeders and even some animal shelters won't let us have a puppy in December. Is this a myth? No myth. Responsible breeders and adoption counselors at shelters and rescue leagues have learned the hard way that animals don't make good Christmas presents. Too many of them are returned—surrendered to shelters or rescue leagues a few weeks or months later. Some breeders, shelters, and leagues now have a moratorium on pre-Christmas adoptions and sales. Others allow you to choose a pet before Christmas but don't allow you to take it home until January.

These policies are good for families as well as pets. Take your son with you when you choose a dog; he will feel good about being involved in the decision, and you will end up with a better match. Years of compatibility are more important than the thrill of a Christmas morning surprise that can last, at best, only a few moments.

You will probably be grateful *not* having a new dog under foot during the holiday season. With a stream of visitors, do you really want to worry about the new dog slipping out the front door? While you're cooking for a batch of relatives, do you really want to get started on the dog's feeding schedule? Who's going to make sure that the dog doesn't eat tinsel, step on a broken ornament, or lift his leg on the Christmas tree? Who has time to walk it, amid the hoopla of holiday gifts and excitement? This is probably the worst time of year to bring a new pet home, because it will be doubly stressful for your family and for the dog.

Give your son a wonderful book about dogs, or a collar and leash, and promise that you will all pick out the dog together—after Christmas. It will be a better gift, and a better holiday, for everyone.

Resources

American Animal Hospital
Association
PO Box 150899
Denver, CO 80215-0899
(800) 252-2242

American Dog Trainers
Network
www.inch.com/~dogs
(212) 727-7257

American Kennel Club
5580 Centerview Drive
Raleigh, NC 27606-3390
(919) 233-9767

Association of Pet Dog
Trainers
PO Box 385
Davis, CA 95617
1-800-PET-DOGS

National Association of Dog
Obedience Instructors
Corresponding Secretary
729 Grapevine Highway
Hurst, TX 76054-2085

National Dog Groomers
Association of America
Box 101
Clark, PA 16113
(412) 962-2711

Project BREED
18707 Curry Powder Lane
Germantown, MD 2987-2014
(301) 428-3675

United Kennel Club
100 East Kilgore Road
Kalamazoo, MI 49001

BOOKS FOR ADULTS

Benjamin, Carol Lea. *The Chosen Puppy: How to Select and Raise a Great Puppy From an Animal Shelter*. New York: Howell Book House, 1990.

———. *Second-Hand Dog: How to Turn Yours Into a First-Rate Pet*. New York: Howell Book House, 1988.

Christiansen, Bob. *Choosing A Shelter Dog*. Carlsbad, CA: Canine Learning Center, 1995. To order, call (800) 354-3647.

Fox, Michael W. *Superdog: Raising the Perfect Canine Companion*. New York: Howell Book House, 1990.

———. *Understanding Your Dog*. New York: St. Martin's Press, 1992.

Kilcommons, Brian, and Sarah Wilson. *Child-Proofing Your Dog: A Complete Guide to Preparing Your Dog for the Children in Your Life*. New York: Warner Books, 1994.

———. *Good Owners, Great Dogs: A Training Manual for Humans and Their Canine Companions*. New York: Warner Books, 1992.

Lane, Marion S. and staff of Humane Society of the United States. *Complete Guide to Dog Care*. New York: Little, Brown, 1998.

McLennan, Bardi. *Dogs and Kids: Parenting Tips*. New York: Howell Book House, 1993.

Pavia, Audrey, and Betsy Sikora Siino. *Dogs on the Web*. New York: Henry Holt, 1997.

Rubenstein, Eliza, and Shari Kalina. *The Adoption Option: Choosing and Raising the Shelter Dog For You*. New York: Howell Book House, 1996.

Siegal, Mordecai. *Understanding the Dog You Love: A Guide to Preventing and Solving Behavior Problems in Your Dog*. New York: Berkley Books, 1994.

Tortora, Daniel F. *The Right Dog For You: Choosing a Breed that Matches Your Personality, Family, and Lifestyle.* New York: Simon & Schuster, 1980.

Weber, Shirley. *Project BREED: A Nationwide Source Book for Rescue of All Breeds of Dogs and Other Species.* Germantown, MD: Project BREED, 1998. To order, call (301) 428-3675.

Wrede, Barbara J. *Before You Buy That Puppy.* Hauppauge, NY: Barron's, 1994.

NONFICTION FOR CHILDREN
Benjamin, Carol Lea. *Dog Training for Kids.* New York: Howell Book House, 1988.

Milton, Joyce. *Wild, Wild Wolves.* New York: Random House, 1992.

O'Neil, Jacqueline. *Kids + Dogs = Fun: Great Activities Your Kids and Dogs Can Do Together.* New York: Howell Book House, 1996.

Popovich, Christine, and Peter J. Vollmer. *How To Play With Your Dog!* Escondido, CA: Super Puppy Press, 1989. Ages 2–5. To order, call (619) 489-1818.

Ryden, Hope. *Your Dog's Wild Cousins.* New York: Dutton, 1994.

Simon, Seymour. *Wolves.* New York: HarperCollins, 1993.

Standiford, Natalie. *The Bravest Dog Ever: The True Story of Balto.* New York: Random House, 1989.

FICTION FOR CHILDREN
George, Jean Craighead. *Julie of the Wolves.* New York: HarperCollins, 1972.

Knight, Eric. *Lassie Come-Home.* New York: Holt, Rinehart and Winston, 1940.

Naylor, Phyllis Reynolds. *Shiloh.* New York: Bantam Doubleday Dell, 1991.

———. *Shiloh Season.* New York: Atheneum, 1996.

Sendak, Maurice, and Matthew Margolis. *Some Swell Pup, or*

Are You Sure You Want a Dog? New York: Farrar, Straus and Giroux, 1976.

Wells, Rosemary. *Lassie Come-Home: Eric Knight's Original 1938 Classic Written for Young Readers.* New York: Henry Holt, 1995.

SIX

Cats

It was Alice who took the phone call that afternoon, from a man with an Eastern European accent. He gave an address, a delicatessen on a major boulevard. He had a kitten, he said, that he had taken away from a bunch of kids. They were "playing doctor" and had cut off one of the kitten's ears. A customer had told him about the all-volunteer cat rescue group that Alice belonged to. He couldn't keep the kitten, could someone come and get it? At least it wasn't crying anymore. It was asleep now.

Alice picked up the kitten, taking it immediately to one of the local vets who provided low-cost assistance to the group. They estimated the little tabby's age at twelve to fourteen weeks and named him Vincent in honor of artist Vincent van Gogh, who also lost an ear. Vincent healed quickly and then moved into a cage in the rescue group's small shelter in a converted garage.

A few weeks later, a ten-year-old girl, accompanied by her mother, toured the shelter. Her parents had promised that she could choose a kitten, and she fell in love with Vincent. Her mother tried to talk her out of it.

"We don't want a cat that isn't perfect," she objected.

"I do," insisted the girl, and her mother gave in.

Vincent went to a wonderful home. His young owner saw

Cats
Facts At a Glance

COST	$6,000–$8,000 over the cat's lifetime
SIZE	7–12 pounds
LONGEVITY	14–16 years
TIME REQUIREMENT	1 hour per day for feeding, playing, grooming, cleaning litter box
SPACE	Enough for litter box, and for cat to climb, see out a window
EXERCISE	30 minutes–1 hour of indoor play daily
EQUIPMENT	Food and water bowls, collar, ID tag, litter box and scoop, scratching post, carrier, toys
ODOR	Very little, if litter box is kept clean
SHEDDING	Usually moderate; varies with type of coat
PHYSICAL CHARACTERISTICS AFFECTING KIDS	Cats can be injured by children; most cats will scratch if they cannot escape a threat; de-clawed cats more likely to bite
TEMPERAMENTAL CHARACTERISTICS AFFECTING KIDS	Many but not all cats like children; become attached to people but retain independence; usually playful; curious, like to observe
PERSONALITY TRAITS	Range from vocal to quiet, from friendly and affectionate to shy and standoffish, from low-key to active and busy
PARENTAL SUPERVISION	Young children should not be left unsupervised with a cat or kitten
LEGAL RESTRICTIONS	Most jurisdictions prohibit free roaming; some require licensing, spaying, and neutering; some landlords and condo associations prohibit cats or limit number allowed

past his physical imperfections and allowed her heart to respond to his sweet and loving personality. Her mother was glad that her daughter taught her to have a more open mind about what makes a "perfect pet."

ORIGINS. The domestic cat, *Felis catus*, belongs to one of three species of the family *Felidae*, whose members are hunters, feeding almost exclusively on meat. Within this family are the lion, tiger, leopard, jaguar, and cheetah. Although *Felidae* lived in proximity to prehistoric humans, cats were among the last animals to be domesticated. It is probable that domestication first took place in the Middle East, when farmers encouraged a small, wild bush cat to remain in populated areas to catch the mice and rats that fed on stored grain.

Most scientists believe that the African wildcat, which looks remarkably like its domestic cousin and still lives on the African continent, is the main ancestor of the domestic cat. Historians agree that domesticated cats lived in Egypt at least thirty-five hundred years ago. For two thousand years, until the fourth century, Egyptians honored cats, considered them sacred, and mummified and buried their remains.

During the Middle Ages, however, the animal once considered sacred was condemned by the Christian church, which decreed that cats were agents of Satan. Cats were sought out, tortured, and destroyed in huge numbers throughout Europe. Apparently no other animal has endured such a pendulum of treatment by humans.

Unlike the dog, the cat has not been bred into many different sizes and shapes for specialized tasks. Cats are roughly similar in size and shape, but their appearance can vary in a number of ways: eyes that are round or almond-shaped, blue, green, gray, yellow, or turquoise; short or long hair of innumerable colors and patterns; body types that range from stocky and short-legged to long-legged and slim; faces that are round or narrow; tails and ears that are short or long.

NEEDS. Myths and misunderstandings about cats abound. According to the Humane Society of the United States, "One of the most widespread misconceptions about cats is that they are aloof, independent animals who don't really form attachments with people." Many people incorrectly believe that cats are so self-sufficient that they need little care.

In fact, cats need daily attention and social interaction almost as much as they need food and water. In return, a cat may be affectionate and form strong attachments to people. Cats are curious, intelligent creatures that need stimulation—another cat or people to play with and a perch by a window from which to watch the world.

They need to exercise, climb, and stretch. They also need to scratch. This is not neurotic or "spiteful," as some people believe, but normal, biologically programmed behavior. (Cats in the wild scratch on tree bark.) Cats scratch with their front claws to mark territory, to remove dead husks from their claws, and probably also to stretch. If you don't want your cat scratching your furniture or carpets, give it an inviting alternative in the form of at least one sturdy scratching post. As cats normally sleep fifteen to eighteen hours a day, they need a place to sleep or doze undisturbed.

CHILDREN AND CATS. *"One time,"* explained eleven-year-old Sarah, *"I was mad at everyone in my family, and there was no one left for me to talk to. I was in my room, and my cat Ashby came and curled up next to me."*

"Yes," chimed in Alice, her eight-year-old sister. *"A cat can cheer you up."*

A cat is a friend, playmate, and comfort. Cats retain their autonomy and a strong sense of their own unique "feline selves"—the capacity to let their human know, "Okay, that's enough attention for now. I'm going to go do my own thing."

Parents need to understand and teach their children how

to handle cats. Mordecai Siegal, author of *The Good Cat Book*, put it this way, "When children play with cats there are guidelines to make the experience safe, loads of fun, and meaningful to their relationship." This is not a complicated process. By reading at least one good book about cats, and sharing it with your children, you can establish the necessary guidelines. Here is a sample of what kids need to learn:

- how to pick up, hold, pat, and play with a cat
- how to read cat body language and understand when a cat is signaling, "Stop!"
- not to disturb a cat when it is eating or sleeping
- not to roughhouse with a cat, or hold or chase it when it wants to get away

COMMITMENT. In recent years, cats have overtaken dogs as the most popular pet in America. Some sixty million cats live in about thirty million homes. One reason for their increased popularity is that cats adapt more easily than dogs to today's busy lifestyles and to townhouse or high-rise accommodations. A cat needs attention every day, but it does not need to be walked outdoors.

Felis catus's increased popularity is not always accompanied by an understanding of, or a commitment to care for, the animal throughout its life. An indoor cat commonly lives to be fourteen to seventeen years old, and it is not unusual to meet a cat that is twenty. This is a *long* commitment. If you get a cat when your child is eight, that cat will still be with you after your child has grown up and left home for marriage, work, or college.

Millions of pet cats and kittens are surrendered to animal shelters every year. Of these, less than half find new homes. The rest, more than three million a year, are euthanized, no matter how healthy and well behaved, because shelters simply run out of space. Studies show that many cats are surrendered because owners lack understanding of cat behavior. Owners who refuse to sterilize their pets complain about the biologically dictated behavior that unsterilized cats inevitably display. Owners who avoid cleaning the litter box complain about cat elimination outside the box (cats don't like to use dirty litter). Parents who permit their child to maul a kitten complain when the kitten grows into a fearful cat that refuses to be handled.

These and other "behavior" problems can be prevented by families who understand their cat and try to meet its needs. A good veterinarian, a good book about cat care, and a commitment to keep your cat throughout its natural life add up to a long, satisfying relationship with your feline.

What You Need to Know About Cats *Before* You Get One

SIZE. Most cats weigh between seven and twelve pounds, although some large, obese cats weigh in at twenty pounds and more.

LONGEVITY. The average life span of a well cared for indoor cat is fourteen to seventeen years and may be longer. Cats that spend time outdoors have shorter lives because of the greater likelihood of injury (from cars, dogs, other cats) and illness due to disease or ingesting toxic substances.

LEGAL RESTRICTIONS. If you live in a rental unit, condominium, or cooperative, or belong to a homeowner's association, carefully read your lease or the covenants governing your association to determine whether cat ownership is prohibited or regulated. Some associations, for example, permit cats as pets but limit to two the number allowed in each unit.

Some local governments require that pet cats be licensed, and most jurisdictions prohibit cats from roaming off of their owner's property. Your local health department, animal control department, or shelter can tell you the regulations affecting your jurisdiction.

COSTS. The care of a cat, excluding extraordinary veterinary expenses, will be $6,500 or more, assuming a life span of fifteen years. If you begin with a kitten, it will cost more because of early veterinary care. Prices, especially for veterinary care, vary by region.

Food for your cat will cost at least $200 a year, if you buy dry food in bulk (the larger the bag, the cheaper it is). If you add pricey canned "gourmet" food, your annual bill will be higher.

Basic equipment includes:

• comprehensive book about cat care	$10–25
• litter (changed weekly)	$100–200 (annual)
• food and water bowls (unbreakable)	$10–20
• comb or brush	$3–10
• nail clipper	$10
• breakaway collar	$5–10
• identification tag	$5–10
• litter box	$3–30
• litter scoop	$2–5
• scratching post	$15–40
• carrier	$20–60
• toys	$0–15 (annual)
• bed (optional)	$15–30
• window perch (optional)	$20–30
• climbing tree (optional)	$75–150

Routine veterinary care, including annual exams and vaccinations, is about $65–$100 a year. Sterilizing your pet is a must: spaying (females) is about $100–$175 (the older the cat, the more expensive); neutering (males) is about $50–$85. Before you get a cat or kitten, call the veterinary clinic that you plan to use and request figures for routine procedures. Some vets offer "kitty packages" for the first year (exam, vaccinations, sterilization). In some areas, low-cost sterilization services are available, usually through the local shelter.

Be sure to set aside, either mentally or in fact, a *veterinary emergency fund* of at least $500. Indoor cats live longer, safer lives than cats allowed outdoors, but even indoor cats can develop health problems that need medical attention.

Most cats and kittens come from shelters, private rescue organizations, or friends—or are strays that find us—so *acquisition* costs are usually minimal. A shelter or rescue group may ask for a donation that only partially covers costs of sterilization, vaccinations, and medical care, sometimes as little as $25, up to $65 in areas where the cost of running a shelter is higher. Purebred cats or kittens can be bought from breeders for $100–$500.

EQUIPMENT. Every cat needs a plastic litter box that is big enough for it to turn around in. Some owners prefer a litter box with a hood, but some cats refuse to use them. Many types of litter are now available. You may want to experiment, but once you find a litter your cat likes, stick with it. A good carrier (not a temporary cardboard one) is a must for trips to the vet. For grooming, a narrow-toothed comb may be sufficient for a short-haired cat. A long-haired cat may also need a brush. Special nail clippers are available for cats. You can make or buy a scratching post in a variety of shapes, sizes, and textures.

Climbing trees, "cat condos," window perches, and cat beds are nice to have, but they are optional. Toys really aren't—cats need to be amused. You can make or buy quite a variety. It's a good idea to get some interactive ones and some that your cat can play with while it is alone. As you gradually form a collection, as most cat owners do, leave a few out to be played with and store the rest, then switch a few stored and "used" toys every few weeks.

SPACE. Cats do not take up much space, although a bored, neglected cat can seem to be always underfoot as it begs for attention. Cats can accommodate comfortably to apartment living if they get enough attention, stimulation, and exercise.

Most cats pick out a favorite spot for dozing, or you can provide a cat bed (with no guarantee that your cat will use it). A litter box (usually about 15 inches by 18 inches) should be placed in a quiet, accessible location. If this is a bathroom, the door should be left open when humans aren't using it.

Cats also need a window on the world. If your cat can sit on a piece of furniture and look out a window, it is less likely to become bored (and hence grouchy or destructive). An alternative is to buy and attach a "window perch." Be certain that the window is closed, or the screen securely fastened, to prevent your cat from falling. Only in cartoons do cats land right side up and unharmed.

TIME REQUIREMENTS. Cats need attention and affection from people, and kittens need more.

Most cats should be fed twice a day. Kittens eat more often. Ask your vet or shelter worker to recommend the food that is best for your pet. *Feeding*, including providing fresh, clean drinking water and keeping bowls clean, takes five to ten minutes a day.

Although cats spend as much as one-third of their waking hours grooming themselves, they still need your help. When a cat cleans itself by licking its body, it inevitably swallows some of its own hair. Hair is not soluble, but most of it passes harmlessly through the digestive tract. Some of it, however, accumulates in the stomach, forming hairballs. Usually these are regurgitated (in my home, almost always on an Oriental rug, never on a bare floor), but in some cases hairballs can lead to more serious digestive problems. To avoid them, *comb or brush* your cat regularly.

A longhaired cat, such as a Persian, needs daily grooming. A shorthaired cat should be brushed about once a week. Grooming takes five to twenty minutes, depending on the cat's coat. Some cats need their claws trimmed every few weeks, a procedure that takes about five minutes. This is a job for an experienced adult or vet.

Cats need *exercise*, for the same reasons that people do: to discharge energy; improve coordination, muscle tone, and circulation; avoid weight gain; and reduce tension and stress. The best way to exercise a cat is to play with it. Play is fun for cats, teaches them to socialize, and helps prevent boredom that might otherwise lead to destructive behavior.

Pet supply stores sell cat toys, or you can easily make up your own games and toys: a string to pull and swing, with a feather or soft object tied to one end, or a ball of scrunched-up paper to throw. Check your cat care book for other suggestions and for games and toys to be avoided because they might be dangerous.

Encourage your child to play with the cat, as this will help create a bond between them and show your child how to play gently. By purchasing a cat tree or other "exercise equipment" from a pet supply store or through catalogs, your cat can exercise and play alone.

Interactive playing with your cat can also help you to *train* it, for example by teaching it that toys (not your furniture or your child's fingers) are for biting and scratching. Cats can be trained to use a litter box and to use a scratching post rather than your furniture. Dr. Michael Fox, a respected authority on animal behavior, has written in *Supercat: Raising the Perfect Feline Companion*, "... cats are highly trainable given the right understanding and attitude, and a well-trained cat makes a more satisfying companion than one raised with the erroneous notion that all cats are untrainable individualists with wills of their own.'' The amount of time you spend training your cat will depend on its personality and your inclinations, for example, whether you want to teach it not to climb on furniture. Assume that you will spend a few minutes every day for the first few months training your new cat.

Cats need a *clean litter box*. At least once a day, the litter needs to be cleaned with a scoop, a procedure that takes a moment or two. The box should be emptied and thoroughly washed once a week, then refilled with clean litter. This takes about fifteen minutes.

SHEDS OR SMELLS? Despite daily self-cleaning, cats do shed, year-round, usually moderately. How much your cat sheds depends on its coat. The more you comb or brush your cat, the less hair it will leave on furniture and carpets.

I have never met a cat that smelled, unless it was sick, had just eaten fish, or had very bad dental problems. A litter box should not smell (or smell very little) *if* it is cleaned daily and if enough litter is used.

CHARACTERISTICS AFFECTING CHILDREN. Children have no pre-wired knowledge of what to do with a cat— and a cat, with its small size, delicate grace, and waving tail, is an extremely inviting object. Can I bounce this like a ball? Can I grab it like a toy? Children need to have answers to these questions before they experiment on the cat. A full-grown cat, after all, weighs only about ten pounds. A kick or a swat can cause real damage.

Kittens are even more fragile and can easily be injured. Even if there is no permanent physical injury, a cat or kitten that is roughly treated is likely to become withdrawn or fearful and more likely to lash out at a child who chases or grabs it.

The swipe of a cat's paw, if the claws are extended, can

be painful and frightening. A bite is even more painful and can easily become infected. Parents must teach their children how to interact with a cat so that these injuries can be avoided.

PERSONALITY TRAITS. As writer Mary Bly commented, ''Dogs come when they are called; cats take a message and get back to you.'' Most cats are not going to roll on their backs for you, let you rub their stomach, shake your hand, or fetch a ball. Cats are playful, but they don't necessarily want to play when you do. They are sensitive and intelligent; they like to observe the world and usually like to explore it, too.

Individual personalities vary, depending on inherited tendencies and environment. Some cats are friendly, people oriented, and affectionate. Others are shy. Some have high energy levels and are active, vocal, and inquisitive. Others are quiet and calm. Some cats like being handled by adults and children, and some don't much like it. Some cats are great lap sitters, and others are not.

NEED FOR PARENTAL SUPERVISION. *Catherine's four-year-old son, Malcolm, was active and curious, given to chasing the cat, cornering him, and grabbing his tail or any other convenient handle. More than once, Malcolm ended up scratched and crying. Catherine punished the cat when this happened and finally had it declawed.*

Quick movements and loud noises startle cats. Being chased frightens them. Being cornered forces them to defend themselves, as they can no longer take the preferred option, which is escape. All of this is cat nature, not bad behavior.

By punishing the cat for normal, predictable behavior, Catherine gave Malcolm permission to tease and hurt it and did nothing to help her son understand, appreciate, or enjoy this pet. Ironically, she also had created a situation where Malcolm is more likely to be bitten, because the cat no longer can defend himself with its paws.

A better option would have been for Catherine to put the cat in a separate room when she could not be present to supervise her son. Infants, toddlers, and children up to the age of six should not be left alone with kittens and cats. They simply don't know when they are hugging too hard and can't always restrain themselves from chasing or grabbing this fascinating animal.

Child's Age and Care of Cat

A child's mental, emotional, and physical development are very individualized. Evaluate what tasks your child can reasonably be expected to perform and what chores she is likely to have time to do. The guidelines I suggest are only guidelines. Use your knowledge of your child and common sense to decide what chores best fit her, and remember that you will have to teach her what to do.

Children **age three to five** can help an adult put away cat food and can fill a water bowl. Give your child a plastic container with a small mouth, filled with cold water, and have her empty it into the cat's bowl. Under your supervision, she can play with the cat.

Children **age five to seven** also can wash the food and water bowls and pour pre-measured dry food into the bowl.

Children **age seven to ten** also can measure and pour dry food, or open a pop-top can and spoon out canned food. Many children this age can exercise the cat by playing with it without supervision.

Children **age ten to twelve** also can scoop the litter box daily and exercise the cat by playing with it.

Children **twelve and up** also can wash out the litter box, change the litter, and groom the cat (but should not clip nails).

Your Family's Pet Resources

Inventory your resources to see if they enable your family to keep a cat.

TIME. Which family member(s) will feed and play with the cat and scoop the litter box daily? Who will groom the cat, change the litter, and wash the box once a week? Who will take the cat to the veterinarian for an annual checkup?

COST. Are you prepared to spend at least $300–$500 a year, for fifteen years or more, to care for a cat? Can you afford a veterinary emergency?

ABILITY. Are your children old enough to help with any of the chores? To "let a sleeping cat lie"?

PLACE AND SPACE. Do you have enough indoor space to place a litter box in an accessible, relatively quiet spot? Is there at least one window that a cat can see out of? Are there legal restrictions against keeping a cat in your home?

HEALTH. Is anyone in your family allergic to cats? How about regular visitors such as a nanny, housekeeper, or grandparent?

TRAVEL. Who will care for the cat when the family travels? If necessary, can you afford to board it?

HOUSEKEEPING. Will spillage or odor from a litter box bother you? What about cat hair on the furniture or carpets?

SPECIAL ISSUES. Do you expect to be moving soon? Can the cat go with you? Do you have other pets, such as a bird or dog, that might have trouble getting along with a cat, and how will you handle that?

In *A Cat is Watching*, animal expert Roger Caras muses, "Cats are a tonic, they are a laugh, they are a cuddle, they are at least pretty just about all of the time and beautiful some of the time. They are demanding, and they are also giving for people who are accepting."

Where to Get a Cat or Kitten

One night during a Chicago winter many years ago, I was walking my collie pup near a small park. It was snowing, and the air was terribly cold. One of the weirdest sounds I had ever heard came from a dark alley. I wanted to hurry on, but my collie insisted on investigating. I was hesitant, but we started down the alley. The sound was coming from a tiny bundle of fur. I thought it was a rat and jumped back. But my collie persevered, and eventually I followed him—to a calico kitten.

Crying loudly, she let me pick her up, and we took her home. Her nose was frostbitten, and her body was wet and trembling.

I called her Kittino, later shortened to Tino. The vet said that she would be fine, although her nose always bore a small dark scar from the frostbite. When she was old enough, she had her vaccinations and was spayed. She was never sick a day in her life, until she developed terminal cancer at age nineteen. She was an incredibly trusting, loving, and lovable cat.

There are many homeless cats in the world. One of them may cross your path some day. Don't assume that because it is a stray, it is sick, dangerous, or unlikely to be a good addition to your family. Polar Bear, one of the most famous cats in the world, found author and animal activist Cleveland Amory on a cold New York City night. Polar Bear became the subject of a series of delightful, best-selling books, *The Cat Who Came for Christmas*, *The Cat and the Curmudgeon*, and *The Best Cat Ever*.

If you find a stray cat, try to find the owners by posting signs in the neighborhood, checking the "lost" column in the newspaper ads and placing a "found" ad (most papers do this for free), and notifying the local animal shelter. Hold back enough information so that callers will have to describe to you some identifying features. This way, you can be certain that you are returning the cat to the real owner.

If no owner is found, if your family is ready for a cat, and this seems to be the right one for you—well, your search has ended before it began. You will have joined the majority of cat owners who were adopted by their cat, rather than the other way around. Take the cat to a veterinarian for a thorough examination, buy your cat books and equipment, and enjoy.

In addition to the cat or kitten that might find your family (and this happens more often than you might think), there are three places to get a cat or kitten: rescue group, animal shelter, breeder. *Do not* buy a kitten from a pet shop, no matter how adorable it is. Reputable breeders do not sell to pet stores. Any kitten you buy in a pet store will be overpriced; far better to save the life of a cat or kitten that you find in a shelter and use the money you save to buy equipment or veterinary care.

A **cat rescue organization** is a private group that provides care to homeless, surrendered, or abandoned cats and kittens until permanent homes are found. In some groups, volunteers provide foster homes, and in others shelters are maintained where cats are kept in cages. A few organizations are fortunate to have enough funding to hire staff, while many are run by volunteers.

These are dedicated cat lovers. They are generous with their time and energy, and they work hard to raise funds to buy food and veterinary care for their charges. They carefully try to match the right feline with the right family, as they want to avoid "returns." They will interview you, not only to make certain that you have the resources to keep a cat but also to help them find the right cat for your family. They may ask to meet your entire family and may want to make a ''home visit'' as well. They require that all cats or kittens that they place be sterilized and charge modest fees to partially cover the cost of these procedures.

To find a cat rescue organization, ask your local humane society or a veterinarian for a reference. Local vets may also know about kittens or cats that need homes. Avoid patronizing an organization that is not recommended by a professional such as your vet.

Local **animal shelters** are, unfortunately, overflowing with healthy cats and kittens needing homes. Shelters are government-funded, privately funded, or both; their quality and size vary from state to state and within states. Despite tight budgets, many are staffed by well-trained, dedicated professionals who are anxious to match your family with the right cat. Usually they will interview you or ask you to fill out a questionnaire. Shelters require that kittens and cats be sterilized and typically charge $35–$55 to help defray expenses.

Although some cats are surrendered to shelters because of behavior problems, many are there for other reasons: The owner has died, is moving abroad, or no longer has the time or money to care properly for the pet. Approximately half of all kittens are surrendered because of an unwanted litter. Adult cats as well as kittens obtained from shelters can make wonderful family pets.

If you want to buy a purebred kitten, look for a reputable **breeder**. You can meet (and begin to evaluate) breeders at a cat show, or obtain lists of breeders from cat clubs and magazines.

Buy only from an established breeder, not a backyard amateur. How can you tell the difference? Good breeders are motivated by love of cats, mostly for the particular breed in which they specialize. They would like to make money, or at least break even, but will put devotion to the breed above profit. A good breeder:

- runs a clean facility
- wants to know about your family, your home, why you want a cat, and how you plan to care for it
- provides a health guarantee
- will not sell you a kitten that is less than eight to twelve weeks old
- provides you with advice and information
- can answer your questions with authority and first-hand experience
- screens for genetic defects and provides written proof of screening
- requires you to spay or neuter kittens intended to be pets
- provides references and a written contract
- breeds just a few litters a year
- wants the kitten back if you decide not to keep it
- will not sell you a kitten if you plan to keep it outdoors

A purebred kitten can cost up to $500 (or more, if it is "show quality"), depending on the popularity of the breed and its availability in the area where you live.

Questions That Parents Ask

What is the best kind of cat to get for a family with children? One that is healthy, friendly, and comfortable around children (some cats definitely seem to prefer adults). The kitten or cat you pick out should be alert and have bright eyes, a glossy coat, and a nose free of discharge. A friendly kitten or cat will not cower away from you, try to hide, or hiss when you pick it up.

Do purebred cats make better pets? Writing in *Cats USA*, Patricia Jacobberger explains that, "A purebred kitten is bred from known pedigreed parentage to conform to a written standard that describes what the ideal example of that breed should look like." There are about forty recognized cat breeds in America, and they make up less than 5 percent of all cats in this country.

A purebred is not necessarily smarter, healthier, or easier to care for than any other cat. What a purebred kitten offers is predictability of appearance. Although individuals within a breed and within a single litter have different personalities, there is some predictability in that area, as well. The popular Persian, for example, is generally sweet, affectionate, and quiet, while a Siamese is more likely to be vocal and active but also affectionate

Do cats and kids really get along? Many children develop strong affection for cats, and vice versa. Infants and toddlers usually cannot handle these pets with the gentleness and restraint needed; parental supervision is important when these youngsters are around cats and kittens.

Isn't a kitten better for a child than a cat? Not necessarily. Kittens are cute and playful but also energetic and inquisitive; they require more monitoring, care, and attention than older cats. An adult cat can make a loving addition to a family and become very attached to a child.

The ASPCA and many cat rescue groups and shelters do not believe that kittens and young children mix. Some shelters will not adopt out young kittens to children under the age of six or seven. This is for the protection of both the child and the kitten. Kittens have sharp, needlelike milk teeth and use them to explore, play, and even express affection. Kittens less than twelve to sixteen weeks old don't seem to understand about retractable claws and become "Velcro kitties" that want to climb up a bare human leg, with claws out. The kitten means no harm, but this can be a painful experience for a child.

An older, calmer cat, especially one that is used to living in a family with children, may be a better choice than a kitten if your children are under seven years of age. Most cats adjust to a new home without much difficulty, and a cat that is used to living with children will probably bond easily with your child.

Will a male or female cat make a better pet for a

child? As long as it is altered, either a male or a female makes a good pet.

It is frequently said that a dog is the best pet for a boy, while a cat is best for a girl. Why is this so? Actually, it isn't so at all. I have known athletic, active boys and quiet, introspective boys who loved their pet cat. I have known shy girls who loved a pet dog just as much as did extroverted, sports-loving girls. My own son is now nine years old. He is athletic, active, and gregarious. He loves and plays with each of our four pets—two dogs, two cats— in a different way. When I asked him which animal was his favorite, he answered me with some indignation, "I love them all the same amount!"

It is true that some cats are so jealous of a newborn baby that they will actually try to smother it? No. This is an old wives' tale. But cats who like warm, cuddly places to sleep may join baby in the crib—not always a happy development for new parents. If your cat snuggles very close to an infant who is too young to move away or push the cat away, it is best to keep them separated until the child is older.

What about stories about cats attacking babies? Cats can become anxious when a new baby arrives. Such a momentous change places stress on everyone, including the family cat. Usually, the cat gets less attention, and its routines—and those of the entire household—go out the window. Reactions range from begging for attention to urinating outside the litter box but seldom include attacks on people. An understanding owner can calm and reassure the cat by seeing that it gets enough attention, and help it get back on track by returning to, or establishing new, routines before the baby arrives.

Can a child be taught to be fully responsible for the care of a cat? Do not get a cat or kitten with the assumption that your child will take care of this pet. No matter how mature and responsible he or she may be, you must factor yourself in, at least as a supervisor and pinch-hitter. A child's age and personality, schoolwork, and extracurricular activities will determine how much help you have to provide.

We have heard that it is good for a female to have "just one litter" before being spayed. Should we do this? Your female cat will not benefit, either in terms of health or personality, from having a litter, but you will be responsible for finding homes for her kittens and also for adding to the cat overpopulation problem.

Will our children benefit from watching our female cat give birth? Veterinarians and animal welfare groups unanimously urge owners to sterilize cats and kittens. With millions of unwanted cats and kittens being euthanized every year, the best lesson you can teach your children about cat reproduction is: "The kindest way is to neuter and spay." There are excellent books and videos, appropriate for children, to teach them about animal reproduction.

Doesn't sterilization make cats fat and change their personalities? Overeating and lack of exercise produce obesity in cats, just as in human beings.

As to personality: Cats that are *not* spayed or neutered are *very* difficult pets. An unneutered male cat will spray a foul-smelling combination of urine and other secretions on your furniture and is more prone than a neutered male to fight and to develop health and behavior problems. An unspayed female in heat will be uncomfortable and grumpy, yowl loudly, stain your furniture and rugs, and be more susceptible to mammary tumors and other serious health problems. Altered kittens grow into healthier, better-behaved cats.

My daughter desperately wants a cat, but my wife is allergic to them. What if we keep the cat in my daughter's bedroom? You will almost certainly end up with a neurotic, unhappy, and possibly destructive cat that won't be much fun as a pet. Cats are curious, active, intelligent creatures that need company, diversion, and stimulation. It is not a good idea to restrict a cat to one room, thereby limiting the amount of attention it receives. Besides, the cat will probably manage to escape its confinement.

Twice as many people are allergic to cats as to dogs, and 30 percent of cat owners are allergic to their own pets. You do have a number of options, which your wife can discuss with her physician.

Most people who are allergic to cats are allergic to a protein found in cat skin and saliva. Presumably, your wife can easily avoid being licked by the cat and can also avoid picking it up. You or your daughter should groom the cat frequently, preferably outdoors, so that as much dead skin as possible is shed outside the home. Keep the cat out of your bedroom at all times. Use a freestanding HEPA (high-efficiency particulate air) filter in as many rooms as possible and a HEPA vacuum cleaner. If your wife is willing, she might consider immunotherapy, a series of shots to decrease sensitivity to particular allergens. A new vaccine for people with cat allergies has recently been developed and is currently being tested.

A last resort is to try to interest your daughter in a non-fur-bearing type of pet.

Isn't there some health threat that cats pose to newborn babies? The threat is to babies in utero in the first trimester, and it comes from toxoplasmosis, a disease that is spread to human beings by an organism that is sometimes found in cat feces, as well as in garden soil and raw meat. If a pregnant woman contracts this disease during the first trimester of pregnancy, the fetus can be damaged.

A pregnant woman who owns cats should be tested for toxoplasmosis, to find out if she is immune. Her pet cats should also be tested for the disease. In any case, a pregnant woman should not clean the litter box, and someone should change the litter every other day. It is not necessary for a pregnant woman to get rid of pet cats: Many women are immune, most cats (especially indoor cats) don't have the disease, and the expectant mother can take precautions to avoid coming into contact with the disease-carrying organism (precautions that include wearing rubber gloves to garden and not eating undercooked meat—good habits for everyone).

Should cats be declawed so that they can't hurt children? In *The New Natural Cat: A Complete Guide for Finicky Owners*, Anitra Frazier explains, "Declawed cats are not good to have around children. They are less secure in their own abilities to escape and will be more likely to bite. Cats with all their claws intact are by far the gentlest and safest companions for young children."

Declawing is not a benign procedure. It involves placing the cat under general anesthesia and surgically amputating the last joints of its front toes, which are then bandaged to prevent hemorrhage. After the anesthetic wears off, the cat experiences pain for some time, especially when it walks. Many shelters refuse to adopt out cats or kittens to owners who plan to declaw them. (In England, declawing is illegal because it is considered inhumane.)

More people declaw pet cats to prevent damage to their furniture rather than to protect their children. Both situations have better solutions. Unless a cat is being chased, hit, teased, or otherwise frightened or abused, there is very little reason for it to hurt your child; most cats, if they don't like what's happening, walk or run away. The best approach is to supervise your child carefully and teach him or her how not to harm, frighten, or annoy the cat.

To prevent your upholstery from being shredded, you can: keep your cat's claws clipped; provide one or more scratching posts, laced with a bit of catnip to make them enticing; teach your cat not to scratch upholstery by covering (temporarily) its favorite objects with aluminum foil, bubble wrap, tape, or contact paper (sticky side up), or other materials that it doesn't like; ask your vet about nail caps, which cover the claws (but last only about six weeks).

If you feel you absolutely cannot live with a cat that has claws, adopt one that has already been declawed.

It is better to get one cat or two? The answer depends on your inclination and resources. Your veterinary and cat food bills will double. You will need to clean the litter box more often (and perhaps find room for a second box), and spend more time grooming and exercising your feline pets. On the other hand, two cats or kittens will keep each other company when no one else is home to entertain them.

Resources

CAT CLUBS

American Association of Cat
Enthusiasts
PO Box 213
Pine Brook, NJ 07058
(201) 335-6717

American Cat Association
8101 Katherine Avenue
Panorama City, CA 91402
(818) 781-5656

American Cat Fanciers
Association
PO Box 203
Point Lookout, MO 65726
(417) 334-5430

Canadian Cat Association
83 Kennedy Road, Unit 1806
Brampton, Ontario
Canada L6W 3P3

Cat Fanciers' Association
1805 Atlantic Avenue
PO Box 1005
Manasquan, NJ 08736
(908) 528-9797

Cat Fanciers' Federation
Juanita Vorhees
PO Box 661
Gratis, OH 45330
(513) 787-9009

Happy Household Pet Cat
Club
Lois Evers
PO Box 334
Rome, NY 13440

The International Cat
Association
PO Box 2684
Harlingen, TX 78551
(210) 428-8046

TO LOCATE A VETERINARIAN
American Animal Hospital Association
PO Box 150899
Denver, CO 80215-0899
(800) 252-2242

BOOKS FOR ADULTS

Caras, Roger. *A Cat is Watching: A Look at the Way Cats See Us*. New York: Simon & Schuster, 1989.

Frazier, Anitra, with Norma Eckroate. *The New Natural Cat: A Complete Guide for Finicky Owners*. New York: Penguin, 1990.

Jankowski, Connie. *Adopting Cats and Kittens: A Care and Training Guide*. New York: Macmillan, 1993.

Johnson, Pam. *Cat Love: Understanding the Needs and Nature of Your Cat*. Pownal, VT: Garden Way, 1990.

Kilcommons, Brian, and Sarah Wilson. *Good Owners, Great Cats: A Guidebook for Humans and Their Feline Companions*. New York: Warner Books, 1995.

Morris, Desmond. *Catwatching: Why Cats Purr and Everything Else You Ever Wanted to Know*. New York: Crown, 1986.

Sandler, Anna. *The Longhaired Cat: An Owner's Guide to a Happy Healthy Pet*. New York: Howell Book House, 1996.

Siegal, Mordecai. *The Good Cat Book*. New York: Simon & Schuster, 1981.

NONFICTION FOR CHILDREN

Evans, Mark. *ASPCA Pet Care Guide for Kids: Kitten*. New York: DK Publishing, 1993.

Olson, Karla. *My First Kitten*. Kansas City, MO: Andrews & McMeel, 1994.

O'Neill, Amanda. *Cats*. New York: Kingfisher, 1998.

Ryden, Hope. *Your Cat's Wild Cousins*. New York: Dutton, 1991.

FICTION FOR CHILDREN

Armstrong, Jennifer. *Chin Yu Min & the Ginger Cat*. New York: Crown, 1993.

Samuels, Barbara. *Duncan and Delores*. New York: Macmillan, 1989. Ages 4–7.

PART THREE

Children and Small, Furry Pets

SEVEN

Small, Furry Pets: Overview

"Mention the word *pet,* and most people think of cats and dogs," comments Susan Wiener, who provides a foster home to as many as twenty assorted rabbits and guinea pigs at a time. But if you live in an apartment, if your family doesn't have time to exercise a dog, or if you are allergic to cats, then a rabbit, guinea pig, or gerbils might be just the right pet for your family. "Most small children love small animals," Wiener wrote in a recent article, but she cautions that, "Surprisingly, . . . smaller creatures may not be the best choice for very young children. They are more delicate and less resilient than a cat or a dog and must be handled with care. However, they make wonderful pets for older children and adults."

These little creatures are increasingly popular. Americans own about 4 million rabbits; 3.5 million hamsters; 2 million guinea pigs; and roughly 2 million rats, mice, and gerbils. These small, furry animals are smarter, and have more personality, than most people realize. They are quiet and gentle. Children love watching, holding, and playing with them. Once you have the proper equipment, they are not expensive to care for, although they do require daily attention.

Each of these animals has distinct characteristics and

Small, Furry Pets
Facts At a Glance

ANIMAL	SIZE	LIFE SPAN (years)	HOW MANY TO GET	HABITAT
Gerbil	2–4 ounces	3–4	2 or more*	Cage or tank
Guinea pig	1–3 pounds	6–8	1 or 2**	Cage
Hamster	3–4 ounces	2–3	1	Cage or tank
Mouse	1–3 ounces	2–3	2 or more*	Cage or tank
Rabbit	2–20 pounds	6–10	1 or 2**	Cage
Rat	10–16 ounces	2–4	2 or more*	Cage or tank

*Seek expert advice about gender combinations; do not overcrowd habitat.
**Require more human attention if kept alone.

needs. Before you decide that one of these is the ideal pet for your family, learn how they are similar and how they are different. Here are some important, common traits:

Rabbits, guinea pigs, gerbils, hamsters, rats, and mice all live in a confined space. This is a defining feature of their existence and of the care they need. As Susan Ginsburg put it in ''Choosing a Pet for Your Child'', ''Life in a cage may be safer than in the great outdoors, but that advantage is diminished by the stress of being a captive in an unnatural environment, so the larger the housing, the better.'' A larger enclosure costs more, but it's worth it. A cage for a guinea pig that costs $60 translates into about 3¢ a day for a guinea pig that lives six years; a large cage, for $100, translates into 5¢ a day. Those extra pennies won't buy you a pack of gum a week, but they will double your pet's living space and joie de vivre.

Because your pet cannot leave the habitat you create for it, it's up to you to make it safe, healthy, and stimulating. Temperatures that are too hot or too cold can be fatal. Cages or tanks (also referred to as aquariums) that are allowed to become damp or dirty cause disease and infections that also can be fatal.

These pets need company. With the notable exception of the golden hamster, these are sociable animals. Their undomesticated ancestors functioned and survived in family groups or larger colonies.

When putting pets together, be careful about over-crowding and of gender combinations; for example, two unrelated adult, male gerbils will fight. Gather expert advice once you have decided on a particular type of pet and then decide how many and what gender. Do not attempt to mix one species with another; putting pet rats and mice together in the same cage will result in fighting and death. Other types of pets—a guinea pig or rabbit—can live alone if the humans in your family serve as that pet's colony, providing lots of daily attention.

Confined pets are easy to overlook. Unlike a dog or cat, they cannot rub up against you, wake you up at night, or grab your ankles to demand attention. Whether you have a single pet or a colony, put the cage or tank where the action is: the family room, living room, even the kitchen if it is large enough and a safe spot can be found. Your pets will get more attention, and your family's comings and goings will serve as entertainment—just think of your family as your pet's favorite live TV show. (Hamsters are the exception. Because they need to sleep during the day, put the hamster habitat away from areas of high daytime traffic.)

Most of us have witnessed the abnormal behavior of zoo animals confined in small cages of concrete and metal bars: Constant pacing is the most obvious example. These animals are stressed by the absence of normal habitat, exercise, stimulation, and interaction with their own kind. Some zoos are trying to improve their lot by providing larger, more natural environments. A confined pet in the home is in a similar situation: It lives in a limited, unnatural environment. When it is ignored, it becomes stressed, and stress can lead to behavioral and health problems.

These pets need exercise. They need to be taken out of their enclosure to exercise and interact with your family. They cannot be trained not to chew and explore, so they require close supervision, another enclosure (such as a playpen or indoor pet yard), and/or a fully petproof room to move around in. Carol Himsel, a veterinarian who treats small pets, has written a list of possible hazards to pet rats if left to roam outside their enclosure. Her list is equally applicable to other pet rodents and rabbits; to petproof a room or area, make certain that you can guard against these hazards:

- drafts
- excessive sunlight
- other aggressive pets
- falling from heights
- falling objects
- open doors and windows
- electrical cords and outlets
- cleaning agents and other chemicals
- drugs in the medicine cabinet
- pesticides and herbicides
- alcoholic beverages
- caffeine
- recliners and convertible furniture
- trapping inside clothes dryers, refrigerators
- mousetraps
- sharp objects in trash
- rancid garbage
- automobile exhaust fumes
- unventilated cars on hot days
- plastic bags
- being stepped on
- swinging doors
- toilets, other containers with water
- wood stoves and fireplaces
- portable heaters
- some houseplants (e.g., philodendrons)

These pets need to gnaw. Guinea pigs, gerbils, hamsters, mice, and rats are rodents. The word *rodent* comes from the Latin word *rodere*, which means "to gnaw." These animals have two pairs of front teeth, upper and lower, called incisors, that grow continuously throughout their lives. Rabbits are not rodents, and they have one, rather than two, pair of incisors. But, like rodents, they need to chew, or their incisors will grow too long. Overgrown teeth can cause serious health problems for all of these pets.

Commercial chew blocks can be purchased, or homemade from cardboard. For some species, nuts and firm vegetables such as carrots help teeth wear down.

These pets may need veterinary care. *Jeff, a second grader, mistakenly picked his gerbil up by the tail, which broke off and bled profusely. Ross's rabbit jumped off a table, where he should not have been, injuring a back leg. Benita's hamster wandered into the moving blades of a fan, which should have been off limits. A guinea pig whose feet were infected was turned in to a rescue organization; the bottom of his cage was filthy. In each of these situations, veterinary care saved the pet's life.*

Small animals can get sick or hurt and need veterinary care. Finding a veterinarian experienced in treating these pets is more difficult than finding a dog or cat vet, because fewer veterinarians are trained in these specialties. Unfortunately, there is no national or regional veterinary directory of specialists; you will need to find one on your own. Check the Yellow Pages and ask animal shelter employees, fellow pet owners, local breeders, veterinarians, and rescue clubs (such as the House Rabbit Society, or a hamster or guinea pig rescue organization) for recommendations. When you find a prospective vet, call and ask questions about his or her specialization. Ask what courses, training, and experience he or she has in treating your type of pet.

Most shelters and rescue groups arrange for veterinary care and "well-pet" examinations before they adopt out a pet. If you acquire your pet from another source, take it for a checkup within a few days of bringing it home. This gives you an opportunity to establish a relationship with your veterinarian and ask questions. If there is something seriously wrong with your new pet's health, you might need to return it before your children become attached to it. Unlike dogs and cats, these small animals do not require periodic vaccinations, but veterinarians who specialize in treating these pets usually recommend a yearly checkup.

Some first-time owners are surprised to learn that their gerbil, rabbit, or hamster can get sick, and many are unaware that these small animals can be effectively treated. Some owners believe that such a small animal should not have money spent on it for veterinary care. Indeed, as shelter workers attest, some owners discard a small pet just *because* it has gotten sick or been injured. Yet these pets, like all others, deserve to be cared for. Ironically, their illnesses and injuries are often the result of improper care that easily can be avoided: dehydration due to lack of water or overexposure to heat, malnutrition due to poor diet, chills and respiratory problems from exposure to drafts, overgrown teeth because of the lack of gnawing materials. If one of these animals does show signs of illness—listlessness, loss of hair, diarrhea, refusal to eat, runny nose— quick veterinary attention is essential because illnesses can be fatal within a day or two.

A child's love for an animal is not dependent on its size or its purchase price. A hamster acquired for nothing can be as cherished as an expensive, purebred dog. Discarding or ignoring an ailing pet signals to a child who loves it that his or her feelings, and this pet's life, are not worth much.

Because treating these small animals is a specialty, veterinary costs may be higher than for dogs and cats. Families that are financially pressed can contact a local shelter or rescue group for advice. Some veterinary clinics provide low-cost services or are willing to arrange for stretched-out payments.

Some people are allergic to these pets, or to their litter. "Allergies" is one of the most common reasons listed on the "give up sheet" filled in by owners who relinquish these pets at shelters. Some parents choose these pets because they hope that a family member who is allergic to dogs or cats can tolerate a small pet kept in a confined space. It is true that a small animal has less fur and dander, because of its size, and without the run of the house it does not rub or drop fur and dander on carpets, upholstery, walls, and drapes. But animal allergens easily become airborne, later landing on furniture and carpets.

Keeping these pets confined twenty-four hours a day, 365 days a year is not an effective defense against airborne allergens, and it is cruel to the animal. A child who is never allowed to pat or play with a pet will not form much of a bond or have much fun with it and will lose interest, while the pet will be timid, unaffectionate, more likely to bite, and just plain sad.

An individual's exposure to airborne allergens can be controlled somewhat. A small pet's exercise can be confined to a single room, preferably one with a washable floor and no upholstered furniture. The allergic family member should not be assigned the task of cleaning the enclosure, nor should the pet be kept in the allergic person's bedroom. If your resources permit it, a High Efficiency Particle Arresting (HEPA) air cleaner can be used, and a HEPA vacuum cleaner will help to remove allergen particles from carpets and floors.

Some people are allergic to one or more types of litter (also referred to as substrate) used in cages (or to the dust it generates), or to the hay that some of these pets need for a proper diet. Since allergies often are multiple, discuss these possibilities with an allergist.

Let your doctor be your guide. Remember that some allergies take a while to build up. Your child may become enchanted with a friend's pet hamster and insist that she has no symptoms after patting it. But the outcome may be different after a week or a month if the hamster lives in your home.

Where to Get a Small, Furry Pet

Animail, the newsletter of the Montgomery County, MD Humane Society, recently announced: "Fifteen guinea pigs! Twenty-seven gerbils, males and females together! Seven more guinea pigs—two pregnant! Eighteen more gerbils! Six more guinea pigs—five pregnant! FORTY-THREE Siberian hamsters! These groups of small animals have all come into the Shelter in recent months, reminding us again that overpopulation of pets is not confined to cats and dogs. Unfortunately, even some otherwise responsible owners who spay and neuter their feline and canine pets may carelessly allow their smaller animals to breed . . . and breed . . . and breed."

Although there are fewer pet rodents and rabbits in America than dogs and cats, they run some of the same risks. Overpopulation is one of them. A pair of fancy rats can deliver a litter of six to twelve pups every month, and so can gerbils. Owners who never planned to breed their pets end up with unwanted litters that a little planned unparenthood could prevent. Don't let your pets breed, unless you want to keep their progeny or have good homes lined up for them in advance—permanent homes where they will be well taken care of.

Loss of interest by children, resistance by a family member, unexpected reproduction, or improper care (resulting in a smelly cage or unfriendly pet) often leads to relinquishment. Before your family elects to get one of these pets, learn about its nature and its needs. Don't give your son a hamster if he really wants a dog. Don't believe it when people tell you that a guinea pig "takes no time," that a rabbit "doesn't cost a thing once you have the cage," or that gerbils "won't be any effort."

Many small pets are discarded, usually within months, because of unrealistic expectations about their behavior or care. The result is a large and growing population of small pets in need of homes. When parents ask me where to get a guinea pig, rabbit, hamster, or other small pet, I recommend the adoption option: re-homing a pet instead of buying a "new" one. By doing this, you save the life of a pet and save a little money into the bargain. With patience and persistence, you can adopt a healthy, lovable small pet. There are three places to find the small pet for you: animal shelter, rescue group, "private placement."

Many people do not realize that small animals are available for adoption through **animal shelters.** Some shelters receive many, others only a few. If, when you first visit or call your local shelter, the type of pet you want is not available, ask to be put on a waiting list or make a return visit.

Because shelters are for the most part locally funded, their resources, quality, size, and procedures vary. Some shelters require prospective owners to be interviewed or fill out a questionnaire. Some charge an adoption fee, and some charge nothing.

Many of these pets are surrendered when they are still young, after a few weeks or months with a family. They usually are given up because their owners have lost interest or because this isn't the pet that the family had in mind to begin with. Recently a guinea pig was surrendered at my local shelter because, as the mother explained, "The kids weren't taking good enough care of it since we got a dog." The guinea pig was only six months old. It is also common for a family to give up a mother and her litter soon after she has delivered, usually because they "never wanted this many," as one man said after dropping off a mother hamster and her ten tiny one-day-old pups.

Rescue groups provide care for small pets that have been surrendered by their owners. Typically, a group will care primarily for one species, but there is also some overlap. Frequently, the group works in cooperation with the local animal shelter.

Rescue groups are made up of volunteers who provide foster homes for surrendered pets and screen prospective adopters. These are knowledgeable people who do their best to match the right family with the right pet and can provide valuable guidance to new owners. They may adopt out for free, or charge a fee to help defray their expenses.

To find a rescue group in your area, ask local veterinarians, shelters, or small-pet owners for suggestions, and check the "Resources" listed at the end of each small pet chapter.

What I dub **"private placements"** are common in the small-pet world. Let people know that you are looking for a pet hamster or guinea pig and that you will provide a good home. Place notices in veterinary offices, your children's school newsletter, the local newspaper, and on bulletin boards. Word of mouth among children and parents may lead to a family whose gerbils have had babies. Often, at the end of the school year, teachers are looking for permanent homes for classroom pets such as guinea pigs and hamsters.

Although the process I have outlined might seem like a lot of work for a small animal, adoption—rather than a quick purchase at a pet shop—is a humane approach with an extra benefit. According to Susan Wiener and others who take care of unwanted guinea pigs, rabbits, hamsters, and other small pets, the most common mistake that families make is buying on the spur of the moment: The animal is inexpensive and small, and somehow the reality of its needs and life span doesn't have time to sink in. The result: a pet that is unwanted a few months later.

If you and your family invest time and effort searching for a small pet to re-home, you will have plenty of time for reflection. You will meet people who know a lot about these pets and who will give you sound advice. You will have time to prepare, and when you find the right animal, you will have the additional satisfaction of rescuing it from homelessness and, possibly, an untimely death. You might also save money by picking up some secondhand equipment at the same time.

If the adoption option doesn't work for you, look for a local breeder of the pet you are interested in. Do not buy from a breeder who wants to ship your pet to you; this practice is stressful for the animals and can result in illness, injury, and death.

It is better to choose and transport your own pet from a reputable local breeder or pet shop. This gives you the opportunity to evaluate the seller, to learn, and to select your family's pet. Both a pet shop and breeder facility should:

- look, smell, and be clean—including inside all animal habitats
- have uncrowded habitats
- have fresh food and clean water in habitats
- have animals that appear healthy and well cared for
- be staffed by people who care about the animals and the type of home you will give them, and willingly provide you with assistance and information

Veterinarians, pet owners, pet clubs, and rescue league and shelter personnel are often a good source of recommendations—or warnings—about local pet shops and breeders. Some shops and breeders develop a reputation for responsible small-pet handling; others develop a reputation for selling sick pets, misrepresenting a pet's age or sex, or giving incorrect information. Unfortunately, many pet shops do not give small mammals the care and attention they need. If you do buy your pet, try to buy it from a responsible seller, for the sake of the pet and your family.

How to Choose a Small, Furry Pet

Once you have decided on the type of pet you want, how do you choose an individual? Evaluating a small mammal's personality so that you can pick out a "friendly" rat or "cuddly" guinea pig is not always easy. Some small pets, such as hamsters and guinea pigs, are reticent until they get to know you. They may ignore you or shy away from you when you first reach for them.

Some guinea pigs become your best friend the day after you bring them home; others may take a week or two to warm up to you. Gerbils, rabbits, hamsters, mice, and rats usually need to get to know you before they respond to your voice, hop onto your hand (gerbils), snuggle in your lap (hamsters), or perch on your shoulder (rats). A good book will tell your child how to introduce himself to each of these pets and coach him through the first few days or weeks when he is teaching a new pet to trust him. The *House Rabbit Handbook* puts it this way: ''Adoptable rabbits come in all shapes. A successful adoption is not due to picking the bunny with the 'best' personality but rather to setting up an environment that brings out the best in the bunny you do bring home.'' When selecting more than one pet at a time—two or more gerbils, rats, mice, guinea pigs, or rabbits—seek expert advice about the best gender and relationship combinations. For example, with gerbils, it's usually recommended to select two young females or males from the same litter.

When selecting one of these pets, try to find a physically healthy one that:

- is active and alert
- is not too thin (unless there is a history of underfeeding)
- seems to be breathing normally (not wheezing or coughing)
- has bright, clear eyes with no discharge
- has no discharge from the nose
- has a full, shiny coat (without bald patches)
- has clean, dry ears
- does not have overgrown teeth
- does not have diarrhea (anal area appears dry, clean)

Once you have brought your small pet or pets home, be prepared for an adjustment period. Your care book should advise you how to tame your pet. Certainly patience will be one of the key ingredients—and one of the hardest for children. These small mammals are much closer, genetically and historically, to their wild ancestors than are dogs or cats. They need to learn to trust people or, if they have already been socialized, they need to get to know you and your family. Many public shelters warn adopters to give new pets at least thirty days to adjust to a new environment. Yet shelter workers from Texas to Massachussets tell stories of small pets returned within three or four days because they "weren't friendly enough."

Be guided by a reliable book or expert about when and how to try to tame, handle, and train your pet. Get expert advice about equipment and nutrition; remember that while these small species have much in common, they also have different physiological and psychological needs. Food or bedding that is right for one type of pet may not be right for another. If you get good advice and follow it, your family will be rewarded by the pleasure of having an affectionate, healthy, interesting pet.

EIGHT

Fancy Mice

"Don't even think about it!"

The woman spoke emphatically to two children, a boy and a girl, who looked about ten and twelve years old. After wandering the aisles of the Upper West Side pet store in Manhattan, the children had stopped, mesmerized, in front of a tank filled with half a dozen tiny, busy, white mice.

"We're not bringing those rats into our apartment, and that's that."

"They're not rats, Mom. They're mice. Look how little they are. They're really cute." The girl lifted the mesh lid off the tank and slipped her hand inside. Three mice immediately climbed into her palm.

"Get your hand out of there! You'll get germs. I don't care what they are. They're vermin. Rodents. Over my dead body. No way. We agreed on a hamster. End of discussion."

This mother obviously didn't realize that hamsters, like rats and mice, are rodents. Her misunderstanding, and her reaction, is not unusual, at least for adults. Children seem more open-minded when it comes to mice, expressing fascination rather than disgust or horror.

ORIGINS. The word *mouse* comes from an old Sanskrit word meaning "thief." The house mouse, descended from

Fancy Mice
Facts At a Glance

COST	$200–$300 for two over their lifetime
SIZE	2–3 ounces
LONGEVITY	2–3 years
TIME REQUIREMENT	30 minutes per day to feed, play with, spot-clean habitat; 10 minutes every other day to change litter; 30 minutes per week to wash habitat
SPACE	Habitat at least 1' × 2' for two (larger for more), placed away from drafts, direct light, noise
EXERCISE	Need climbing structure in habitat
EQUIPMENT	Cage or tank with lid, food bowl, hanging water bottle, bottle brush, nest box, toys, exercise equipment, chew blocks, litter, bedding
ODOR	Yes, unless litter and cage are kept clean
SHEDDING	Not noticeable
PHYSICAL CHARACTERISTICS AFFECTING KIDS	Very small and frisky, sometimes hard to handle; fragile, easily injured if dropped or squeezed; rarely bite, and bite usually is not painful
TEMPERAMENTAL CHARACTERISTICS AFFECTING KIDS	Playful, active, curious, sociable, need interaction with other mice
PERSONALITY TRAITS	Timid with people unless handled frequently, gently, quietly; can become friendly, trusting
PARENTAL SUPERVISION	Very young children (preschool) should not handle; young children should be supervised when handling
LEGAL RESTRICTIONS	Some species of mice are illegal to own as pets in some states and jurisdictions; some landlords prohibit all pets

wild field mice, attached itself to humans as long as eight thousand years ago, stealing food from storerooms, barns, and houses. Like their wild cousins in the *muridae* family (of which there are five hundred different species), house mice live in colonies and usually forage at night to escape human and other predators.

Humans usually regard the mouse as a pest but occasionally have considered it sacred and even worshiped it. A four-thousand-year-old Cretan temple honors these tiny creatures because, according to legend, they enabled Crete to win a crucial battle by chewing through the leather straps of the enemy army's shields. In ancient Egypt, white mice were considered good luck. During the Middle Ages, mice were used in numerous medicines, and more recently mice have been used extensively in scientific and medical research.

While people no doubt have caught and kept wild mice as pets for thousands of years, the mouse "fancy"—keeping mice as pets and selectively breeding for desired traits—began in the seventeenth century. The fancy became popular in Japan in the eighteenth century and in Europe in the nineteenth. In the United States, mice first became popular as pets in the 1950s.

Fancy mice have been bred for gentleness, friendliness, and appearance. Their hair may be short, long, curly, or frizzy. There is even a hairless mouse. Fancy mice display a great assortment of colors and patterns: beige, cinnamon, chocolate, pearl, cream, black, white, silver, spotted, tricolor, and others.

NEEDS. House mice live communally, usually in dark areas such as attics or basements, and search for food at night. They escape predators by running, climbing and hiding. The needs of their descendants, fancy mice, are dictated by this inheritance. Pet mice need a large enough habitat to allow them to exercise and toys or "furniture" such as ropes and ladders to climb. As communal animals, they need to live with at least one other of their own kind. As burrowing animals, they need an inch or so of substrate on the floor of their enclosure. As rodents, they need safe chewing materials.

A mouse habitat should include at least one snug hiding place and, if possible, an area of shaded or dim light. Loud noises and bright lights signal danger in the wild and can cause stress and panic in pet mice.

Mice are susceptible to respiratory problems if their habitat becomes damp or cold. Put their enclosure in an area with external temperatures in the range of 70° to 75° Fahrenheit and quickly remove wet bedding or leaking water bottles.

Mice need frequent, gentle handling to teach them to trust and socialize with human beings.

CHILDREN AND FANCY MICE. Fancy mice are wonderful pets to watch. One owner described them as being ''like a tankful of fish, but more fun because they are so busy and playful.'' Three or four mice in a large tank (twenty-gallon size or larger) equipped with a miniature gym of steps, ladders, planks, and trapezes will put on an entertaining show for children.

A mouse weighs about the same as a chicken egg and is only slightly less fragile. An excited child easily can injure it by squeezing too tightly. Because they are so delicate, mice are not good ''holding'' pets for children who cannot control their muscle coordination or understand the need for gentleness. Children who are old enough to handle these pets carefully and quietly—usually by age nine or ten—will be able to play with them.

COMMITMENT. Once you have acquired a habitat and play equipment, pet mice are inexpensive and easy to care for. They do require daily attention: fresh food and water; a warm, dry, clean cage, with proper substrate; and friendly handling.

What You Need to Know About Fancy Mice *Before* You Get One

SIZE. A fancy mouse weighs about one ounce.

LONGEVITY. Pet mice live two to three years, occasionally four.

LEGAL RESTRICTIONS. Most landlords accept small, confined pets, but some do not. In some states, the only pet mouse that is legal is the fancy mouse *(Mus musculus)*; other, more exotic species (deer mice, spiny mice, harvest mice, and others) may be illegal where you live.

COSTS. The care of three or four pet mice, barring veterinary emergencies, will be about $200–$300 over their lifetimes. The cost depends on prices in your region; the type of enclosure, litter, and food you choose; and the number of toys and other items you buy.

Food will cost about $1 a week. Commercial pellet diets or "lab blocks" provide the necessary nutrition. This can be supplemented with small amounts of fresh, washed fruits and vegetables.

Litter, which should be changed frequently, is another ongoing expense. The cost will vary from $1 to $2 a week, depending on the kind you use, whether you buy it in bulk, how large the enclosure, and how often you change it.

If they have not already had one, take your mice for a *veterinary checkup* soon after you bring them home, which will cost from $25 to $50 each. Set aside, either mentally or in fact, a *veterinary emergency fund* of $100 per animal.

Your *acquisition* costs will be small. Perhaps you will find baby mice for free. Or you can buy from a breeder or a pet store. Many pet mice—usually white ones—are used

Basic equipment includes:

• comprehensive book(s) about mouse care	$10–20
• cage, condo, or tank (20-gallon size or larger)	$30–50
• tank cover (depending on size)	$15–25
• nest or hide box	$0–6
• food bowl	$3
• hanging water bottle	$7–10
• bottle brush	$0–3
• chew blocks	$0–10 (annual)
• toys, exercise equipment	$0–20 (annual)
• rubber gloves (for spot cleaning)	$3
• carrier (optional)	$10–15

as "feeder" mice for reptiles; they also are sold as pets, usually for $1–$3.

Mice bred specifically for the "fancy" are more varied in appearance and more friendly, both because of selective breeding and because their breeder is likely to have handled them. Mice from a good breeder usually are less stressed and healthier than mice sold in pet stores and somewhat more expensive.

EQUIPMENT. The enclosure is the most important piece of equipment. Some mice fanciers prefer to use a cage, but it is not always easy to find a cage with mesh or bars close enough together. Cages provide better ventilation than tanks, but less protection from drafts. Large multilevel cages provide plenty of opportunity for climbing and games. Floors should be solid, not mesh or wire, or covered with Plexiglas or a similar material to prevent injury.

If you use a glass tank, select a large one, spacious enough for "furniture" and exercise. Cover the top with a tight-fitting mesh lid. Tanks are heavy, which make them harder to clean than cages. They also provide poor ventilation, allowing ammonia from waste products to build up; this can pose a health threat to the mice and create an unpleasant odor.

Follow the advice of your mouse care book about recommended litter, chewing, and nesting materials. Many items, including toys, a nest box, and nesting materials or bedding, can be homemade, and most mice enjoy an exercise wheel. Food bowls and sipper bottles are available at pet supply stores.

SPACE. A twenty-gallon tank is adequate, but bigger is better. Put the habitat away from drafts, direct sunlight, bright indoor lights, loud noises, and heating or air-conditioning vents.

TIME REQUIREMENT. *Feed* twice a day, on a regular schedule. Remove old food, wash the bowl, and put down fresh food. This takes about five minutes. Every other day, empty, clean, and refill the water bottle and provide a small amount of fruit or vegetables. These two tasks take about five minutes.

Mice groom themselves and each other and are fastidious about keeping themselves clean, but a family member will need to *clean the enclosure. Spot-clean* daily, wearing rubber gloves to pick up droppings (two or three minutes); *change litter* every other day (five to ten minutes); thoroughly *wash and dry* the enclosure and put down fresh litter once a week (twenty minutes).

If you want your mice to be "holding" pets, they need to be *played with*, at least once a day so that they will be people-oriented and friendly.

SHEDS OR SMELLS? Mice smell more than rats do, and male mice have a stronger odor than females. To avoid an unpleasant odor in your home, clean the cage thoroughly and often.

CHARACTERISTICS AFFECTING CHILDREN. Mice are frisky, active, playful, sociable, and acrobatic. They can be injured by rough handling. Children must be old enough to approach them calmly and to lift and hold them gently.

PERSONALITY TRAITS. Most fancy mice are friendly. Some are skittish; others are calm and laid back. Patience, gentleness, consistency, and kindness turn most mice into trusting pets.

NEED FOR PARENTAL SUPERVISION. Children under nine years old need supervision when handling mice. It is

---

Child's Age and Care of Fancy Mice

With parental supervision:

Children **age to three to five** can put food pellets in the bowl, put prewashed vegetables or fruit in the cage.

Children **age five to seven** also can hand-feed vegetables and treats, and help an adult wash vegetables, fruit, and bowl.

Children **age seven to ten** also can empty, clean, and refill water bottle, spot-clean cage (wearing rubber gloves), change litter.

Children **age ten to twelve** also can hold mice, help an adult cut up fruit or vegetables, wash cage or tank.

Children **twelve and up** can clean and wash enclosure and equipment.

better for these children to watch mice play than to try to hold them, because a wriggling, nervous mouse can escape or be grasped so hard that it is injured.

Your Family's Pet Resources

Inventory your resources to see if they enable your family to keep pet mice.

TIME. Which family members will feed and play with the mice and spot-clean the cage daily? Who will change the litter twice a week? Who will wash and clean the cage once a week?

COSTS. Your initial acquisition costs, including equipment and a veterinary checkup, will be at least $100. Can you afford this and an annual expenditure of up to $100 for two years?

ABILITY. Are your children old enough to play with these pets, and if not, will they be satisfied watching them play? Are your children old enough to help with any chores?

PLACE AND SPACE. Do you have room for a good-size enclosure? Can it be placed away from bright lights, loud noises, drafts, and direct heat and still be "where the action is"? Are there legal restrictions against keeping these pets in your home?

HEALTH. Does anyone in your family have allergies that may be triggered by these pets or their litter?

TRAVEL. Who will care for these pets when the family travels? Can you afford to pay someone to do this?

HOUSEKEEPING. Will spillage from a cage bother you? How about the smell?

SPECIAL ISSUES. Is anyone in your family afraid of mice or opposed to having them as pets? Will you take them with you if you move?

According to Betsy Sikora Siino in *You Want a What for a Pet?!*, "Mice are some of the tiniest pets you may have. They weigh almost nothing, and they are very adaptable, alert and fun to watch. In fact, many equate the keeping of mice with the keeping of fish in an aquarium. Keep several together in a large habitat, and they can provide hours of relaxing observation."

Questions That Parents Ask

Can a tiny animal like this be much of a pet? Both children and adults become very attached to these little creatures. With their soft fur, bright eyes, and front paws that they use like hands, fancy mice are beguiling and amusing. Depending on your child's age and abilities, he or she may be able to hold and carry these pets. A very young child may have to be content with being an observer; whether that is possible, you will have to decide.

Aren't mice smelly and dirty? Mice are fastidious about self-grooming and even groom each other. Male mice do give off a musky odor, and a mouse cage or tank will smell if not cleaned. A nontoxic, absorbent litter can help reduce odor.

Can children be bitten by mice? A mouse that is frightened by loud noises or quick movements, or by being squeezed too tightly, will bite in self-defense.

Can mice really get veterinary treatment when they are sick? Yes, if you find a veterinarian qualified to treat them.

My wife can't stand the thought of pet mice, but my daughter and I think it's a neat idea. Any suggestions? You could invite your wife to visit a breeder with you.

Maybe when she sees how cute and friendly fancy mice are, she will change her mind. If not, it's better to give up the plan for now and try to find a small pet that the three of you can all enjoy.

A friend whose mice have had babies wants to give us one. If we give it a lot of attention, it will be happy alone, won't it? Not really. No matter what your good intentions, it's not possible for you to be a twenty-four-hour-a-day companion. These pets are so small and inexpensive to keep, and so in need of companionship of one of their own kind, that it doesn't make sense not to get two. Seek expert advice about age and gender combinations before trying to introduce two strange mice to each other.

Is it okay to keep the habitat in our son's bedroom? He spends a lot of time there, playing, doing homework, and using the computer. Although willing to play during the day, mice are basically nocturnal and likely to be playing and making noise during the night. They may keep your son awake. If your son plays loud music or computer games, this can be stressful for mice.

Can we leave our mice at home for a few days while we go on vacation? You can leave your mice overnight, with a clean cage, plenty of fresh food and water, and dim lights, in a room with a stable, comfortable temperature. If you will be away longer, ask or pay someone to come into your home to clean the cage and provide food and water. Leave detailed, written instructions and emergency phone numbers.

Resources

American Fancy Rat & Mouse
Association
9230 64th Street
Riverside, CA 925509-5924

Rat & Mouse Club of
America
13075 Springdale Street
Suite 302
Westminster, CA 92683

Northeast Rat & Mouse Club
International
96 Liberty Road
Bernardsville, NJ 07924

BOOKS FOR ADULTS
Bielfeld, Horst. *Mice: A Complete Pet Owner's Manual*.
Hauppauge, NY: Barron's, 1985.

Randolph, Elizabeth. *Rabbits and Other Furry Pets*. New York:
Fawcett Crest, 1992.

Siino, Betsy Sikora. *You Want a What for a Pet?! A Guide to
12 "Alternative" Pets*. New York: Howell Book House,
1996.

NONFICTION FOR CHILDREN
Henrie, Fiona. *Mice and Rats: Junior Petkeeper's Library*. New
York: Franklin Watts, 1980.

Pope, Joyce. *Taking Care of Your Mice and Rats*. New York:
Franklin Watts, 1990.

FICTION FOR CHILDREN
Avi. *Poppy*. New York: Orchard Books, 1995.

Cleary, Beverly. *The Mouse and the Motorcycle*. New York:
Avon Books, 1965.

Steig, William. *Abel's Island*. New York: Farrar, Straus and
Giroux, 1976.

———. *Doctor DeSoto*. New York: Scholastic, 1982.

White, E. B. *Stuart Little*. New York: HarperCollins, 1945.

NINE

Fancy Rats

Best Friends Magazine recounts this folk tale: "Another well-known story is of a farmer who chased two rats out of his farmhouse and went after them with a club. He caught up with them walking side by side, quite slowly. Looking closer he saw they were holding a straw in their mouths. Then he realized that one of the rats was blind and the other was guiding his companion with the straw. The farmer went home and put away the club."

I don't know if the tale is true, but according to owners of pet rats, it could be. Rat expert Ginger Cardinal has written: "Rats have compassion for their fellow rats: Often a rat who is paired with another that has a disability, whether it is physical or mental, will be very kind to the other rat. Usually, help is offered with food, cleaning and general care. The first rat . . . seems to understand that the other rat is at a disadvantage."

Rats suffer from bad press. What could be worse than being blamed for the plague that decimated entire populations during the Middle Ages? In fact, fleas that infested black rats were the actual carriers of the disease, and fancy rats are descended from the Norway, or brown rat, not the black rat.

"I think of rats as miniature dogs," a veteran animal

Rats
Facts At a Glance

COST	$400–$600 for two over their lifetime
SIZE	10–16 ounces
LONGEVITY	2–4 years
TIME REQUIREMENT	30 minutes per day to spot-clean cage, feed, play with, exercise; 20 minutes every other day to change litter; 30 minutes weekly to wash cage
SPACE	Tank or cage, at least 2 square feet per pet, 9" high, placed away from drafts and direct sun
EXERCISE	Need to climb and exercise in enclosure; need to be exercised outside of enclosure daily
EQUIPMENT	Tank or cage, hanging water bottle, bottle brush, bedding, litter, food bowl, chew toys, hide box, play toys, exercise wheel
ODOR	Cage or tank will smell if not cleaned often
SHEDDING	Not noticeable
PHYSICAL CHARACTERISTICS AFFECTING KIDS	Small, can be difficult to hold if active; fragile; can easily be injured if squeezed; rarely bite
TEMPERAMENTAL CHARACTERISTICS AFFECTING KIDS	Gentle, sociable, playful, curious, intelligent, active; need interaction with other rats and stimulation
PERSONALITY TRAITS	Usually friendly, trusting, playful; trainable if handled gently and often
PARENTAL SUPERVISION	Young children should be supervised when handling
LEGAL RESTRICTIONS	Some landlords prohibit all pets

shelter employee told me. "They are smart, trainable and friendly, and become attached to you. But they are a lot less work, on a daily basis."

"Of all my clients, those with pet rats seem the most dedicated to their pets," said a veterinarian in Boston.

Contrary to popular beliefs, rats are affectionate, clean, and less likely than dogs to transmit disease. Debbie Ducommon described them in *Critters USA* as "social butterflies that love to be with people and beg to come out of their cages to play or be petted. Rats are smart enough to play games with their owners such as tag, hide-and-seek, tug-of-war and peek-a-boo."

ORIGINS. Rats probably originated in Southeast Asia. By the Middle Ages, they had reached Europe by traveling aboard ships, and a few centuries later they reached North America the same way. Domestic rats were bred from Norway rats as early as the seventeenth century and used extensively in scientific and medical research beginning in the nineteenth century.

Fancy rats have been selectively bred for intelligence, gentleness, and appearance. They come in a multitude of coats: twenty-eight different colors and seven different patterns, at last count. Colors range from basic white, black, beige, brown, and agouti to exotic shades of lilac, amber, pearl, fawn, and cinnamon, in combinations of two or more colors. Most rats have a smooth coat, but there also are hairless rats, "rex" or wavy-haired rats, and even a Manx or tailless breed.

NEEDS. Fancy rats are smart and active; they need attention, mental stimulation, and exercise. Their wild ancestors lived in colonies, and these pets inherited the social need to live with at least one other of their own kind. As rodents, they need safe, nontoxic materials to chew.

It is important that the habitat be spacious and not overcrowded. (Overcrowding can lead to aggression in these otherwise peaceable animals.) Rats need to exercise and explore outside of their enclosure every day. Ratproofing a room can be a challenge, as noted previously on pages 110–111.

To protect rats from respiratory infections and pneumonia, the habitat should be kept dry, clean, and warm. A cold or drafty room, even for a few hours, can spell doom. A dirty enclosure generates ammonia that not only smells but also can become toxic.

CHILDREN AND FANCY RATS. Fancy rats are excellent pets for children age eight and up. They bond easily and closely. Considered the most intelligent of the small mammals, they are active and playful. Most rats can be trained to use a litter box.

Because of their small size, rats are fragile and easily injured if squeezed, dropped, or improperly handled. Children under the age of eight can enjoy watching rats play or play with them under close parental supervision.

Like other animals, pet rats will bite if threatened or roughly handled. They have small, sharp teeth, and their bite can be painful. Children need to learn not to poke their fingers into the cage and how to pick up and hold a fancy rat: A rat should not be lifted or held by the tail.

COMMITMENT. Once you have acquired a roomy cage or tank and some play equipment, pet rats are inexpensive and easy to care for. They do require daily attention.

What You Need to Know About Fancy Rats *Before* You Get One

SIZE. A typical pet rat is seven inches long, with a tail of equal length, and weighs one pound or less.

LONGEVITY. Pet rats usually live two to four years, but some live five years and even six.

LEGAL RESTRICTIONS. Some landlords prohibit pets of all kinds.

COSTS. The care of two fancy rats, barring veterinary emergencies, will be about $400–$600 over their lifetimes. This will vary with prices in your region, size of enclosure, type of litter and food, number of toys, and other items.

Food will cost about $50 a year or less for two. Commercial diets in the form of pellets, mixed grains, blocks, or cubes prepared for small rodents meet basic nutritional needs. Cost does not include fresh fruits, vegetables, eggs, or nuts, which should be added to the commercial diet.

Another ongoing expense is *litter*, which needs to be changed frequently. The cost will vary, depending on size of the habitat, number of rats, whether they are trained to use a litter box, the type of litter, and whether you can buy in bulk. This will cost from $5 to $10 per month, or from $60 to $100 per year.

Basic equipment includes:

- comprehensive book(s) about fancy rat care — $10–20
- tank or cage (medium or large) — $50–100
- tank cover (depending on size) — $15–30
- hide box — $0–15
- food bowl — $3
- hanging water bottle — $7–10
- bottle brush — $0–3
- chew blocks — $0–10 (annual)
- toys, exercise equipment — $0–20 (annual)
- rubber gloves (for spot cleaning) — $3
- carrier (optional) — $15–30

Take your fancy rats for a well-pet checkup soon after you bring them home, which will cost from $25 to $50 each. Be sure to set aside, either mentally or in fact, a *veterinary emergency fund* of $100 per animal.

Your *acquisition* costs will be small. A shelter or rescue group may let you have pet rats for free or for a token donation. Breeders sell rats for between $10 and $20. If you patronize a pet store, pet rats may be available for as little as $2–$3 each, or $5 for a well-socialized pet.

EQUIPMENT. The most important piece of equipment is the habitat. A cage allows better ventilation than a tank, but it is not always easy to find a cage that is both safe for rats and escape-proof. A multiplatform cage with access ladders or stairs is ideal. The floor should not be mesh or wire, which can cause injuries; Plexiglas can be used to cover mesh flooring.

A tank is heavier and somewhat harder to clean than a cage and may need cleaning more often to prevent ammonia buildup. If you use a tank, the bigger the better (a ten-gallon size is not large enough); a tight-fitting screen lid is mandatory. Consult your comprehensive rat care book before choosing litter, because some types, such as pine or cedar shavings, can be harmful.

Chewing materials, nesting boxes and bedding or nesting material can be store-bought or made from nontoxic materials. An exercise wheel is recommended, although you probably will not find any made specifically for pet rats, and hamster wheels are too small. Look for a solid one that is large enough for a guinea pig. Furniture for agile rats to climb on, over, and through can be purchased or made. A food bowl and water bottle, and an old toothbrush or a baby bottle brush to clean it, will complete your setup.

SPACE. The minimum rule of thumb is two square feet of floor space per rat, but the bigger the better. A large multistoried cage is ideal for two rats. Place the enclosure "where the action is," so that they can entertain—and be entertained by—your family, away from drafts, direct sunlight, heating and air-conditioning vents, bright lights, and loud noises. Because rats are naturally nocturnal, they may be noisy at night, so a bedroom is not usually a desirable location.

TIME REQUIREMENT. *Feed* pet rats twice a day, on a regular schedule. Remove old food, wipe out the bowl, and put down commercial food once a day. This takes five minutes or less. Empty, clean, refill, and check the water bottle, and provide some dried fruit or nuts, or washed, cut fresh fruit or vegetables once a day. This takes ten to fifteen minutes.

Rats groom themselves frequently and keep their bodies clean without help. To keep their cage clean, *spot-clean* it or the litter box daily using a scoop or rubber gloves (this takes two or three minutes). Thoroughly *wash and dry the enclosure* and put down fresh litter once a week (this takes about half an hour).

Rats need stimulation, interaction, and *exercise*. They should be taken out of their enclosure daily for playtime and be allowed to explore and exercise in a safe area for at least an hour. One pastime enjoyed by children and pet rats alike is maze running: Children construct mazes out of blocks or toys for their pets to negotiate.

SHEDS OR SMELLS? A cage or tank that is not cleaned regularly and frequently will smell.

CHARACTERISTICS AFFECTING CHILDREN. Fancy rats are friendly and gentle, and they rarely bite. They have sharp nails, which inadvertently can hurt when the rat is being held.

Children who are too young to correctly lift or hold a

rat can unintentionally injure it. Children eight years and older usually can learn how to handle a pet rat.

PERSONALITY TRAITS. Most rats are fun-loving, curious, acrobatic, and busy. Individual rats have distinct personalities. Kathleen described "two pet rats with similar backgrounds and very different personalities. Both had been in a classroom where children were allowed to poke pencils at them and tease them. One of these rats is now quite aggressive, and the other is extremely timid. Once they get to know and trust you, though, both are fine."

NEED FOR PARENTAL SUPERVISION. Children of all ages can enjoy watching the antics of these pets inside their habitat. Children under the age of eight need supervision when handling these pets. Pet rats outside of their enclosure should be monitored by adults.

Child's Age and Care of Fancy Rats

With parental supervision:

Children **age three to five** can put food into a clean bowl, put prewashed vegetables or fruit in the enclosure.

Children **age five to seven** also can put litter into a clean enclosure, hand-feed treats, refill and hang water bottle, and help an adult wash vegetables and fruit.

Children **age seven to ten** also can empty and clean water bottle, spot-clean cage (wearing rubber gloves).

Children **age ten to twelve** also can help an adult clean and wash cage, cut up fruit or vegetables.

Children **age twelve and up** also can clean and wash cage, equipment.

Your Family's Pet Resources

Inventory your resources to see if they enable your family to keep fancy rats.

TIME. Which family member(s) will spot-clean the enclosure or litter box, feed, and play with these pets daily? Who will clean the enclosure each week?

COST. Your acquisition costs, including equipment and veterinary check, will be around $150. Can you spend this much, plus annual expenditures of about $100? For three or four years? Can you afford to pay for a veterinary emergency?

ABILITY. Are your children old enough to help with chores? Are they old enough to carefully handle fancy rats without dropping or squeezing them?

PLACE AND SPACE. Do you have room for a large habitat? Can it be placed away from heat, drafts, direct sun, bright lights, and loud noises and still be "where the action is"? Can you ratproof at least one room so that your pets can exercise in it every day? Are there legal restrictions against keeping these pets in your home?

HEALTH. Does anyone in your family have allergies that may be triggered by these pets, or by their litter?

TRAVEL. Who will care for this pet when your family travels? If necessary, can you afford to pay someone to pet-sit?

HOUSEKEEPING. Will spillage from the cage bother you? How about the need to ratproof a room so that these pets can exercise?

SPECIAL ISSUES. Are there family members who fear or dislike this animal, making it more likely that it will be given away or not well cared for? Will you take it with you if you move?

Writes Ginger Cardinal, "Rats are delightful creatures that are often misunderstood. . . . They are affectionate, loyal, social and very clean. They are quite personable and enjoy being handled. They make wonderful pets for adults and children alike."

Questions That Parents Ask

My wife hates the idea of pet rats, but our two children are begging for some. If the kids play with them every day, can we keep these pets in the garage? No. Pet rats will almost certainly die from the cold if they are banished to a garage. If someone in your family really hates the idea of a pet rat, try to come up with an alternative that, at a minimum, everyone at least feels comfortable with.

Pet rats are cute and smart, but don't they smell really bad? These pets do not have much odor, but their enclosure or litter box will smell if not cleaned frequently. A dirty enclosure also causes health problems.

Don't pet rats have fleas and other parasites? Rats can get fleas, but they are less likely to get them than are dogs or cats—and usually it is the family dog or cat that brings the fleas into the house to meet the rats. Like dogs and cats, rats can be bothered by other external parasites, such as mites or lice. A veterinarian can recommend the best treatment.

I know that pet rats are prettier than the wild ones, but aren't they just as dirty? Domestic rats groom and clean themselves, the way cats do, so they actually are clean pets. What they cannot do is clean their habitat.

Can we leave pet rats alone while we go on vacation?

You can leave these pets alone, in a clean enclosure, for two days (one night). Leave plenty of food and fresh water for them; double-check to make certain that the sipper on the water bottle is working properly, because rats can dehydrate quickly and die without access to water. A good precaution is to hang an extra bottle of fresh water next to the regular one. Make certain that the temperature will remain constant and comfortable around your pets' enclosure, and that it will not be exposed to bright light or loud noises.

If you will be away more than two days, ask someone to come to your home to clean the enclosure, provide fresh food and water, and play with your pets. An alternative is to take your pets to a friend's home, or board them with a veterinarian or kennel, preferably in their own enclosure to reduce the stress of a strange environment. Ask around for references before you choose a kennel, and leave detailed, written instructions.

We've read that rats are nocturnal. Does this mean that our child can't play with them during the day? Left to their own devices, rats are nocturnal, but they enjoy human interaction and usually are happy to play during the day. Because rats also tend to be active and noisy at night, it's not a good idea to put their habitat in a bedroom.

We've heard that rats are sickly pets. Is this true? Not really, although, unfortunately, chronic respiratory infection has become endemic in the pet rat population. No cure has been found yet, although breeders are trying to breed pets that are resistant. Antibiotic treatment can help.

Tumors are also common, especially in females, but usually they are benign. Spaying reduces the incidence of tumors.

Should we get a male or female? Either will make a good pet, but two will be happier together than one alone. Check with an expert or a good book about gender combinations. Be careful when you buy your pets; it is not unusual for pet shops to mis-sex rats and to unknowingly sell pregnant females.

Resources

CLUBS

American Fancy Rat & Mouse
Association
PO Box 2589
Winnetka, CA 91396-2589

American Rat, Mouse &
Hamster Society
13317 Neddick Avenue
Poway, CA 92064

Midwest Rat and Mouse Club
7409 Cimmaron Station
Columbus, OH 43235

Northeast Rat & Mouse Club
International
603 Brandt Avenue
New Cumberland, PA 17070

Rat & Mouse Club of
America
13075 Springdale Street
Suite 302
Westminster, CA 92683

Rat, Mouse, & Hamster
Fanciers
188 School Street
Danville, CA 94526

The Rat Fan Club
857 Lindo Lane
Chico, CA 95973

There are fancy rat clubs in many states. Ask a national or regional club, local owner, breeder, or veterinarian for information.

BOOKS FOR ADULTS

Cardinal, Ginger. *The Rat: An Owner's Guide to a Happy Healthy Pet.* New York: Howell Book House, 1998.

Ducommon, Debbie. *Rats! A Fun and Care Book for Today's Pet Owner.* Mission Viejo, CA: Bowtie Press, 1998.

Himsel, Carol A. *Rats: A Complete Pet Owner's Manual.* Hauppauge, NY: Barron's, 1991.

Siino, Betsy Sikora. *You Want a What for a Pet?! A Guide to 12 "Alternative" Pets.* New York: Howell Book House, 1996.

NONFICTION FOR CHILDREN

Henrie, Fiona. *Mice and Rats: Junior Petkeeper's Library*. New York: Franklin Watts, 1980.

Pope, Joyce. *Taking Care of Your Mice and Rats*. New York: Franklin Watts, 1990.

FICTION FOR CHILDREN

Conly, Jane Leslie. *Rasco and the Rats of NIMH*. New York: HarperCollins, 1986.

———. *R-T, Margaret, and the Rats of NIMH*. New York: HarperCollins, 1990.

O'Brien, Robert C. *Mrs. Frisby and the Rats of NIMH*. New York: Aladdin, 1986.

Seidler, Tor. *A Rat's Tale*. New York: Farrar, Straus & Giroux, 1986.

TEN

Gerbils

"Gerbils are cute and soft. They are not too hard to take care of. It is fun to hold them—I like to hold them against my cheek. I would say this is a good pet because they are fun to play with," says eight-year-old Gregory Smith.

The Smiths—Gregory, his eleven-year-old brother Nicholas, his mother and father—have owned gerbils for two years. When I asked Greg whose idea it was to get gerbils, he thought for a moment and then said, "Our whole family's." When I asked him who took care of the gerbils, he again replied, "Our whole family."

Greg's brief comments explain why the Smiths' gerbils have fared so well, and why the family enjoys them so much. These family pets live in two large tanks in the family room and receive lots of attention and care.

About a year ago, I was privileged to pet-sit for Squeaker, Frisky, Hot Chocolate, Arctic, and Mousy. Like Greg, I was entranced. I liked to sit and watch them, and sometimes they paused to watch me, but usually they were busy chewing, digging, burying, climbing. When I put my hand into the tank, they rushed over to sniff it and let me pick them up. Greg is right—they *are* soft.

ORIGINS. Known variously as "antelope rats," "desert rats," and "yellow rats," some ninety different species of

Gerbils
Facts At a Glance

COST	$500–$600 for two over their lifetime
SIZE	3–4 ounces
LONGEVITY	2–4 years
TIME REQUIREMENT	30 minutes per day to feed, play with, exercise; 30 minutes every 1 to 2 weeks to clean cage
SPACE	Tank at least 26" × 11" × 11" for two, placed away from drafts and direct sun
EXERCISE	Need to dig, climb inside tank; should be taken out of tank daily to exercise (closely watched)
EQUIPMENT	Tank, cage, or gerbilarium; hanging water bottle, bottle brush, food bowl, chew toys, hide box, play toys, litter
ODOR	Very little, if tank and litter are kept clean
SHEDDING	Not noticeable
PHYSICAL CHARACTERISTICS AFFECTING KIDS	Small, easy to handle; fragile, can be injured if squeezed or dropped; can nip
TEMPERAMENTAL CHARACTERISTICS AFFECTING KIDS	Gentle, sociable, playful, curious, active, need interaction with other gerbils
PERSONALITY TRAITS	Some are shy; usually become friendly and trusting if handled gently and often
PARENTAL SUPERVISION	Young children should be supervised when handling
LEGAL RESTRICTIONS	Illegal to own or bring gerbils into California; some landlords prohibit all pets

gerbils live in the deserts of Asia and Africa. Although the Latin name for the tiny gerbil is *Meriones unguiculatas*, or "little clawed warrior," the Mongolian gerbil that is popular in the United States is friendly and not aggressive. Nearly all American pet gerbils descended from twenty pairs that Japanese scientists took from the Mongolian desert in 1935. In 1954, Japan sent twenty-two pairs descended from the original twenty to the United States for medical research. In the 1960s, a few pet shops began to sell these cute rodents, and their popularity has increased ever since.

Gerbils weigh less than half a pound and have a body that is about four inches long, plus a tail of similar length. Unlike rats, they have fur-covered tails with a tuft on the end, and their hind legs are bigger than their front legs. Colors include gray, black, agouti, reddish brown, and spotted. Their large, dark eyes are fetching.

NEEDS. *Arriving one morning at my son's second-grade classroom for my weekly volunteer stint, I noticed a new addition: a ten-gallon tank inhabited by a dark brown gerbil. Having recently concluded several weeks of gerbil-sitting for the Smiths, I considered myself a gerbil pro and offered to clean Chocolate's tank. I did not know what I did not know.*

Delighted to have an audience—a small circle of attentive children—I discoursed on gerbil history and care as I reached into the tank and held my hand out for a friendly sniff.

Chocolate bit me! And it hurt, it really hurt. The children erupted with laughter. They had known what to expect, but of course no one wanted to spoil the fun by warning me.

I went back to the books. I learned that in the wild, gerbils live in family groups or colonies. They need companionship of their own kind and gentle, consistent handling. The five Smith gerbils were friendly because they lived together and because the boys played with them daily. Chocolate had been left on his own. Without human or gerbil friendship, he had become suspicious and neurotic.

Keeping one gerbil by itself is cruel. Two or more—preferably siblings of the same sex that have been together since birth—will be healthier and happier living together. Expert advice is needed about gender and age combinations, because not all gerbils get along together.

Gerbils are burrowing animals and need to dig, so their habitat must contain an appropriate litter or substrate. Seek expert advice about which materials to use and which to avoid. As rodents, gerbils need to gnaw, so chewable materials must be available at all times.

Gerbils are active and curious. A range of safe toys that you can cycle through their cage is one way to satisfy their urge to climb in, over, up and through things. With proper precautions, gerbils should be taken out of their cage and allowed to exercise, preferably every day. One room that is relatively easy to gerbilproof is the bathroom. (Close toilet lid, remove electrical cords and toxic materials such as soaps and cosmetics.)

CHILDREN AND GERBILS. Gerbils are delightful pets for children: quiet, clean, playful, friendly. It's fun to watch them hide inside a cardboard tube, then demolish it with their teeth. They can learn to recognize a child's voice and will eagerly hop onto a child's hand.

COMMITMENT. Gerbils are ideal "first pets" and ideal second, third, fourth, and fifth pets. Children love them, and they are relatively easy to care for, but they do need daily attention.

What You Need to Know About Gerbils *Before* You Get One

SIZE. Adults are about eight inches long, including the tail, and weigh two to four ounces.

LONGEVITY. Gerbils live three to four years, occasionally five.

LEGAL RESTRICTIONS. It is illegal to own or bring gerbils into California. Check your local animal control laws and your lease before you bring gerbils home.

COSTS. The care of two gerbils, barring a veterinary emergency, will be about $400–$600 for both over the course of their lives. Costs vary depending on longevity, the type of enclosure and bedding, number of toys or treats, and regional variations in prices.

Basic equipment includes:

- comprehensive book(s) about gerbil care $10–25
- cage or tank $30–60
- screen lid (depends on size of tank) $15–30
- hide box $0–10
- food bowl $3–5
- hanging water bottle $7
- bottle brush $0–3
- chewing materials $0–10 (annual)
- toys $0–20 (annual)
- rubber gloves (for cleaning enclosure) $3
- carrier (optional) $30

Food will cost $50–$75 a year for two. This includes a customized seed and cereal mixture available in pet stores but does not include the fresh fruits or vegetables that you occasionally may give gerbils.

Litter will be $50–$150 a year, depending on the type you use, whether you buy in bulk, size of the tank, and how often you change it. If you want to fill a gerbilarium or tank with a burrowing mixture (peat moss, sterilized topsoil, straw) so that your pets can dig tunnels, your costs will be higher. The costs of *nesting materials*—cardboard, white paper, small rags, or hay—to put inside the hide box will be negligible.

If your gerbils have not had one, take them for a "well-pet" checkup soon after you bring them home. This will cost from $25 to $50 each. Set aside, either mentally or in fact, a *veterinary emergency fund* of at least $100 per gerbil.

Your *acquisition* costs will be small. Because gerbils breed frequently and easily, it should be easy to find a pair for free. Call your local shelter first; if there are no gerbils for adoption, ask for suggestions on where to look and spread the word of your interest. If you end up buying gerbils in a pet shop, you will pay about $5 each.

EQUIPMENT. Gerbils can live comfortably in an aquarium, provided it is large enough and is kept clean. Ten gallons is the minimum size; twenty or thirty gallons is better. A wire mesh lid must be securely attached to the top. You can create a gerbilarium by partially filling a large tank with burrowing material.

Gerbils also can live in a cage, provided that the bars are close enough together to prevent escape and cannot be chewed through; the bottom should be solid, not mesh or wire. A cage that is enclosed on three sides provides gerbils with a sense of security. A cage with several stories and connecting ladders provides exercise and diversion.

A nest box, chewing materials, toys, a few inches of litter, a small amount of nesting material, and a food bowl and water bottle complete your setup. Be guided by an expert or your pet care book to determine which products are safe and healthy.

SPACE. The minimum-size cage or tank has a floor area of about 250 square inches and is eleven or twelve inches deep. A bigger habitat is preferable.

The tank, cage, or gerbilarium should be kept dry and placed away from television and stereo speakers (loud noises can cause stress), drafts, direct sun, radiators, and heating or air-conditioning vents. In the desert, gerbils escape extreme temperatures by burrowing underground, an option not available to them in a tank, so the air temperature around them should be kept in the range of 60° to 70° Fahrenheit.

TIME REQUIREMENT. *Feeding* gerbils takes about ten minutes a day. Remove old food, wipe out the bowl, and put down about a tablespoon of custom gerbil food per gerbil each day. It's best to do this at the same time every day. Empty, clean, and refill the water bottle. You may give your gerbils a small amount of fresh, washed fruit or vegetables one or two times a week.

Gerbils need *attention* and *exercise*. They need to be played with and petted or handled for at least fifteen minutes every day. They need to be let out of their enclosure, into a gerbilproof area, or else supervised as they scamper about and exercise—ideally for thirty minutes a day or more.

Gerbils need a clean, dry habitat. *Change the litter* every ten to fourteen days and thoroughly *wash and dry the entire tank* or the cage bottom before putting down new litter. This takes twenty to thirty minutes. Gerbilariums need to be emptied and cleaned less often—every four to six weeks—and it will take longer to empty and clean them. Extreme care must be used if there are baby gerbils, especially with a gerbilarium. Because even a ten-gallon tank (but not a cage) weighs eleven pounds, it may be too heavy or unwieldy for a small child to lift and clean without considerable help.

SHEDS OR SMELLS? Gerbils produce very little odor. A habitat that is not cleaned regularly will smell eventually.

CHARACTERISTICS AFFECTING CHILDREN. Gerbils are playful and gentle. They rarely nip. Young children can inadvertently hurt this small, fragile animal by squeezing or dropping it.

PERSONALITY TRAITS. In general, gerbils are energetic, friendly, and playful, and they respond well to humans who handle them regularly.

NEED FOR PARENTAL SUPERVISION. Children under the age of seven, and perhaps even up to age ten, need supervision when handling gerbils. Gerbils are very active, and children are tempted to grab or squeeze them, with potentially disastrous results.

Child's Age and Care of Gerbil

With parental supervision:

Children **age three to five** can put pre-measured food, prewashed fruit or vegetables in the bowl.

Children **age five to seven** also can clean bowl, refill and hang water bottle, help an adult wash vegetables or fruit.

Children **age seven to ten** also can empty and clean water bottle, put litter and nesting material in clean cage.

Children **age ten to twelve** also can help an adult clean and wash cage, cut up fruit or vegetables.

Children **age twelve and up** also can clean and wash cage.

Your Family's Pet Resources

Inventory your resources to see if they enable your family to keep a gerbil colony.

TIME. Which family member(s) will feed and play with the gerbils daily? Who will clean the tank or cage every two weeks, or more often if necessary?

COST. Can you spend at least $80–$100 in initial expenditures for equipment and well-pet exams? Spend $100 a year for food and bedding? Pay for a veterinary emergency?

ABILITY. Are your children old enough to help with any chores? Are they strong enough to lift and clean a tank? Are they old enough to handle a gerbil without harming it?

PLACE AND SPACE. Do you have room for a tank or cage, away from heat, drafts, and loud noises—but not away from the family? Are there legal restrictions against gerbils in your area?

HEALTH. Does anyone in your family have allergies that could be triggered by gerbils, or by their litter?

TRAVEL. Who will care for this pet when your family travels?

HOUSEKEEPING. Will spillage from a cage bother you? How about the need to gerbilproof a room or area so that these pets can exercise?

SPECIAL ISSUES. Are there family members who fear or dislike this animal because it is a rodent? Will this prevent the gerbils from receiving good care, or make it likely they will be given away?

*   *   *

In *Taking Care of Your Gerbils: A Young Pet Owner's Guide*, Helen Piers concludes with these thoughts for young owners: "You will get a lot of fun keeping gerbils as pets. In return, give them the best possible life you can. Remember, they do not have the freedom to come and go as they like and find their own food and nesting places, as in the wild. They depend on you for everything they need."

Questions That Parents Ask

Is it better to have one gerbil or two? It is better to have at least two—they need each other. Try to get two siblings of the same gender that are used to living together, or gerbils of the opposite sex that are too old to breed; if you get young gerbils of the opposite sex, be prepared to separate the offspring by sex into separate tanks so that they will not continue to breed, or else have good, permanent homes lined up for the babies.

Is a tank or cage better? Either can be a good habitat, if it is spacious and well maintained with appropriate substrate and "furniture."

Can we leave our gerbils home alone for a few days, with food and water, while our family takes a vacation? You can leave your gerbils for up to three days. Be sure the tank is clean, dry, and secure, with plenty of gnawing, litter, and nesting materials. Put down a supply of fresh food and make sure the water bottle is functioning. Don't turn off all air conditioning or heat unless you are certain that the room temperature for your gerbils will be safe.

Our daughter is allergic to dogs and cats. If we keep two gerbils in an aquarium, and don't put the aquarium in her bedroom, will she escape an allergic reaction? You need to discuss this question with your daughter's physician. Allergies are unique to each individual. It's possible that having gerbils in the house won't bother your daughter. But because allergies tend to build up over time, it's also possible that your daughter may not have adverse reactions in the first weeks or months but develop them over time—after she has become very attached to her pets.

Resources

BOOKS FOR ADULTS
Gudas, Raymond. *Gerbils: A Complete Pet Owner's Manual.* Hauppauge, NY: Barron's, 1986.

Sproule, Anna and Michael. *Know Your Pet Gerbils.* New York: Bookwright Press, 1989.

Wexler, Jerome. *Pet Gerbils.* Morton Grove, IL: Albert Whitman, 1990.

NONFICTION FOR CHILDREN
Piers, Helen. *Taking Care of Your Gerbils: A Young Pet Owner's Guide.* Hauppauge, NY: Barron's, 1993.

FICTION FOR CHILDREN
Manes, Stephen. *The Great Gerbil Roundup.* New York: Harcourt Brace Jovanovich, 1988.

ELEVEN

Guinea Pigs (Cavies)

A sad lesson is recounted by Horst Bielfeld in *Guinea Pigs: A Complete Pet Owner's Manual*: "I did not keep a guinea pig again . . . until my oldest son was five years old. This was a young male that we named Maximilian. The children loved him dearly. Indeed, our youngest daughter embraced him so passionately one day that the delicate animal did not survive her demonstration of affection. That was an important, if bitter, lesson for us all. Guinea pigs enjoy being petted and cuddled, and children can also be allowed to carry them around. . . . Youngsters often do not know their own strength; and where dogs and cats will fight back by biting and scratching if they are squeezed too hard, guinea pigs remain passive."

With their rotund little bodies and short legs, guinea pigs have been described as "furred ostrich eggs with legs." They make squeaking and chirping noises and a sound that has been described as "a cheap car alarm." There are few animals more endearing to children and adults.

ORIGINS. The guinea pig is not a pig, is not related to pigs, and does not come from Guinea. It is actually a rodent called a cavy, belonging to the family *Caviidae,* which originated in South America. Wild cavies live in groups.

Guinea Pigs (Cavies)
Facts At a Glance

COST	$1,300–$4,000 over the cavy's lifetime
SIZE	1–3 pounds
LONGEVITY	5–6 years
TIME REQUIREMENT	1 hour per day to feed, groom, exercise, play, spot-clean cage; 30 minutes each week to wash cage
SPACE	Cage at least 2' × 2' for one cavy (larger for two), placed away from drafts and direct sun
EXERCISE	Should be allowed out of cage once a day, closely watched
EQUIPMENT	Cage, food bowl, hanging water bottle, bottle brush, litter, chew block, hide box, nail trimmer, brush or comb
ODOR	Cage and litter will smell if not kept clean
SHEDDING	Yes, but mostly inside cage
PHYSICAL CHARACTERISTICS AFFECTING KIDS	Small, fragile; can easily be injured if dropped or squeezed; can nip, scratch
TEMPERAMENTAL CHARACTERISTICS AFFECTING KIDS	Gentle, sociable, need interaction with people or another cavy; usually like to be handled; usually calm
PERSONALITY TRAITS	Friendly and playful if handled gently and often; can be timid
PARENTAL SUPERVISION	Young children should be supervised when handling
LEGAL RESTRICTIONS	Some landlords and condo associations prohibit all pets

Long before Europeans reached the Americas, South and Central American Indians had domesticated cavies. They were used for food and also apparently as sacrificial animals; guinea pig mummies have been found in Inca tombs. European explorers and traders brought cavies back to Europe, probably as pets, as early as the sixteenth century.

Various explanations have been offered for the name *guinea pig*. Both the Dutch and English seamen who first brought cavies to Europe called them "pigs," probably because of their chubby bodies and the squealing noises they make. It is possible that "guinea" came from the English coin of that name, indicating that in the early years of their sale in Europe, these little animals cost a guinea each.

There are about a dozen recognized guinea pig breeds, but mixed cavies are equally adorable and healthy. Cavies vary somewhat in size and shape, but the most noticeable differences are in the coat. Colors include gold, black, white, agouti, chocolate, beige, cream, red, and gray, or a mix of two or three of these colors. Guinea pig hair ranges from short and smooth, the most common, to long and silky, to "rosette"—whorls of hair found in rough-haired, or Abyssinian, guinea pigs.

NEEDS. *One of the saddest creatures I ever encountered was a dejected guinea pig named Norman, who belonged to a neighborhood family. The oldest boy, Alex, was seven. He had begged for a furry pet, and although he suffered from asthma and multiple allergies, his parents gave in and bought Norman. His mother's solution to the allergy problem was to put Norman's cage in the basement. There he lived, alone and ignored. Alex's mother remembered to feed him, change his water, and clean his cage on a fairly regular basis, because she passed by him on the way to the laundry room. For Alex and the rest of the family, out of sight was out of mind. Norman might be remembered once or twice a week and get a few pats. Because he was rarely handled, Norman was shy and easily frightened. What a* *depressing existence for this animal, and an uninspiring experience for Alex.*

These adorable little creatures need to socialize. They like to be petted, and this is especially important if you have only one. Exiling your cavy to a basement or garage not only isolates it but also exposes it to drafts that could kill it.

In addition to attention, food, and water, cavies need to stay dry and warm, with room temperature of about 65° to 70° Fahrenheit. They need exercise outside of the cage every day in an enclosed exercise area or a cavyproof room, where temptingly chewable electrical cords or other dangerous objects have been removed or covered. Proofing a room usually is not difficult, because cavies do not jump or hop; they stay low to the ground. But it is risky to give your cavy the free run of the house, lest it be stepped on, and it should never be left on a chair, bed, or table because a fall can cause serious injury.

CHILDREN AND GUINEA PIGS. These are wonderful pets for children who are old enough to handle them gently. They are sweet, cute, and cuddly, although not all guinea pigs like to be held. They can become very attached to their humans, making small squeaking sounds of greeting. Children need to be taught how, and how *not*, to lift and hold a guinea pig.

COMMITMENT. Guinea pigs often are recommended as an ideal "first pet" for young children. Parents are told that these "low-maintenance" pets require minimal expenditure of money and time. But "low-maintenance" does not mean food and water and nothing more. Guinea pigs need attention 365 days a year.

What You Need to Know About Guinea Pigs *Before* You Get One

SIZE. Adults are about eight to ten inches long and weigh from one to four pounds.

LONGEVITY. Cavies live to be about six years old, but some live to be eight and even ten.

LEGAL RESTRICTIONS. Some landlords prohibit pets of all kinds.

COSTS. The care of a guinea pig, barring a veterinary emergency, will be roughly $1,300 to $4,000 over its lifetime, depending on prices in your region and your consumer choices about cages, litter, and other items.

Food will cost about $75–$100 a year for one cavy. This includes guinea pig pellets and hay. Because vitamin C is critical to cavy nutrition and health, pellets should be vitamin C–fortified and not stored for long periods of time. Not included in this cost are the fresh vegetables and fruit, which you should give your pet daily.

Another ongoing expense is *litter*, which needs to be changed often and can cost from $100 annually to $500, depending on the type, whether you buy it in bulk, how large the cage, and how often you change it.

If it has not already had one, take your new cavy for a well-pet check soon after you bring it home. This will cost from $25 to $50. Set aside, either mentally or in fact, a *veterinary emergency fund* of at least $100 per cavy.

Your *acquisition* costs will be small. With patience and persistence, you may find a guinea pig for free. A shelter or rescue group may request a donation to help offset their costs. If you buy a guinea pig, it may cost from $15 to $25; a purebred will cost more.

Basic equipment includes:

- comprehensive book(s) about guinea pig care $10–20
- cage $60–100
- hide box $0–15
- food bowl $6
- hanging water bottle $7
- bottle brush $0–3
- chew block $0–10 (annual)
- cat nail clippers $9
- cat or child's soft brush (for short hair) $3–6
- pet comb (for long hair) $7
- rubber gloves (for spot cleaning cage) $3
- portable enclosure (optional) $60–100
- pet gate (optional) $20–50
- carrier (optional) $30

EQUIPMENT. Your cavy needs a cage, not an aquarium or tank, because good ventilation is important to its health. The cage should have a plastic tray (not mesh or wire, which can cause injury) at the bottom. Cover the tray with litter; consult a cavy expert, a vet, or comprehensive care book to help you choose the right kind.

Your cavy will also need a food bowl and sipper bottle, and a brush to clean the bottle. The cage should include a hide box, which you can buy or make; a chew block; and, if there is room enough, a brick that helps keep nails from becoming overgrown as the cavy climbs over it. For grooming, you need nail clippers (small ones for cats that are found in pet shops), a pet comb for long hair, or a medium-to-soft pet brush (such as used for cats or children) for short hair.

SPACE. The minimum size cage for a single cavy is two square feet, but a bigger cage is preferable. The more cavies, the larger the cage must be: at least two square feet per animal. The cage should be located away from drafts, direct sunlight, heating and air-conditioning vents, stereo speakers, televisions, and other loud noises.

When you are deciding where to put the cage, keep in mind that litter (including some waste material) can get thrown out of it as your guinea pig moves around inside. It's a good idea to put newspaper under the cage and not a good idea to put the cage on your best carpet.

TIME REQUIREMENT. *Feeding* takes about fifteen minutes a day: Clean the food bowl; wash and fill the water bottle; put down fresh pellets, hay, and washed, fresh vegetables or fruit.

Some cavies need help *grooming* themselves. Those with long hair require daily combing, which takes five to ten minutes. Those with short hair need grooming less often. Trim your pet's nails about every month or two; this takes about ten minutes.

Guinea pigs need *exercise*. Let your cavy hop around outside its cage for at least one hour a day. Pet and play with it every day for at least thirty minutes.

Spot-clean the cage by hand (wearing rubber gloves) at least once a day, removing damp or soiled litter. This takes five minutes or less. *Change litter* every other day, or more often if it is wet or smells. This takes about ten minutes. Once a week, throw out old litter, *thoroughly wash and dry*

the cage, and put down fresh litter. This takes about thirty
minutes.

SHEDS OR SMELLS? Guinea pigs shed. How much you
notice this will depend on how long your cavy's hair is, its
color, and how much you hold it and allow it to explore
outside the cage.

A guinea pig cage that is not cleaned regularly and thoroughly will smell unpleasant, as guinea pigs generate a lot
of waste.

CHARACTERISTICS AFFECTING CHILDREN. Guinea
pigs are docile and gentle. They rarely nip and do not use
their claws for defense.

Children under the age of six or seven can inadvertently
hurt a guinea pig by squeezing it too tightly or by dropping
it.

PERSONALITY TRAITS. Young guinea pigs are frisky and
skittish; they become calmer as they grow older. Personalities vary from very friendly to somewhat retiring. A single guinea pig, if given plenty of TLC and handled
regularly, can become attached to a child or adult. A cavy
that is ignored or roughly handled will be timid and can
become depressed.

NEED FOR PARENTAL SUPERVISION. Very young children, usually those under the age of seven, need supervision
when handling cavies. One expert suggests that children
under the age of ten may not be able to safely handle a
cavy without parental supervision.

Your Family's Pet Resources

Inventory your resources to see if they enable your family
to keep a guinea pig.

Child's Age and Care of Guinea Pig

With parental supervision:

Children **age three to five** can put a handful of hay in the cage, put pellets in the bowl, put pre-washed vegetables or fruit in the cage.

Children **age five to seven** also can hand-feed vegetables and treats and help an adult wash vegetables or fruit, clean bowl, refill and hang water bottle.

Children **age seven to ten** also can empty and clean water bottle, spot-clean cage (wearing rubber gloves), put down fresh litter, help groom.

Children **age ten to twelve** also can help an adult cut up fruit or vegetables, clean and wash cage, groom.

Children **age twelve and up** also can clean and wash cage.

TIME. Which family member(s) will feed and play with the guinea pig daily? Who will groom it? Who will spot-clean the cage daily and wash it weekly? Change the hay twice a week?

COST. Your initial acquisition costs, including equipment and veterinary checkup, will be about $100–$150. Can you spend this much, plus annual expenditures of at least $200? For six years or more? Can you pay for a veterinary emergency?

ABILITY. Are your children old enough to help with any chores? Are they old enough to safely handle a cavy?

PLACE AND SPACE. Do you have room for a large cage? Can it be placed away from heat, drafts, and loud noises and still be "where the action is"? Can you cavyproof at least one room? Are there legal restrictions against keeping a cavy in your home?

HEALTH. Does anyone in your family have allergies that may be triggered by this pet, or by hay or litter?

TRAVEL. Who will care for this pet when your family travels? If necessary, can you afford to board it or pay someone to care for it?

HOUSEKEEPING. Will spillage from the cage bother you? How about the need to cavyproof a room so that this pet can exercise?

SPECIAL ISSUES. Do you and your children find this pet enjoyable and interesting for its own sake, or is it intended to be a substitute for a larger animal? Will you take it with you if you move?

* * *

A recent article about ''Captivating Cavies'' concludes, ''If you enjoy a clean, responsive pet that you can hold in your hands; if you are committed to having that animal as a part of your life for about five years ... chances are a cavy could be the critter for you.''

Questions That Parents Ask

Is it better to have one guinea pig or two? Some experts believe that a cavy should not live alone. Others believe that a single guinea pig can live a good life and be an affectionate, friendly pet if it receives plenty of attention. Two females usually can get along fine, but two males usually cannot, unless they have been neutered. Do not put a male and female together unless at least one has been sterilized.

Two cavies need a bigger cage than one living alone.

They still need daily attention from their humans and exercise outside the cage.

Will a male or female make a better pet for our child? Either will be a good pet.

Can we leave our guinea pig home alone for a few days, with plenty of food, while our family takes a vacation? No. Someone needs to give your guinea pig daily care, but this needn't prevent you from taking vacations. The best option is to find a friend with whom you can leave your cavy, cage and all. Your pet will have the security of a familiar cage and company as well as care.

The next option is to have a friend or a professional pet-sitter come to your home at least once a day to care for your guinea pig. Ask a vet or another pet owner for recommendations, or check the Yellow Pages under pet-sitters. Ask for and check references and satisfy yourself that your pet will be well taken care of. Leave a memo containing detailed information about your guinea pig and its care, and emergency phone numbers.

A final option is to use a boarding kennel that accepts small caged pets. Many kennels accept only dogs and cats, so you might have to do some research. Ask your vet or other small-pet owners for suggestions, and check the Yellow Pages. Before you use a kennel, satisfy yourself—by asking for references, or visiting the kennel and asking questions—that your pet will receive good care. Some veterinary clinics also board small, confined pets. This is a good option if you already have a relationship with a vet whom you trust.

How do we choose a guinea pig that will make a good pet? Look for a healthy animal: one with clear eyes, nose, and ears, and a full, shiny coat. Many guinea pigs are shy with strangers, making it difficult to determine which will be the friendliest. It usually takes a few days of consistent, gentle attention in a new home for a guinea pig to unbend.

Why would a guinea pig ever need a vet? Guinea pigs do get sick sometimes, even with the best of care. They can suffer from respiratory infections, urinary tract infections, and parasites such as fleas and mites. Symptoms such as listlessness, loss of appetite, diarrhea, loss of hair, coughing, or sneezing should receive attention from a veterinarian experienced in treating cavies. Overgrown or misaligned teeth also require veterinary attention.

Resources

CLUBS

Cavy Breeders Association
3034 Forest Oaks Drive
Orange Park, FL 32073

Dallas Cavy Fanciers
1721 East Frankford Road
Apartment 1211
Carrollton, TX 75007

Golden State Cavy Breeders
Association
3727 North Ranchford Court
Concord, CA 94520

North Carolina Cavy Breeders
Association
4991 Breedlove Road
Glenville, NC 28736

Ontario Cavy Club Inc.
90 St. Vincent Street North
Stratford, Ontario
Canada N5A 6H4

There are regional or local cavy clubs in almost every state. Ask a local cavy owner, veterinarian, or breeder for information. Some of the books noted below include lists of clubs.

RESCUE ORGANIZATIONS

Home for Unwanted and
Abandoned Guinea Pigs
3772 Pin Oak Circle
Doraville, GA 30340

House Rabbit Society (assists
in cavy rescues)
PO Box 1201
Alameda, CA 94501
(510) 521-4631

BOOKS FOR ADULTS

Behrend, Katrin. *Guinea Pigs: A Complete Pet Owner's Manual.* Hauppage, NY: Barron's, 1990.

Bielfeld, Horst. *Guinea Pigs: A Complete Owner's Manual.* Hauppauge, NY: Barron's, 1983.

Pavia, Audrey. *The Guinea Pig: An Owner's Guide to a Happy Healthy Pet*. New York: Howell Book House, 1997.

Randolph, Elizabeth. *Rabbits and Other Furry Pets: A Complete Guide to the Purchase and Care of Rabbits, Mice, Gerbils, Hamsters, and Guinea Pigs*. New York: Fawcett Crest, 1992.

BOOKS FOR CHILDREN
Evans, Mark. *ASPCA Pet Care Guide for Kids: Guinea Pigs*. New York: Dorling Kindersley, 1993.

King-Smith, Dick. *I Love Guinea Pigs*. Cambridge, MA: Candlewick Press, 1994.

TWELVE

Hamsters

"We had to move my hamster out of my bedroom," confided Susan. *"I really liked having her there, but she made such a racket at night with her exercise wheel that I couldn't sleep."*

"I know!" said DeVaughn. *"That's how I learned what 'nocturnal' meant. My hamster sleeps all day and plays all night."*

"Mine wakes up to play after dinner," said Susan. *"It's so cute. She lives in the family room, and we have this routine. I go in there after dinner and she's standing up with her front paws on the side of the cage, like she's saying hello. I just love it."*

The hamster is the most popular pet rodent in America, popularity that partly may be due to the fact that the hamster has no tail and thus escapes association with its rodent cousins. While the guinea pig also lacks a tail, it is considerably larger, longer-lived, and more expensive to keep. The hamster is a fetching creature with charms of its own: cute, clean, acrobatic, and friendly.

ORIGINS. The name *hamster* comes from the German word *hamstern*, which means "to hoard." A hamster has cheek pouches that it can stuff with food. In this way, the wild

Hamsters
Facts At a Glance

COST	$300–600 over the hamster's lifetime
SIZE	3–4 ounces
LONGEVITY	2–3 years
TIME REQUIREMENT	30 minutes per day to feed, play with, spot-clean cage; 10 minutes every other day to groom, refill bottle; 30 minutes every week to clean cage
SPACE	At least 30 × 16 × 16 cage or 20-gallon tank, placed away from drafts and direct sun
EXERCISE	Needs exercise wheel, things to climb
EQUIPMENT	Tank or cage, wheel, bedding, litter, hide box, gym or playground, food bowl, hanging water bottle and brush, comb
ODOR	Very little, if cage and litter are kept clean
SHEDDING	Not noticeable
PHYSICAL CHARACTERISTICS AFFECTING KIDS	Small, fragile; can easily be injured if squeezed or dropped; will bite if startled or frightened
TEMPERAMENTAL CHARACTERISTICS AFFECTING KIDS	Solitary; nocturnal, will not play during the day; curious, active
PERSONALITY TRAITS	Can be friendly, trusting, playful if handled gently and quietly; some are shy
PARENTAL SUPERVISION	Children under 10 should be supervised when handling
LEGAL RESTRICTIONS	Illegal in Hawaii; some landlords prohibit all pets

hamster carries food back to its burrow, where it is hoarded. A solitary creature, the wild hamster seeks relief during the day from the desert's heat in extensive underground burrows. Burrows also provide protection from predators, as do the hamster's nocturnal habits, speed, and climbing ability.

Syrian hamsters are the most popular pet hamsters in America. They are all descended from a single family that was found in the Syrian desert in 1930 by a zoology professor at the Hebrew University of Jerusalem, who brought the mother hamster and her litter back to Israel. Later, he sent some of the progeny to England, and eventually some of these were sent to the United States for medical research. Before long researchers began taking these cute little animals home, and their popularity as pets gradually spread.

Before selective breeding resulted in a variety of hair colors and lengths, most hamsters were reddish gold in color, and many still are, hence the common name "golden hamster." Today, hamsters can be found with short, wavy, satin, or long hair and in a variety of colors and patterns: white, cream, beige, brown, black, gray, pied, harlequin, and panda.

Dwarf hamsters, as the name implies, are a smaller version of this small animal. Because of their fragility, they are not recommended pets for young children. More exotic species—Chinese, Russian, Tibetan—have recently been introduced into the United States but are not yet widely available.

NEEDS. A hamster needs to live alone *and* needs human attention daily. It needs to climb and exercise; an exercise wheel is mandatory. The hamster is nocturnal; it does need to be allowed to sleep during the day. A hamster wakened from a sound sleep is not a happy animal and may bite in irritation.

CHILDREN AND HAMSTERS. Hamsters are adorable, active, entertaining, and inquisitive. Children who are old enough to accept that this pet will sleep during the day, and use patience to tame this little creature, will have a friendly pet.

Hamsters are small and easily injured and can deliver a painful bite when irritated or frightened. They are usually not good pets for children under ten.

COMMITMENT. A hamster is relatively inexpensive and easy to care for. In addition to a roomy, healthy environment, a hamster needs attention and fresh food and water every day.

What You Need to Know About Hamsters *Before* You Get One

SIZE. A hamster is typically five inches long and weighs three to four ounces.

LONGEVITY. A hamster usually lives two to three years, and sometimes longer.

LEGAL RESTRICTIONS. Hamsters are not permitted to be kept as pets in the state of Hawaii. Some landlords prohibit all kinds of pets.

COSTS. The care of a hamster, barring a veterinary emergency, will be about $300–$600 over the course of its life, depending on prices in your region and your consumer choices about the enclosure, litter, equipment, and other items.

Food will cost about $1 a week. A commercial diet specifically for hamsters should be purchased in small quantities because food that sits on the shelf loses nutritional value. Cost does not include hay and supplemental fresh food such as fruits and vegetables.

Another ongoing expense is *litter*. Materials such as sawdust and pelleted or torn paper—but not pine or cedar chips—can be used. The cost varies from next to nothing if you have plenty of used paper (especially packing paper or something similar without ink on it) to $5 or $10 a month, depending on the size of the enclosure, how often you change the litter, and whether you buy in bulk. Nesting material can be made from torn-up tissues, paper towels, clean cotton rags, or hay.

Basic equipment includes:

• comprehensive book(s) about hamster care	$10–20
• tank or cage (medium or large)	$40–80
• tank cover (depending on size)	$20–30
• hide box or nest	$0–10
• food bowl	$3
• hanging water bottle	$5–7
• bottle brush	$0–3
• chewing materials	$0–10 (annual)
• exercise wheel	$10
• toys, furniture, gym equipment	$20–80
• rubber gloves (for spot cleaning)	$3
• portable enclosure (optional)	$60
• used toothbrush or hamster comb (optional)	$0–5

If it hasn't already had one, take your hamster to the veterinarian for a well-pet check soon after you bring it home. This may cost $25 to $50. Set aside, either mentally or in fact, a *veterinary emergency fund* of $100.

Your *acquisition* costs will be small. A shelter or rescue group may let you have a hamster for free or for a small donation, or you may find a friend whose hamster has had a litter. Breeders sell hamsters for about $5–$10.

EQUIPMENT. A large aquarium-type tank (twenty- or thirty-gallon size) with a tight-fitting mesh lid is an option that some experts recommend. Because hamsters are skilled escape artists, the lid must fit securely. A large hamster cage with a solid floor also serves as a good habitat, especially if it has more than one story connected by ladders or stairs. The cage bars must be close enough together to prevent escape. A cage is easier to clean and provides better ventilation than a tank but also less protection from drafts.

A hamster needs about two inches of clean, dry bedding to burrow in and things to gnaw on—hay, cardboard, hard wood, nuts, and firm vegetables. As a private animal, it needs a "cave" or nest box to retreat to and sleep in. A food bowl, water bottle, and exercise wheel complete the setup. Gyms and playgrounds can be elaborate, store-bought items consisting of connecting tubes and tunnels, or homemade from cardboard boxes and tubes. Playgrounds or gyms are hard to clean and should be used for daily exercise, not as a full-time habitat.

SPACE. The cage or tank should be as spacious as possible, located away from direct sunlight, bright lights, loud noises, and drafts, in a temperature range of 65° to 80° Fahrenheit. A ten-gallon tank or small hamster cage of the type commonly found in pet stores is barely adequate.

Because a hamster exercises, plays, and makes noise at night, its habitat does not belong in a bedroom.

TIME REQUIREMENT. Hamsters should be *fed* once a day, on a regular schedule. Remove hoarded food that is likely to mold or rot, clean the food bowl, and put down new food. This takes five or ten minutes, including washing and cutting fresh vegetables or fruit. The water bottle should be emptied, cleaned, refilled, and checked every other day. This takes about five minutes.

Hamsters groom themselves and like to be clean. An animal that begins to look bedraggled or dirty probably is sick and should be taken to the vet. A long-haired hamster needs help *grooming* that long, glamorous hair, which takes ten minutes or less every day or two. You can buy a special hamster comb, or use a soft baby brush or clean, used tooth-brush.

Hamsters need a clean, dry cage. Wearing rubber gloves, *spot-clean* the cage every day, removing soiled or damp litter. (A hamster usually chooses one particular area as a "litter box.") This takes five minutes or less. Once a week, empty the litter, thoroughly *wash and dry the cage*, and put down new litter. This takes twenty to thirty minutes.

Hamsters need plenty of *exercise*. This need can be met in part by a wheel inside the enclosure. In addition, care-fully hamsterproof a room, as described on pages 110–111, and give your hamster the run of the room for a while every day. Or put your hamster in a pet enclosure, playpen, or "gym" each evening for playtime.

Handle, *play with*, and talk quietly to your pet for a few minutes every day. A hamster that receives consistent, gen-tle handling will trust you and be friendly.

SHEDS OR SMELLS? A cage or tank that is cleaned regu-larly and frequently should not smell.

CHARACTERISTICS AFFECTING CHILDREN. A hamster wants to be left alone during the day. It will sleep more and more as it gets older. A hamster that is poked, fright-ened or wakened suddenly may bite. A child can play with a hamster in the evening or at night.

PERSONALITY TRAITS. Hamster personalities vary. Most are quite active, but some are more laid-back than others. Some like to be cuddled and held, and others do not. Hamsters are curious, seemingly possessed of endless stamina during their waking hours.

NEED FOR PARENTAL SUPERVISION. Children under the age of ten need supervision when handling these small pets. Unsupervised, young children can enjoy watching a hamster play in a gym or exercise on a wheel.

Child's Age and Care of a Hamster

With parental supervision:

Children **age three to five** can put food in a clean bowl, put nuts, prewashed vegetables or fruit in the enclosure.

Children **age five to seven** also can help an adult wash vegetables, fruit, and food bowl; refill and hang water bottle.

Children **age seven to ten** also can help an adult cut up fruit or vegetables; hand-feed fresh foods, nuts, and treats; empty and clean the water bottle.

Children **age ten to twelve** also can spot-clean the cage (wearing rubber gloves), help an adult wash the cage or tank.

Children **age twelve and up** also can clean and wash enclosure, equipment.

Your Family's Pet Resources

Inventory your resources to see if they enable your family to keep a hamster.

TIME. Which family members will feed and play with this pet and spot-clean its enclosure daily, and refill the water bottle every other day? Who will wash the enclosure each week?

COST. Your acquisition costs, including equipment and veterinary checkup, will be about $100. Can you spend this much, plus an annual expenditure of $50–$150? Can you pay for a veterinary emergency?

ABILITY. Are your children old enough to play gently with this pet, and, if not, will they be satisfied to watch it? Are your children old enough to help with chores?

PLACE AND SPACE. Do you have room for a good-sized enclosure? Can it be placed away from drafts, radiators, bright lights, air conditioners, loud noises, and heavy daytime activity? Can it be placed in a location where a noisy hamster will not disturb your family at night?

HEALTH. Does anyone in your family have allergies that may be triggered by a hamster, or by its litter?

TRAVEL. Who will care for this pet when your family travels? Can you afford to pay someone to do this?

HOUSEKEEPING. Will spillage from a cage bother you?

SPECIAL ISSUES. Is anyone in your family afraid of hamsters, or opposed to having one as a pet? Will you take it with you if you move?

*   *   *

A recent article in *Critters USA* notes, ''The cheek pouch-filling technique is only one of several traits that makes the hamster an enjoyable, delightful pet. They are fun to watch as they go about their daily routine.''

Questions That Parents Ask

We have heard that hamsters make wonderful pets for children and also that they are terrible pets for children.

Which is it? The answer depends on you and your children: your resources and commitment, their ages and personalities. Hamsters sleep all day and play at night. Some children can't abide this and are bitten when they try to wake a sleeping hamster. Some children are too young to be quiet enough, calm enough, and gentle enough to handle a hamster without hurting it, or getting hurt themselves. For these children, hamsters are not a good pet.

Can a hamster be trained to use a litter box? In many cases, yes, if the habitat is large enough to accommodate a small litter box in one corner, if you provide a litter that appeals, and if you keep it clean.

Can we leave our hamster at home while we go on a family vacation? You can leave your hamster alone overnight provided it has a clean cage, adequate food, clean water, plenty of toys, and a safe room temperature. If you will be gone longer, you need to make other arrangements. You can take your hamster, in its habitat, to a friend who will care for it, or have a friend come to the house every evening to spot-clean the cage and food bowl, change the water, put down fresh food, and play with your hamster. If no friends or neighbors are available, ask veterinarians, fellow hamster owners, and rescue and shelter personnel to recommend a professional pet-sitter or veterinary clinics or kennels that board small pets. To assure yourself of the quality of care your pet will receive, talk to the people who will care for it and ask for and check references.

Resources

CLUBS

American Rat, Mouse and
Hamster Society
13317 Neddick Avenue
Poway, CA 92064

Rat, Mouse and Hamster
Fanciers
188 School Street
Danville, CA 94526

Chubby Cheeked Hamster
Association
12060 SE 112th Avenue
Belleview, FL 34402

BOOKS FOR ADULTS

von Frisch, Otto. *Hamsters: A Complete Pet Owner's Manual.*
Hauppauge, NY: Barron's, 1994.

NONFICTION FOR CHILDREN

Evans, Mark. *Hamster: ASPCA Pet Care Guides for Kids.* New
York: DK Publishing, 1993.

Piers, Helen. *Taking Care of Your Hamster: A Young Pet
Owner's Guide.* Hauppauge, NY: Barron's, 1992.

FICTION FOR CHILDREN

Inkpen, Deborah. *Harriet.* Hauppauge, NY: Barron's, 1998.

THIRTEEN

Rabbits

Emma began asking for a pet when she was four. For a year her parents resisted.

"Her friends at school had pets, or claimed they did, and so she wanted one," explained her mother, Janet. "I don't think she cared what kind of pet. We definitely weren't going to get a dog or a cat, so when she said she wanted a rabbit, that sounded like a good idea."

Emma and her parents picked out a dwarf rabbit that she named Tuffy.

Janet, who takes care of Tuffy, described what happened next. "Emma lost interest within a week, once she realized that she couldn't hold the bunny and carry it around like a doll."

As Carolyn Mixon wrote in *Rabbits* magazine, "rabbits rarely conform to the cute-and-cuddly stereotype in children's stories. . . . They are physically delicate animals, which means they can be hurt by children picking them up. Because rabbits feel frightened when people pick them up, they kick and struggle, so children can also get hurt. Rabbits . . . may either run away or try to bite when approached too quickly and too loudly. Stress-related illnesses are common. For these reasons, many children, especially young

Rabbits
Facts At a Glance

COST	$1,200–$4,000 over the rabbit's lifetime
SIZE	2–20 pounds
LONGEVITY	6–10 years
TIME	1 hour per day to feed, groom, play with, spot-clean cage or scoop litter box; 35 minutes per week to wash litter box, cage; 20 minutes a month to trim nails, clean hide box
SPACE	Cage at least 3' × 3' for one dwarf rabbit (larger for two or for larger rabbits), placed away from heat, drafts, loud noise
EXERCISE	Need to exercise out of cage at least 3–4 hours per day
EQUIPMENT	Cage, food bowl, hay rack, hanging water bottle, bottle brush, hide box, toys, salt lick, chew block, comb or brush, nail clippers, litter
ODOR	Litter box and cage will smell if not kept clean
SHEDDING	Yes, varies with type of coat
PHYSICAL CHARACTERISTICS AFFECTING KIDS	Smaller rabbits fragile, easily injured; not easily handled; may bite, scratch, kick if frightened
TEMPERAMENTAL CHARACTERISTICS AFFECTING KIDS	Sociable, need interaction with people or another rabbit; may not like to be lifted or held
PERSONALITY TRAITS	Become trusting, friendly if handled gently and often; can be timid
PARENTAL SUPERVISION	Children under 7 should be supervised when handling
LEGAL RESTRICTIONS	Some landlords prohibit all pets

children, find it difficult to interact with a rabbit and soon lose interest.''

Rabbits are charming, inquisitive, quiet, affectionate, sociable, and fun. They are excellent pets for those who understand them and give them the care they need.

ORIGINS. Scientists for many years classified rabbits as rodents, but now they classify them as lagomorphs. While rodents have one pair of upper incisor teeth, lagomorphs have two. Actually, lagomorphs are more closely related to hoofed animals than to rodents.

Rabbits predate humans by millions of years. Stone Age people depicted rabbits, which they used for meat and fur, in cave paintings, and rabbits were domesticated for these purposes around 500 B.C. They were not kept as pets until the eighteenth century.

Today, there are more than forty-five breeds of domestic rabbits and a limitless range of cross-breeds. Rabbits vary greatly in size from two-pound dwarfs to twenty-two-pound giants. Ear type varies: from tall and upright, to small, upright and pointed, to large floppy ears that hang down (known as ''lops''). Colors run the gamut: silver, black, white, brown, gray, agouti, tortoise, harlequin. Some coats are marked with a dark ''saddle'' or a white ''collar,'' others with spots or patches. Hair type varies: from ''normal,'' which is about one inch long, to rex, which is shorter, to satin, to very long Angora coats.

NEEDS. Wild rabbits live in colonies. They dig and inhabit complex warrens of burrows and connecting tunnels that are used for sleeping, raising young, and hiding from predators. They are naturally crepuscular, sleeping during the day and grazing at dawn and twilight. Many animals hunt them: humans, coyotes, foxes, owls, hawks, cats, dogs, and ferrets.

Domestic rabbits have inherited their ancestors' sociability. A pet rabbit left alone for long periods of time will be bored and depressed and may become destructive and aggressive. A rabbit can find companionship with another rabbit (consult an expert about gender combinations), other types of pets such as a guinea pig (with supervision), or people. It is not easy for people to give a rabbit all the companionship that its nature craves.

Rabbits need attention, stimulation, and exercise. The more you handle your rabbit in a nonthreatening way, the more it will trust you. Give it toys to help prevent boredom, and let it out of its cage to exercise for several hours every day, in a bunnyproof room or area.

Although they are not rodents, rabbits need to gnaw, a need that can be met by chew toys and hard foods such as carrots. An unsupervised, uncaged rabbit will gnaw on furniture, woodwork, carpets, even telephone cords.

CHILDREN AND RABBITS. Parents are often surprised to learn that rabbits rarely make good pets for young children. Most children want to hold and cuddle a rabbit. Most rabbits do not want to be held or cuddled, probably because they associate being grasped, lifted, or carried with being caught by a predator.

Because they are fun to watch and play with, rabbits are excellent pets for adults and older children, who should be taught how to play with and pick up a rabbit (never by the ears). Some experts believe that children should be at least seven years old before parents bring home a bunny.

COMMITMENT. *The woman in the pet shop was buying rabbit food.*

"This rabbit keeps backing up to the bars of the cage and spraying urine outside. How can I make him stop?" she asked.

Uneasily, the shop owner said, "Well, he probably needs to be neutered."

"You don't understand," the woman said. "This is a rabbit, not a dog or a cat. Why would I have to do that?"

"Some rabbits just do better when they're neutered," I

broke in, *"and a vet could tell you if there's something else wrong."*

"I never thought I'd need a vet for a rabbit," the woman said dispiritedly. *"No one told me I'd have to spend real money."*

The popularity of rabbits as pets has soared in the past ten years. But the last decade also has seen increasing numbers of pet rabbits surrendered to shelters and rescue groups, or turned loose to succumb to starvation, thirst, heatstroke, or predators.

Many people do not understand the nature or needs of a rabbit before buying one. Caring for a rabbit calls for a considerable daily time commitment. In addition to a clean cage, fresh water, and a balanced diet, rabbits need attention and exercise.

What You Need to Know About Rabbits *Before* You Get One

SIZE. Dwarf breeds weigh from two to four pounds. Small breeds weigh from four to eight, medium breeds from nine to twelve, and giant breeds can weigh up to twenty pounds and more. Mixed breeds come in all sizes.

LONGEVITY. Domestic rabbits that live indoors usually live six to eight years, and some live as many as ten and twelve years.

LEGAL RESTRICTIONS. Some landlords prohibit pets of all kinds. Check your lease before bringing home a bunny.

COSTS. Taking care of a rabbit can range from $1,200 to $4,000 over its lifetime, depending on the size of your rabbit, prices in your region, and your choices about type of cage, food, substrate, litter, number of toys, and other items.

Food costs $100–$300 a year, depending on the size of

the rabbit. This includes alfalfa or timothy hay and a commercial pelletized diet that should be bought in small quantities to maintain nutritional quality. This does not include the fresh vegetables that rabbits need daily, or the small amounts of fruit or other treats that should be offered every few days.

Litter for the litter box is an annual expense that varies with the number and size of rabbits and size of the litter box. It may cost $50–$150 a year. Consult an expert before buying litter, because some types are unhealthful for rabbits.

Some owners place newspapers in the bottom of the cage, and others add *substrate* of straw or pelleted paper. Cost will vary from nothing to $100 or more annually.

Your rabbit will not need vaccinations, but it should be spayed or neutered, a one-time *veterinary expense*. The surgery is less expensive for males and costs $50 to $175. Many shelters adopt out rabbits only after they have been sterilized and charge an adoption fee or no fee. Rescue groups and shelters can refer adopters to low-cost spay/neuter clinics.

Take your rabbit for a well-pet veterinary checkup soon after you bring it home. This visit typically costs $25–$50 and gives you an opportunity to establish a relationship with a vet and ask questions.

Acquisition costs vary. Shelters and rescue groups adopt out for free or for a donation to help cover costs. If you buy a rabbit from a reputable breeder, you will probably pay $20 on up.

EQUIPMENT. Your rabbit should live in the largest possible cage, preferably one with a solid bottom. If the bottom is wire mesh, cover part of it with a resting board made of solid material such as Plexiglas. Some owners convert medium or large dog cages to rabbit use by doing this. Cages and carriers can be purchased in pet shops or through catalogs.

Buy or build a hide box (made of a material safe for

Basic equipment includes:

• comprehensive book(s) about rabbit care	$10–20
• cage	$50–120
• hide box	$0–40
• litter box	$3–10
• litter box scoop	$2–5
• hay rack	$5–8
• food bowl	$3–5
• water bottle	$5–10
• bottle brush	$0–3
• chew toys or wood	$0–10 (annual)
• salt lick	$1
• toys	$0–20 (annual)
• rubber gloves (for cage cleaning)	$3
• brush or comb	$4–6
• nail clipper	$3–10
• carrier	$20–30
• mesh or wire indoor pet gate (optional)	$25

rabbits to chew) that fits your rabbit's size, with a small towel inside for bedding. You can use a cardboard box and keep replacing it if your rabbit chews it up.

Rabbits can use a cat litter box, or smaller boxes made

especially for rabbits and ferrets. Some cat litters are toxic to rabbits.

The water bottle should be the sipper type, hung on the side of the cage. Use a clean, used toothbrush or baby bottle brush to clean it. A hay rack that attaches to the side of the cage holds timothy or alfalfa. The food bowl should be of a heavy material, such as earthenware, that won't tip or splinter. Choose a size that is appropriate for your rabbit's size and cage.

Some rabbits like a salt lick. They need things to chew, such as nontoxic wood. Toys can be homemade, as long as they are not sharp, toxic, or made of a material that will splinter. Paper bags or cardboard boxes to climb in, rolls from paper towels, balls, and squeaky toys are popular.

Grooming materials can be found in pet shops. A fine-toothed flea comb works well on rabbits with short hair. A dog comb with wider teeth or a slicker brush is needed for long-haired rabbits. Cat nail clippers or human nail clippers can be used to trim nails.

SPACE. A single dwarf rabbit should have a cage that measures at least two by three feet, with enough head room to stand on its hind legs without its ears touching the top of the cage. A larger rabbit (or more than one) needs a larger cage.

Rabbits like company, so put the cage in a location where your family spends time, such as the family room. Place it well away from loud noises such as blaring TVs, radios, or stereo speakers. Avoid drafts, direct sunlight, and heating and air-conditioning vents; temperatures between 60° and 70° Fahrenheit are fine, but warmer temperatures, especially over 80°, spell danger. Try to assure that your rabbit receives about twelve hours of light and twelve of darkness. Do not banish it to a darkened garage or basement, which also is likely to be damp and cold—all elements that threaten its health.

Because rabbits need a lot of exercise, you will need to carefully rabbitproof at least one room.

TIME REQUIREMENT. *Feed* your rabbit twice a day. In the morning, clean the food bowl; put down pellets, vegetables, and fresh timothy or alfalfa. In the evening, replenish the hay and vegetables and clean and refill the water bottle. This takes about five minutes morning and evening. Every few days, give your rabbit a small amount of fresh, washed fruit.

Clean the litter box daily with a scoop. This takes two or three minutes. Empty the box, thoroughly wash and dry it, and refill it with clean litter once a week. This takes about fifteen minutes.

Spot-clean the cage once a day. This takes five minutes or less. Once a week, wash and dry the bottom of the cage (including the resting board, if the cage has a wire bottom). This takes about twenty minutes. Thoroughly wash inside the hide box once a month. This takes about ten minutes. If your rabbit does not use a litter box, change newspapers or substrate frequently.

Let your rabbit out of its cage to *exercise* every day for a minimum of three to four hours; young rabbits need more exercise than older ones. Rabbits can get into a lot of mischief indoors, so refer to your rabbit care book as well as pages 110–111, for guidance about rabbitproofing a room.

Your rabbit needs daily *attention* from its human family. The easiest way to do this is to get down on the floor to play with and pat it. Do this at least twice a day, for twenty to thirty minutes.

Rabbits are clean animals, but they need your help with *grooming*. Like cats, rabbits lick their coats, swallowing hair in the process. Unlike cats, rabbits cannot regurgitate the hair, and this can pose a serious health problem. Comb long-haired varieties, such as Angoras, daily. Brush or comb rabbits with shorter hair every two or three days and more often when they are shedding. Grooming may take ten to thirty minutes, depending on hair length.

Rabbits need to have their nails trimmed, usually about every two months. Take your rabbit to a veterinarian, or have your vet teach you to do it; actual trimming takes five to ten minutes, if your rabbit is used to this procedure and accepts it calmly.

SHEDS OR SMELLS? Rabbits have little odor. All rabbits shed; how much they shed, and how much you notice, depends on hair length, thickness, and color. A cage or litter box that is not cleaned frequently will smell.

CHARACTERISTICS AFFECTING CHILDREN. Rabbits are active and playful. They usually do not like to be held or cuddled, but often they like to sit or sleep next to a person. They generally feel most secure on the floor. A rabbit that feels threatened might bite, scratch, or kick.

Children who are too young to correctly handle a rabbit can unintentionally injure it. Children older than seven are more likely to have the patience and coordination to handle a rabbit.

PERSONALITY TRAITS. Rabbit personalities range from outgoing, to shy and retiring, to aggressive. Dwarf breeds are usually active and excitable, some larger breeds are known for being mellow, and lops are often people-oriented. Within each breed and within each litter (whether pure or mixed), babies display a range of personalities.

NEED FOR PARENTAL SUPERVISION. Children under the age of seven need close supervision when handling these pets, and older children may also require supervision. Bunnies outside of their cage should be monitored by adults.

Your Family's Pet Resources

TIME. Which family members will feed and play with the rabbit twice a day? Who will scoop the litter box or spot-clean the cage daily? Who will wash the litter box and cage

---

Child's Age and Care of Rabbit

With parental supervision:

Children **age three to five** can put hay in the hay rack, put pellets in the food bowl, put prewashed vegetables or fruit in the cage, pat the rabbit while it sits next to a parent.

Children **age five to seven** also can clean the food bowl, refill and hang the water bottle, help an adult wash vegetables or fruit.

Children **age seven to ten** also can empty and clean the water bottle, pick up and replace newspaper, scoop litter box, pet and play with the rabbit.

Children **age ten to twelve** also can help an adult cut up fruit or vegetables, groom, wash the cage.

Children **age twelve and up** also can clean and wash the cage and litter box, groom the rabbit (but not clip nails).

---

weekly and clean the hide box each month? Who will groom the rabbit, trim its nails?

COST. Your initial acquisition cost, including equipment, spaying or neutering, and veterinary checkup will be $200–$300 for one rabbit. Can you afford this, plus annual expenditures of at least $150? For six to ten years? Can you afford veterinary care if the rabbit is sick or is injured?

ABILITY. Are your children old enough to play with a rabbit? Are they old enough to help with chores?

PLACE AND SPACE. Do you have room for a large cage? Can it be placed away from heat, drafts, and loud noises and still be ''where the action is''? Can you bunnyproof at least one room so that your pet can exercise safely? Are there legal problems with keeping a rabbit in your home?

HEALTH. Does anyone in your family have allergies that may be triggered by this pet, its litter, or the hay that is part of its diet?

TRAVEL. Who will care for your rabbit when the family travels? If necessary, can you afford to board it or pay someone to care for it?

HOUSEKEEPING. Will spillage from the cage bother you? Odor from a litter box? Will you mind bunnyproofing a room?

SPECIAL ISSUES. If your child can not cuddle and carry this pet, will you keep it and give it the attention it needs? If you move, will you take the rabbit with you?

In *House Rabbit Handbook*, Marinell Harriman announces: "What a great surprise it is to new rabbit people that they have an intelligent creature in their midst with an inquisitive mind that is constantly looking for activity. Rabbits are comprised of paradoxes that make them extremely entertaining—inquisitive yet cautious, skittish yet confident, energetic yet lazy, timid yet bold."

Questions Parents Ask

We have heard that rabbits are the ideal family pet, especially in a home where both parents work. Is this true? Rabbits are charming, interesting animals and can make wonderful pets, but they are not ideal for every family. A rabbit needs a spacious cage and plenty of exercise and stimulation. It should not be left in a cage around the clock or unattended for many hours. Both the cage and litter box need to be cleaned, and the rabbit groomed. A rabbit may be ideal for you if you have the time and resources to devote to it.

What is the best kind of rabbit to get for a family with children? This depends on the age and personality of your children. Baby rabbits are too delicate for most children. Dwarf breeds tend to be very active and often dislike being held, while some larger rabbits actually like it. A mixed breed will make as good a pet as a pure breed, if you like its temperament. Consistent, gentle handling helps produce family-friendly bunnies.

Isn't a small rabbit a better choice for a small child? Not necessarily. The smaller the rabbit, the more fragile and easily hurt. The smaller the child, the harder it is to understand a rabbit's nature and, if necessary, refrain from trying to grab, hold, and carry it. Smaller rabbits tend to be more active and may be even less receptive than a large rabbit to being cuddled.

Is it better to get a baby bunny? There are a number of advantages to adopting an adult bunny. Its personality and size are known quantities, making it easier to choose the rabbit that matches your family. Adults tend to be calmer and easier to handle and are past the baby phase when they try to dig and chew everything in sight. It is easier to litter-train an adult, particularly if it has been spayed or neutered.

I've seen pet rabbits do really annoying things, like spray urine. Will litter training stop this? Spraying is related to sexual maturity, not litter box training. Male rabbits (bucks) that have not been neutered and female rabbits (does) that have not been spayed will engage in this and other unpleasant habits. This behavior will gradually disappear a few weeks or months after spaying or neutering. Altered rabbits are healthier, calmer, and less aggressive.

Should we get one rabbit or two? If you have room for a large enough cage, and can afford food and other costs for two, by all means get two rabbits, especially if your pets will be left alone for eight or more hours a day. They will keep each other company and be twice as much fun for your family. Consult an expert about age and gender combinations. Two bucks, for example, usually cannot live together peacefully.

Does a rabbit need veterinary attention? Yes. Rabbits should be spayed or neutered. Unspayed females are prone to uterine cancer. Both males and females are less cranky after being altered and are easier to litter train.

Rabbits that do not receive sufficient fresh water and a proper diet that includes timothy or alfalfa hay can develop digestive problems. Overexposure to heat can cause heat-stroke. Lack of chewing materials can result in overgrown teeth, which can make it impossible for a rabbit to eat. Rabbits living in cages with wire floors can develop sores on their feet and hind legs. Even a well-cared-for rabbit can get sick or injured and need veterinary care.

Do purebred rabbits make better pets? When you buy or adopt a purebred, you are buying predictability. You have a good idea of how big a youngster will grow to be and some clues to its personality. Mixed breeds are just as cute and healthy, but they are less predictable. If you adopt or buy an adult, you know just what you are getting, whether it is a pure or mixed breed.

How do we choose a rabbit? Consult your rabbit care book (or take it with you) to learn how to distinguish a healthy rabbit. Responsible breeders, shelters, and rescue groups will not sell or adopt out a sick animal and should inform you about past health problems.

If a rabbit is healthy, spend some time observing it and trying to get to know it. Does it seem to have the type of personality that your family will enjoy?

Can we leave our pet rabbit alone for a few days while we take a vacation? You can leave your rabbit alone overnight, in a clean cage, with plenty of food, fresh water, and toys. If you are going to be away longer, arrange for a trustworthy person to come to your home to feed and water your pet, clean the cage, and monitor it while it exercises outside the cage. This could be a professional sitter, whose references you have checked, or a friend or neighbor you trust.

Another alternative is to take your rabbit, cage and all, to a friend's home, veterinary clinic, or boarding kennel to be looked after. Unless you are already familiar with the vet or kennel, ask a lot of questions about the care your pet will receive, check references and visit the facility to make certain that it is clean and that the personnel are caring and knowledgeable.

Resources

CLUBS AND RESCUE GROUPS
House Rabbit Society (HRS)
National Headquarters
PO Box 1201
Alameda, CA 94501
(510) 521-4631
www.rabbit.org
Can provide list of state and
regional HRS locations.

BOOKS FOR ADULTS
Harriman, Marinell. *House Rabbit Handbook: How to Live with an Urban Rabbit*. Alameda, CA: Drollery Press, 1995.

Pavia, Audrey. *The Rabbit: An Owner's Guide to a Happy, Healthy Pet*. NY: Howell Book House, 1996.

NONFICTION FOR CHILDREN
Evans, Mark. *Rabbit: ASPCA Pet Care Guides for Kids*. New York: Dorling Kindersley, 1992.

FICTION FOR CHILDREN
Howe, Deborah and James. *Bunnicula: A Rabbit-Tale of Mystery*. New York: Aladdin, 1976.

Lawson, Robert. *Rabbit Hill*. New York: Puffin, 1944.

Williams, Margery. *The Velveteen Rabbit*. New York: Derrydale Books, 1986.

FOURTEEN

A Footnote About Ferrets

The little girl, perhaps eight years old, returned to stand in front of the ferret cage. An irresistibly adorable head poked up from the hammock.

Above the cage, which was strategically positioned in the pet shop window, a sign read, "Do not put fingers in the cage." Another sign read, "Do not take ferrets out of the cage."

The girl spoke softly to the kit, who hopped out of the hammock and approached her with interest. She poked a finger into the cage for him to sniff—then screeched when he nipped it. As she tore her finger away, the startled ferret forgot to let go.

Her mother, who had been buying dog food, ran to her side and nearly fainted at the sight of blood dripping from her daughter's finger. She began berating one of the shop employees for having such a "dangerous animal" on display. As I left the store, she was threatening a lawsuit.

Ferrets are not dangerous. If properly handled and trained, they are affectionate and friendly. These days, humans pose more of a threat to them than the other way around. These adorable, playful little animals are increasingly popular as pets. Unfortunately, many ferrets are bought on impulse by people who are unaware of their nature and needs. The result, predictably, is that more and more ferrets are being surrendered to shelters and rescue organizations.

Of all the confined, furry pets that I write about, ferrets are the most expensive to buy and maintain and, in my view, require the most attention and care. Because of their growing popularity, some are bred in ferret farms or mills, or by amateur backyard breeders under inhumane conditions. Ferrets from these sources are usually sold through pet shops, sometimes at too young an age, and do not always receive proper handling or socialization. As a result, they may nip or bite unless gently socialized and trained.

As appealing as they are, I give ferrets a footnote here rather than a full discussion because I believe that they are best suited to families that:

- do not have young children
- have experience with pet ownership
- have plenty of time to devote to daily pet care

Ferrets need a lot of exercise and supervision. Compared to other small confined pets, keeping a ferret clean is more of a challenge, and their odor is more obvious. Quite a few local jurisdictions, as well as California, Hawaii, and the District of Columbia, prohibit ferret ownership. Ferrets are natural predators: Given the opportunity, they will hunt and kill other small pets such as birds, gerbils, rabbits, hamsters, and guinea pigs as well as mice and rats.

Together with the mink, sable, otter, badger, and skunk, the ferret belongs to the weasel family *mustelidae*. A ferret weighs from twelve ounces up to five pounds. Females are smaller than males. A domestic ferret typically lives seven to nine years and occasionally as long as eleven or even twelve. Most people are familiar with ferrets that have a raccoonlike mask, but other ferrets are all white, and some are silver or cinnamon.

Ferrets were first dometicated by the Egyptians as early as 3000 B.C. They were introduced into Europe much later, possibly by the Crusaders in the twelfth century, and exported to America soon after colonization.

Ferrets sleep about fifteen hours a day, but when they are active, they are *very* active and curious. They need a spacious, escape-proof cage to live in (never a tank!), preferably with two or three stories and connecting ladders, and a solid floor. These fun-loving animals are intelligent and sociable; they need lots of toys, attention, and playtime. They need to roam outside the cage for at least four hours a day and preferably more. It is cruel to leave a ferret locked in a cage twenty-four hours a day. Because they are so inquisitive and busy, it takes quite an effort to ferretproof a room or rooms, and even then the ferret needs supervision. The most common cause of ferret health problems is accidents (such as getting sat on after climbing under a chair cushion) and ingestion of toxic materials, rubber, or plastic.

Ferrets are carnivores with a high metabolism. They need almost constant access to high-protein food; commercial dog or cat food is not adequate. Owners need to regularly clean their ferret's ears and teeth, clip its nails, and bathe it. Ferrets should not be declawed.

Ferrets require an annual veterinary checkup and distemper and rabies vaccinations and boosters. It is imperative for ferrets to be spayed or neutered. An unneutered male (a hob) smells bad, will be aggressive, and be prone to health problems. An unspayed female (a jill) can become fatally ill when she goes into heat if she is not bred.

Ferrets, especially males, have a strong musky odor that many people find offensive. Unsterilized ferrets of both sexes give off a particularly strong odor when in heat or rut. Sterilization greatly reduces the odor in both sexes, although some pets continue to give off at least some aroma. While ferrets can be descented surgically, most ferret aficionados believe that this is neither necessary nor desirable.

Because of their tendency to nip if startled or frightened, their talent as escape artists, and their fragility, ferrets are not recommended for families with young children. Although these animals are neither mean nor inherently dangerous, they can inflict serious injuries.

If you do want to pursue the idea of ferret ownership, I recommend that you contact a local rescue organization. People who run these organizations are extremely knowledgeable and can help you learn about ferrets and recommend qualified veterinarians and reputable breeders. I strongly recommend acquiring a ferret through adoption from a rescue organization or shelter, where you are most likely to find adults rather than kits. An older ferret may be a good choice, as it tends to be more mellow and calm. Pamela Grant, co-founder of Pet Pals Ferret Rescue and Adoption, recommends an adult as a first ferret because:

- Most are already trained not to nip and to use the litter box in their cage.
- Their personalities are established. Some rescue operators provide personality profiles.
- They are fully grown, and children won't lose interest because they grow from the "hold in your hand" size.

Resources

CLUBS AND RESCUE ORGANIZATIONS

American Ferret Association
PO Box 3986
Frederick, MD 21705

Ferret Fanciers Club
713 Chautauga Court
Pittsburgh, PA 15214

League of Independent Ferret
Enthusiasts
9330 Old Burke Lake Road
Burke, VA 22015

North American Ferret
Association
PO Box 1963
Dale City, VA 22193

STAR Ferrets
PO Box 1714
Springfield, VA 22151-0714
Will provide free list of ferret
shelters, breeders, clubs,
veterinarians by state.

United Ferret Organization
PO Box 606
Assonet, MA 02702

BOOK

Shefferman, Mary R. *The Ferret: An Owner's Guide to a Happy Healthy Pet.* New York: Howell Book House, 1996.

PART FOUR

Children, Wings, and Fins

FIFTEEN

Birds

"Listen, my children, and you shall hear / Of the midnight ride of Paul Revere." The recitation of Longfellow's poem was being given, not by the family's third-grader, but by a three-year-old budgie (or budgerigar, commonly known in America as a parakeet). Budgies have been known to master hundreds of words and phrases and even memorize poems.

Some birds sing, others talk, some are extremely affectionate, and all are intelligent. No other animal living on land sports such a palette of gold, yellow, red, blue, green, white, silver, gray, brown, black, orange, and every imaginable shade in between.

Parents find pet birds "full of personality" and "great company." Children have good things to say, as well: "hilarious," "fun to play with," "sits on my shoulder," "helps me with my homework by stealing my pencil."

Called "our sisters of the sky" by St. Francis of Assisi, birds have long fascinated us because of their unique ability to travel through the air. Scientists, dreamers, and inventors from Daedalus to Leonardo da Vinci to the Wright brothers studied birds to unlock the mystery of flight. Of all the animals, poets have turned most often to birds for inspiration and expression.

Birds
Facts At a Glance

COST	$1,000–$10,000 over the bird's lifetime
SIZE	1 ounce to 3 pounds
LONGEVITY	10–50+ years
TIME REQUIREMENT	20–30 minutes per day to feed, clean cage, spray or shower bird; 1 to 2 hours per day out-of-cage time and attention for some species; 30 minutes per week to wash cage, perches, toys
SPACE	Cage at least 40" × 20" × 32" for one canary or budgie, larger for two birds or for a larger bird, placed away from drafts and direct heat
EXERCISE	Some species, such as cockatiels and budgies, need daily exercise outside of cage; others need plenty of room to move inside cage
EQUIPMENT	Cage, perches, spray or birdbath, water bottle or dish, food dish or feeder, toys, brushes for cleaning cage, out-of-cage perch or gym
ODOR	Little or none, if cage is kept clean
SHEDDING	All birds shed old feathers
PHYSICAL CHARACTERISTICS AFFECTING KIDS	Small, fragile; can easily be injured if panicked, squeezed; can bite if feeling threatened
TEMPERAMENTAL CHARACTERISTICS AFFECTING KIDS	Sociable, need attention and interaction with another bird or human; some are trainable
PERSONALITY TRAITS	Range from noisy and aggressive to curious and playful, to affectionate, to quiet and gentle
PARENTAL SUPERVISION	Parents should supervise children under 10 and should supervise a bird outside the cage
LEGAL RESTRICTIONS	Federal and international law prohibits importation of certain species; some states prohibit sale or ownership of certain species; some local laws regulate noise by birds

Samuel Taylor Coleridge, in an epic poem known to most schoolchildren, *The Rime of the Ancient Mariner*, tells of a large bird, an albatross, that brings good luck to a stranded ship and returns "every day, for food or play." But a mariner kills the albatross, thereby dooming himself and his shipmates. Coleridge closes with a plea that still resonates with animal lovers:

> *He prayeth best, who loveth best*
> *All things both great and small;*
> *For the dear God who loveth us,*
> *He made and loveth all.*

ORIGINS. A theory supported by many paleontologists holds that birds descended directly from dinosaurs. The fossil of a feathered animal named archaeopteryx found in Europe that may have been the first bird had teeth and claws. Archaeopteryx became extinct 120 million years ago but, fortunately, birds survive on every continent, adapting to many different environments. They are waders, swimmers, predators, and prey, and their size, color, body shape, wings, bills, feet, and tails have developed accordingly.

Birds may have been the first animals kept by people solely for the fun of it—not to hunt, herd, protect, or provide food. Both the early Egyptian and Chinese civilizations left drawings and records of pet birds. Alexander the Great, who loved birds and kept a pet parakeet, is considered the founder of aviculture, and Aristotle wrote extensively about birds. During the Roman Empire, nobles frequently kept pet birds in large aviaries, and birds subsequently became popular pets throughout Europe (Henry VIII had a favorite parrot), reaching the height of their popularity during the eighteenth century.

The first American bird club was founded in 1927, but bird keeping did not become particularly popular in the United States until the 1950s. During that decade, the diminutive and personable parakeet was introduced (from Australia, via Europe), and since then interest in other species has grown. Today, birds are the third most popular pet in America (not counting fish), after cats and dogs. Unfortunately, the importation of exotic species of birds into the United States and other countries for sale as pets, together with habitat loss, has decimated some species and threatens to extinguish others. Recent international treaties and federal laws attempt to slow the carnage.

Birds are a hobby to many people who do not own one. According to *Popular Science* magazine, fifty-four million people hike or travel to bird-watch each year, and another nine million watch birds at a home feeder. If birds appeal to you, but you can't keep one as a pet, you have many other opportunities to enjoy them.

NEEDS. Wild birds live in flocks and are extremely sociable. This sociability enables them to bond closely with a human owner, but it also means that they require a good deal of interaction with that human or else with another bird. Says Dr. Kenneth Welle of the University of Illinois College of Veterinary Medicine in *Bird Life* magazine, "It is inhumane to put a bird in a cage and give it no social contact." He suggests that owners plan to spend at least one hour twice a day interacting with their bird. He notes that, "Most birds get social time with the 'flock' just by being out of the cage and on a perch in the same room with people. You could take a portable perch around with you as you go from room to room. . . . You also need to give them something to do—a toy to play with or something to gnaw on."

Wild birds sleep, perch, fly, build nests, evade predators, forage for food, raise their young. They are intelligent and active. Pet birds need mental and physical, as well as social, activity. *The Complete Book of Parakeet Care* advises that "a parakeet that is not allowed out of its cage languishes and gradually loses interest in its surroundings. It may overeat or start plucking its feathers out of boredom. . . . Anyone unwilling or unable to spend considerable time keeping a parakeet company and to create conditions that reflect its natural needs at least partially by allowing for flying, playing, gnawing, bathing, and preening should not keep birds at all.'' Like the parakeet, most species kept as pets need time outside the cage daily, and most enjoy a bath or shower.

In the wild, young birds are raised and trained by their parents. Says Dr. Welle, ''For domestically raised birds, owners are essentially the parents; they need to set limits and teach what is socially acceptable to prevent behavior problems.'' First-time bird owners are often surprised to learn that their bird needs training. (The exceptions are birds such as finches, that are kept in pairs and interact primarily with each other.) Birds that are not trained are less fun as pets, less content, and more likely to develop behavior problems such as screaming or biting.

Birds need consistent care. Because their bodies are small and their metabolic rate high, they need frequent access to food and water. A small bird left without food or water for twenty-four hours can starve or dehydrate.

CHILDREN AND BIRDS. *"Abby! Hello! Marty! Bad boy!"* *These words greeted Abby and her brother as they entered the house after school each day. Giggling with delight, they would run to the living room, where their pet budgies lived. Personable, cheery, and animated, the birds amused and entertained them until their mother arrived home from work. This pet was a compromise between Abby's allergies and Steve's desire for a snake. Abby and Steve were enamored of the birds and making plans for a summer outdoor aviary for them.*

Abby never outgrew her allergies or her love of birds, and she became a dedicated wild bird watcher, a hobby that her husband later "caught" from her.

Many children become attached to pet birds and find them to be charming, entertaining companions. Birds most often recommended for families with children are budgies, cockatiels, and canaries. Children enjoy watching or listening to canaries and can hold and play with budgies and cockatiels, two species that need time outside the cage. Children who want to handle a bird need to be old enough—usually at least seven years old—to be gentle and patient.

COMMITMENT. "Many people who buy birds don't understand how much attention they need," says veterinarian Ann Piety. "Birds are very smart and very social. They need a lot of mental stimulation and a lot of interaction."

Adds Moira Gingery, an animal advocate who finds homes for birds given up by their owners, "People buy a bird because they think it isn't much work. They give it up when they discover it *is* work, or because it won't talk or sing or do what they expect it to do. You have to want a bird for everything that a bird is, not just because you want it to talk." A pet bird demands a substantial daily time commitment, for many years.

What You Need to Know About Birds *Before* You Get One

SIZE. Depending on the species, birds vary in size from four to thirty-six inches in length, weighing from one ounce to three pounds.

LONGEVITY. Depending on the species and quality of care, a pet bird can live ten to fifteen years (canaries, parakeets), up to twenty to thirty years for a cockatiel, fifty years for an African gray parrot or macaw, and eighty years for an Amazon parrot.

LEGAL RESTRICTIONS. Many states, including Hawaii, Ohio, Georgia, New Jersey, Kansas, and Wyoming, regulate the importation and/or breeding of certain species. Some local zoning ordinances include guidelines about exotic species and about noise that may apply to birds.

The illegal importation of endangered birds unfortunately continues, threatening the existence of nearly one thousand species. As many as one-half of wild-caught birds die in the process of capture, and many of the survivors die during transport. Those that arrive in America are badly stressed and often diseased. Before you buy a bird, ask bird clubs and avian vets for references to make certain that you are buying a captive-bred, not an illegally imported, bird from a reputable source. Most domestically bred birds sold commercially will have a closed metal band around one leg, placed there when the bird was a baby. All parakeets must be banded, and some states require closed banding of domestically raised birds offered for sale.

COSTS. The cost of purchasing and caring for a bird throughout its life ranges from $1,000 up to $10,000 and more, depending on the species.

Food may cost as little as $50 a year for a small bird such as a canary or parakeet, and more for a large one. Each species has different nutritional needs. Contrary to popular belief and practice, seed is not an adequate diet. Pelletized bird food available through shops and catalogs provides a more healthful diet and can be supplemented with small amounts of seed, fresh vegetables, and fruit.

Experts recommend using newspaper, butcher block paper, paper towels, or paper tray liners on the floor of the cage and recommend against using shavings or litter. The annual cost of *substrate* is nothing for old newspapers.

Veterinary costs include a well-pet checkup for your bird by an avian vet soon after you acquire it. A checkup costs $35–$55, but if blood work is also recommended, this adds $30–$50. Be guided by your veterinarian's recommendation concerning the frequency of follow-up exams; for some birds, exams are annual and cost $35–$100.

Because signs of weakness or illness attract predation, birds are programmed to hide them. Should your bird show symptoms such as lethargy, vomiting, refusing to eat, or huddling on the floor of the cage, take it to a veterinarian immediately. By the time such symptoms become evident, the bird is already very ill. Set aside, mentally or in fact, at least $150 to pay for a *veterinary emergency*.

Consult your avian veterinarian for advice as to whether your bird should have its wings clipped or nails or beak trimmed. To avoid inadvertent injury to the bird, many owners prefer to have a vet do this. The cost for *grooming* ranges from about $30 to $60 and frequency varies. If you plan to do this yourself, ask your vet to train you.

Basic equipment includes:

- comprehensive book(s) about bird care $10–25
- cage $50–500
- water dish or bottle $5–20
- food dish or feeder $5–15
- brushes for cleaning cage $5–15
- perches $5–20
- swing $5–35
- spray bottle or birdbath $3–15
- cuttlebone and/or mineral stone $2–5
- toys $3–25
- out-of-cage perch or playground $5–200

Acquisition costs vary tremendously. Shelters and rescue groups adopt out birds for free or for a modest fee to help cover costs. If you buy from a breeder, price varies with the species, coloration, age, and sex; hand-fed, hand-raised birds cost more. A parakeet may cost $15–$20, and a large parrot may cost $5,000 and more. Canaries typically fall in the $75–$100 range, hand-raised cockatiels are about $100 and up, and zebra finches cost around $10 each.

EQUIPMENT. "No cage is too large," says veterinarian Ann Piety, a remark echoed by many experts. At a minimum, the cage must be taller than the bird and allow it to spread its wings and move about. For a three-foot-long parrot, with an equally impressive wingspan, this minimum is large indeed. Two birds require a larger cage than one. After you decide on the species and number of birds that you want, consult an expert about minimum cage size and try to exceed it.

Spacing between bars ranges from about ¼ inch for small birds such as parakeets and canaries, to ½ inch for cockatiels, to 1 inch and more for large parrots. Cockatiels and budgies like a cage with some horizontal bars so that they can grasp and climb them. Avoid wooden cages and cages with paint that may contain lead. The cage should have an easy-to-clean pull-out tray at the bottom. A steel brush comes in handy for cleaning the bars, and a toothbrush or baby bottle brush can be used to clean a water bottle.

Birds need diversion inside the cage. Preferred toys vary with the species and individual and may include bells, ladders, tassels, cords, ropes, and chew toys. Attach a cuttlebone or calcium stone to the side of the cage to provide calcium and beak conditioning.

Perches are important to a bird, who spends its entire life, waking or sleeping, standing on one. Every bird needs more than one perch or branch of a diameter correctly sized to its feet. Buy perches of different shapes, sizes, and materials, with some horizontal and some angled. Perches for birds outside the cage range from a simple wooden perch on top of the cage, to a portable tabletop perch, to elaborate freestanding "gyms" or "playgrounds" that may include food and water dishes and a tray to collect droppings and spilled food.

Food and water containers are available in several designs and materials. Usually, a water bottle and feeder that attach to the side of the cage are recommended, but check with an expert before deciding what type is best for your bird. Avoid using containers that can be bitten and splintered.

Most birds love to bathe or shower. Some will hop into a shallow pan or saucer, others use a birdbath that attaches to the cage, and some take showers with their owners. A bird shower can be a simple plastic spray bottle.

SPACE. Your bird's cage is its primary environment, where it spends most of its time. Get the biggest cage you can afford and have room for. A tall bird, such as a macaw, needs a tall cage; a flighted bird such as a canary needs less height and more width; climbers, such as cockatiels, like to have height so that they can climb ladders and ropes. A cage for a canary or budgie should measure at least 40 inches long by 20 inches deep by 32 inches high; for a cockatiel, at least 40 by 28 by 52; and for a pair of lovebirds, 48 by 38 by 24. The inside of the cage should be properly furnished with food and water dispensers, perches, and toys, but not be overcrowded.

Birds like activity, so put the cage where your family congregates. One caveat: Do not put it in the kitchen, because fumes from Teflon pans can kill a bird. Fireplace and cigarette smoke also are harmful. Birds do not like to be low to the ground, so place the cage on a stand or shelf at eye level; most large cages are made with stands or legs.

Although birds in the wild survive temperature extremes, pet birds are not conditioned to do so. Place the cage in a well-ventilated area, away from drafts or other temperature fluctuations caused by heating or air-conditioning vents. A bright, sunny location is good, as long as the cage does not overheat. Your bird also needs darkness for sleeping. Do not leave it in a hallway or other area where lights are left on at night, or consign it to a dark room or basement where it gets less than ten or twelve hours of daylight.

Some pet birds must have daily time outside the cage. Broken bones and other injuries result when they crash into windows, walls, furniture, and ceiling fans. Whether or not its wings have been clipped, a bird taken out of the cage should be supervised and the room birdproofed.

"Imagine if a 2-year-old child, who tests everything by putting it in his or her mouth, could fly, and you'll have a good idea of what's involved in 'birdproofing' your home," writes Elaine Radford in *BirdTalk*. Precautions include drawing shades or curtains over windows, covering mirrors, closing doors, and turning off ceiling fans. To prevent drowning, cover or remove bowls, pans, or glasses containing liquids, and empty sinks or tubs. Prevent access to fireplaces, stoves, cleaning materials, cosmetics, and soaps. (Several experts recommend keeping birds out of bathrooms and kitchens, because of the many hazards they present.) Many common household plants are poisonous if eaten by birds; obtain a list of these from a book, veterinarian, or club and remove them from any room your bird is allowed to visit.

SHEDS OR SMELLS? A birdcage that is regularly cleaned should not smell, and a healthy bird does not smell. All birds lose old feathers, replacing them with new ones, a process known as molting. Most wild birds molt once a year. The frequency and extent of molting in pet birds varies with the species, the individual bird, its health, and its living conditions. Some continually lose and replace a few feathers year-round, and others molt lightly two or three times a year. Whether molting or not, all birds "shed" feather dust and dander; some species, such as cockatiels, cockatoos, and African grays, create more dust than others.

"Birds are messy," says my neighbor, Diana, mother of *four kids and two birds. "They always manage to kick seed and whatever through the bars, not to mention feathers and dust. The kids don't seem to mind. Heck, they don't notice. I'm the one doing the cleaning."*

"I am convinced that when I walk into the kitchen on a sunny Saturday afternoon with Dodger, my Timneh African grey, he and I see two very different things. While I see a clean vinyl-covered floor, he sees a fresh canvas," writes Sally Carette in *Bird Talk* magazine. If housekeeping is an issue for you, small birds such as parakeets, finches, canaries, or lovebirds make less of a mess than large birds. You can buy "mess catchers" such as skirts or trays to place under or around the cage and help contain the mess. Birds that exercise outside the cage do not become "potty trained" and leave droppings on carpets and furniture.

TIME REQUIREMENT. The species and number of birds you have determine the amount of time you spend caring for them. Two lovebirds, canaries, or finches will keep each other company. One lovebird, cockatiel, or budgie needs at least one hour of *attention* a day and an hour (preferably more) of *exercise* outside the cage daily.

Daily chores should be done on a consistent schedule. Empty food and water containers and thoroughly *clean* them before *refilling*, which takes about ten minutes. *Change* the paper in the bottom of the cage daily and clean soiled perches. This takes five minutes or less, unless you have an elaborate gym or playground. Spray or shower your bird, or give it a shallow dish to bathe in. This takes five to ten minutes.

Once a week thoroughly *wash* and dry toys, perches, and the cage bottom and *scrub* the bars with a metal brush. This takes twenty to forty-five minutes, depending on the size of the cage and number of accessories. Once a month, wash the cage and accessories with a safe disinfectant and replace gnawed twigs and branches.

CHARACTERISTICS AFFECTING CHILDREN. Birds have light bones that are easily injured if grabbed or squeezed. Children, particularly young children, seem to find it hard to resist poking their fingers through the bars of a cage. This is an invasion of the bird's territory, and it may bite those fingers out of fear. Even a small lovebird can draw blood, and a large bird can inflict serious damage. For this and other reasons, large birds such as macaws are not recommended for families who want a bird to interact or play with young children.

PERSONALITY TRAITS. Each species displays a general cluster of characteristics, but each individual has a unique personality. Some of the large parrots are known for being loud, brassy, and aggressive. Cockatiels are usually thought of as curious and playful. Canaries are active and perky. Doves are generally quiet and gentle. Budgies are affectionate. Lovebirds like to chatter. The quality of life that you give your bird will also shape its personality.

NEED FOR PARENTAL SUPERVISION. *"Our first cockatiel was named Sweetie,"* related Sylvia. *"The kids adored him. He could imitate perfectly the sound of the telephone and the microwave, and he would call the dog and the poor thing would come running every time. One day, the kids took him out of his cage, which he was used to. I guess they forgot about him and left the screen door open. He flew right out, never to be seen again, and we were all devastated."*

Children under the age of seven should be supervised when interacting with a bird, to protect both the bird and child from possible harm. Parents should supervise a bird outside of the cage and thoroughly birdproof a room before a bird is allowed into it. It is all too common for birds to be stepped on, grabbed by the family dog or cat, or fly out an open door.

Your Family's Pet Resources

Inventory your resources to see if they enable you to keep a bird.

TIME. Which family member(s) will feed the bird, give it a shower, change cage papers, supervise it outside the cage daily? Who will clean the cage weekly?

Child's Age and Care of Bird

The type of bird you have, and your child's physical and mental development, will help you decide what chores are appropriate for your child. With parental supervision:

Children **age three to five** can hand-feed treats (to a small bird), put pre-measured food into the feeder, help an adult pick out toys, and put away food.

Children **age five to seven** also can talk quietly to the bird, wash the food container, refill the water bowl or bottle, and help an adult change cage paper.

Children **age seven to ten** also can change cage paper, help an adult train the bird, wash the cage, and wash and cut up fruits and vegetables.

Children **age ten to twelve** also can clean the cage, water bottle, perches, and food dishes; feed and water the bird; play, pet, and interact with it; give it a bath or shower.

COST. Can you afford at least $150 in initial acquisition expenses, plus annual expenditures of $100 or more? Can you pay for a veterinary emergency?

ABILITY. Are your children old enough to help with chores? To remember to keep doors and windows closed when the bird is out of its cage? To handle the bird gently?

PLACE AND SPACE. Do you have room for a large cage in a location where there is plenty of human activity yet is away from drafts and vents? Are you willing to birdproof at least one room?

HEALTH. Is anyone in your family allergic to bird dust or feathers?

TRAVEL. Who will care for the bird when the family travels? Can you afford to pay someone to do this, or to board your bird?

HOUSEKEEPING. Will food, feathers, and dust around the cage bother you? What about droppings from a bird outside the cage?

SPECIAL ISSUES. If you move, will you take the bird with you?

*   *   *

"The reason birds are popular is simply because they can become excellent pets. If birds were not extremely fascinating and lovable, they would never have charmed so many people," writes T. J. Lafeber in *Let's Celebrate Pet Birds! How to Understand, Care For and Live Happily with Birds.*

Where to Get a Pet Bird

Jake jumped off the side of the garbage truck as it slowed to a halt. He had worked this route for three years but was unprepared for what he saw when he yanked the top off the garbage pail: a birdcage, listing sideways—with a bird in it. The bird was alive and moving, perched precariously on a swing. It cringed in fear when Jake gently lifted the cage.

People discard birds because they lose interest in them, don't want to care for them, or develop allergies. Some birds begin to screech or bite if they don't receive enough attention, and owners give them up because of this behavior. There are three places to find pet birds, including those in need of re-homing.

Bird **rescue and rehabilitation groups** are springing up around the country, some specializing in a particular species. These are nonprofit groups run by volunteers. Typically, these groups obtain veterinary care for the bird, and a volunteer provides a foster home. While in the foster home, the bird receives optimum physical care, attention, and training that usually resolves behavior problems. These groups screen potential adopters, working to match the right bird with the right family. Rescue groups usually charge an adoption fee to help cover costs. To find a group, ask your local animal shelter, avian club, or avian veterinarian.

Although some people believe that older birds cannot be "recycled," this is rarely true. A good rescue group is made up of people who understand birds, and they will not place a bird in a home unless they believe that both the bird and the family will benefit. Not all birds needing adoption have problems, as noted in *Bird Talk* magazine: "The most common reasons for deciding to give up a bird are that the owner is no longer able to manage the responsibility of bird ownership or cannot devote enough time to play with the bird. In such instances, the bird may have been an excellent pet. As a result, many top-quality previously owned birds find themselves up for adoption."

Some local **animal shelters** that never used to receive birds now take in several a week. Not all shelters are able to keep and care for birds. Some do keep them "in-house," and others find volunteers to provide foster homes. Shelters may adopt out for free or charge a fee to help cover costs. Some shelters have adoption counselors who screen prospective owners and try to match the right bird to the right family.

Local **breeders** sell birds for profit. Some sell directly to the public, and some sell through specialty pet shops. Ask bird club members and avian vets to recommend responsible breeders, or shops that specialize in and have a reputation for taking good care of pet birds. You can meet and talk to breeders at local shows and clubs.

Do not buy a bird through the mail, or one that has to be shipped to you; you will not get a chance to select your own bird, and shipping is very stressful for the animal. Do not buy a bird in a variety store, large pet shop, or chain pet shop: These birds have been indiscriminately bred by mass-market breeders, and store employees rarely have the training to care properly for them. Many of these birds are sick by the time they are sold.

A responsible breeder will have clean, uncrowded cages and active, healthy birds, and will willingly give you:

- references that you can check
- plenty of information about the bird and how to care for it
- lots of time to visit with and select the right bird
- a written sales agreement, including a "right of return" period during which you can take the bird to your vet, and receive a full refund if the bird is unhealthy

Take time with your children to research birds and make some decisions about species and variety before you go to select one, because you will face many choices. For example, some canaries are bred primarily for their beauty, others for their song, and within each type there are several varieties. When choosing an individual, look for signs of a healthy bird, one with:

- feathers that are smooth, clean, and shiny, not matted
- eyes that are clear and bright, with no discharge
- beak and nails that are clean, normal in shape, and not overgrown
- a straight, upright body, not one that is hunched over or huddled
- alert demeanor, not apathetic or lethargic

Spend time observing and interacting with the bird. Whether the bird is a baby being offered for sale by a breeder, or an adult being re-homed by a rescue group, ask questions about its history and care and encourage your children to be involved with the selection process. Many times there is an attraction or bonding with one bird out of a group.

Birds are sensitive to change. The experience of being caught and removed from a familiar cage, put into a carrier, and driven to a new cage in a strange environment in your home is frightening. It may take days or weeks for a bird to lose its fear and settle into new surroundings. Seek advice about how to help your new bird adapt to your home.

Questions That Parents Ask

Can we leave a pet bird alone when our family spends weekends at the beach? A bird should not be left unattended for more than a day because of its need for fresh water, food, and a clean cage, not to mention attention. If your family travels frequently, the best option is to find a knowledgeable, reliable caretaker who can come to your home regularly, preferably twice a day, to care for your bird and establish a relationship with it. Some birds travel well and go along on family vacations. Others are boarded with breeders, veterinary clinics, or professional sitters. Ask for suggestions from clubs, rescue groups, and other owners, and check references before leaving your bird with someone you do not know.

Our son wants a bird because a friend of his has one. I'm allergic to cats, and we aren't allowed to have dogs in our apartment. Does it make sense to get a small bird to begin with, and then a bigger one later if this works out? Although a small bird costs less and lives in a smaller cage, it still needs daily attention. A small or medium-size bird can live for ten, fifteen, or twenty years—a long-term commitment.

Don't get a bird as an experiment. Get a bird if you're convinced it's the best type of pet for your entire family, and choose a species and individual whose personality appeals to your son.

My husband and I work full time, and our

fourteen-year-old daughter comes home to an empty apartment. Would a pet bird provide her with some companionship without adding chores to our already impossible schedules? A bird can be a wonderful companion, and most landlords who ban dogs and cats do permit birds that are not noisy. Be certain that your daughter wants such a pet. Each day, she will need to give it food, water, and attention and change the cage paper. Someone should clean the cage once a week.

Won't a child lose interest in a bird pretty quickly? This depends on the child and the bird—and the parents. A child who learns from you, other owners, and books how to tame a bird or teach it to talk will have an affectionate, interesting pet. Birds that sing or simply look beautiful and busy also provide hours of diversion. Children become extremely attached to pet birds, who often display funny, quirky personalities.

Is a six-year-old old enough to have a pet bird? If you want your six-year-old to assume primary responsibility for the care of a bird, the answer is no. If you plan to care for the bird and teach your child to help you, the answer may be yes. However, birds should not be chased or teased, as they can panic and injure themselves. It is difficult for the average six-year-old to control his or her exuberant feelings, so you will have to supervise until your child is old enough to remain relatively calm and quiet when playing with or around a bird.

Our daughter wants a pet bird, and my husband thinks she should keep it in her bedroom for it to really be "hers." Is this a good idea? Birds thrive on action and activity, and a bedroom is usually either empty while your daughter is in school, or quiet and dark while she is asleep. Your daughter may interact more with the bird and feel closer to it if its cage is kept in the living, family, or recreation room. If her pet is a cockatiel or budgie, it can come out of its cage to keep your daughter company in her room.

We live in an apartment and want to get a bird for our daughter, who is eight. What is the best kind of bird

to get? The type of bird you choose should depend on your daughter's personality and wishes and your family's interests and resources. It's best to rule out large parrots that can inflict serious injuries and are expensive and often noisy.

Budgies, or parakeets, are still the number-one bird in America, for good reason. They are pretty, small, inexpensive, gregarious, and altogether delightful. Some budgies talk, but unless you buy or adopt one that is already talking, there is no guarantee that yours will. They like to play and take baths, and they need human interaction and supervised exercise outside of the cage. If you cannot give a budgie lots of companionship, buy two; they will be happier, although they will not bond as closely with your family.

Our children are interested in a pet bird, especially a parrot. Friends of ours were nearly evicted because their parrot made so much noise. Are all birds noisy? Not all birds are noisy, but some can really scream. Training a bird not to scream is possible, but it's not guaranteed, takes time, and may require professional intervention. Conures, cockatoos, and some parrots can make lots of noise. Species such as canaries, budgies, and lovebirds may sing or vocalize but are not loud.

Our son is a bit of a roughneck, but he loves animals. What if we start with a pet bird, to see if he can learn to be gentle? It is a mistake to try to "teach" gentleness by providing a child with a small, frail pet. It is cruel to both the animal and the child. Most children are not rough because they want to do harm but because they lack self-control or don't yet understand the consequences of their actions. A normal child who accidentally injures or kills a pet suffers fear and guilt, although the real problem is not his behavior but lack of parental supervision or a mismatch between child and pet. A child who actually seems to enjoy hurting animals or displays no emotional reaction to their pain may have a problem that requires professional help.

Resources

TO LOCATE A VETERINARIAN
Association of Avian Veterinarians
PO Box 299
East Northport, NY 11731
(516) 757-6320

CLUBS AND SOCIETIES

American Budgerigar Society
1704 Kangaroo
Killeen, TX 76543

American Cockatiel Society
9527 60th Lane North
Pinellas Park, FL 33782

American Federation of
Aviculture
3118 West Thomas Road
Suite 713
Phoenix, AZ 85017

Avicultural Society of
America
17347 Aspenglow
Yorba Linda, CA 92686

Bird Adoption and Placement
Center
Dept. BT
171 Daniel Drive
Alamo, CA 94507

Bird Clubs of America
Dept. BT
PO Box 2005
Yorktown, VA 23692

State and local bird clubs for people of all ages sponsor shows and
events and can provide local references to breeders. Some clubs operate or can refer you to a bird rescue or adoption organization. Some
local shelters can also provide rescue or adoption referrals. Magazines
such as *BirdTalk* and *Birds USA* carry information about clubs, meetings, and shows.

BOOKS FOR ADULTS

Alderton, David. *Looking After Birds*. New York: Sterling
    Publishing, 1997.

Erickson, Laura. *Sharing the Wonder of Birds with Kids*.
    Duluth, MN: Pfeifer-Hamilton, 1997.

Gallerstein, Gary A., D.V.M. *The Complete Bird Owner's Handbook*. New York: Howell Book House, 1994.

Lafeber, T. J., D.V.M. *Let's Celebrate Pet Birds: How to Understand, Care For and Live Happily with Birds*. Odell, IL: Lafeber Company, 1989.

Skutch, Alexander. *The Minds of Birds*. College Station, TX: Texas A & M University Press, 1998.

von Frisch, Otto. *Canaries: How to Take Care of Them and Understand Them*. Hauppauge, NY: Barron's, 1991.

Wolter, Annette. *Cockatiels: How to Take Care of Them and Understand Them*. Hauppauge, NY: Barron's, 1991.

————. *Parakeets: A Complete Owner's Manual*. Hauppauge, NY: Barron's, 1990.

Wolter, Annette, and Monika Wegler. *The Complete Book of Parakeet Care: Expert Advice for Pet Owners on Keeping Parakeets Happy, Healthy, and Safe from Harm*. Hauppauge, NY: Barron's, 1994.

NONFICTION FOR CHILDREN

Arnosky, Jim. *Crinkleroot's 25 Birds Every Child Should Know*. New York: Bradbury Press, 1993.

Evans, Mark. *ASPCA Pet Care Guide for Kids: Birds*. New York: Dorling Kindersley, 1993.

Gans, Roma. *How Do Birds Find Their Way?* New York: HarperCollins, 1996.

Reid, Struan. *Bird World*. Brookfield, CT: Millbrook Press, 1991.

Sill, Carolyn. *About Birds: A Guide for Children*. Atlanta: Peachtree Publishers, 1991.

FICTION FOR CHILDREN

Baur, Deborah. *Rosie the Talking Parrot Learns About Friendship and Love*. Pittsburgh: Dorrance, 1997.

King-Smith, Dick. *Mr. Potter's Pet*. New York: Hyperion, 1996.

Smith, Dale. *What the Parrot Told Alice*. Nevada City, CA: Deer Creek Publishing, 1996.

Ward, Helen. *The King of the Birds*. Brookfield, CT: Millbrook Press, 1997.

Wells, Rosemary, and Greg Shed. *The Language of Doves*. New York: Dial Books, 1996.

SIXTEEN

Fish

Diana lay on her bed in the darkened room. It seemed to her years since she had last been allowed to play outside. First, the horrible playground accident: her head crashing onto the wooden post, the splinters in her eye. The hospital. Operations. Bandages. Now, at least, she was at home and her eye uncovered, but she had been ordered to stay inside and out of bright lights. She couldn't even read. Surely, she was going to die of boredom.

It was her uncle who brought her an aquarium and the glorious, graceful fish. He set it up for her on a table next to her bed. Her sister added the miniature castle and sunken pirate ship. Her mother promised that they would shop for underwater plants. She watched the fish by the hour, named them, talked to them, and made up stories about them. Even after she was allowed to play outside and life returned to normal, she loved the fish and never tired of watching them, especially at bedtime.

Although fish share the planet with us, their aquatic home is so alien to human life that almost inevitably they intrigue us. When we create a miniature environment for fish in a home aquarium, we have a window on creatures of the animal kingdom that are as different from us as could be in the way they breathe, move, and even sleep. They

Fish
Facts At a Glance

COST	$150–$250 to set up an aquarium; $20–$50 per year
SIZE	1–12 inches
LONGEVITY	2–10 years
TIME REQUIREMENT	Several hours to set up aquarium; waiting period of weeks to fully stock it; 5 minutes a day to feed fish, check equipment; 20–30 minutes weekly for partial water change, related cleaning, and maintenance
SPACE	20- or 30-gallon tank, placed away from direct sunlight, heat, drafts, on sturdy stand
EXERCISE	Fish need large enough tank
EQUIPMENT	Tank, stand, filtration system, air pump, air hose, air stone, gravel, slate/wood/stones, siphon and hose, algae scraper, hood with lights, net, bucket, scrub brush, thermometer, power strip, plants, test kits, conditioner, heater (for tropical fish)
ODOR	None if tank is kept clean
PERSONALITY TRAITS	Vary from shy and timid to dominant and aggressive toward other fish
PARENTAL SUPERVISION	Young children should be supervised around tank's electrical equipment
LEGAL RESTRICTIONS	Check lease and home or apartment insurance

dress in brilliant polka dots and neon stripes, in every rainbow color. It is no wonder that children and adults alike find themselves enthralled when watching fish.

Parents ask, "Are fish pets, or is fish keeping a hobby?" It is either or both, as long as you keep in mind that fish are alive and entitled to care and respect. There are more fish kept in American homes as pets—perhaps 100 million—than any other type of animal. If you think of fish keeping as a hobby, it is the second most popular in the country, after photography.

Many factors explain this popularity. Fish are quiet; exercise themselves; don't need to be walked, trained, or patted; don't drool, shed, or trigger allergies; don't wake you up at night, chew on your furniture, or mess on your rugs.

Fish keeping is science, entertainment, and not a lot of work. As noted by Mike Wickham in *Aquarium Fish* magazine, "it would be difficult to find a hobby that has a better ratio of time spent enjoying it to time spent maintaining it."

ORIGINS. Fish live in the oceans that cover more than two-thirds of Earth's surface and in the lakes, ponds, streams, and rivers that punctuate the continents. Fish, like mammals, are vertebrates—they have backbones—but they predate land-dwelling animals by hundreds of millions of years. There are as many species of fish as there are species of amphibians, reptiles, birds, and mammals combined.

Humans have captured fish for food since prehistoric times and began raising fish domestically to use as food thousands of years ago. Fish were first kept as pets or for ornamentation in outdoor ponds or pools perhaps three thousand years ago. Goldfish became particularly popular in China, and later in Japan, and were selectively bred for appearance. Around the fifteenth century, ornamental fish were brought inside to live in clay aquariums.

Goldfish were exported to Europe in the sixteenth century. In 1853, the London Zoo opened the first public aquarium, triggering a fish-keeping craze. Twenty-five years later, the first recorded shipment of goldfish was sent to America.

NEEDS. Each species, in adapting to a particular environment, has developed specialized physiology and behaviors. The most critical adaptation is to water, which varies in temperature, depth, plant life, movement (still or running), salinity (fresh or salt), and mineral, chemical, and acid content.

Pet fish breathe, swim, eat, rest, excrete, and breed in a closed environment. For them to survive, it must approximate the natural habitat where the fish or its ancestors originated. The fish keeper must provide water with the correct level of salinity, alkalinity, or acidity (pH level), and hardness or softness. Chlorine and metals such as lead or copper that frequently arrive with tap water are toxic to fish and must be removed or reduced to acceptable levels.

Pet fish can be kept in an outdoor pond, or indoors in an aquarium. Indoor aquarium fish are the focus here. Because saltwater fish, also known as marine fish, are more difficult to keep, families just beginning the aquarium adventure are advised to begin with freshwater rather than marine fish.

Children and beginners soon discover that freshwater fish offer nearly limitless opportunities for discovery and enjoyment. Although 70 percent of Earth's surface is covered with salt water, and only 1 percent with fresh water, more than 40 percent of all twenty thousand known fish species live in fresh water. They fall into two categories: those that live in cold or temperate water and those that live in warm or tropical water.

Julio was nearly as excited as his seven-year-old daughter, Gloria. He had never had a pet as a child, and now, after much discussion, they were heading home with a pair of goldfish. He laughed happily as the little girl renamed them for the third time in less than ten minutes.

When they reached home, they carefully followed the

instructions that the clerk had given them about acclimating the goldfish to their new environment.

A week later, both fish were dead. Gloria cried and cried. She had lovingly decorated the bottom of the bowl with gravel collected from the driveway and added a small plastic Goofy toy, one of her favorites. The clerk at the variety store had not told them to dechlorinate the tap water, had not warned them not to add objects that could contaminate the water, had not explained about the nitrogen cycle, in fact had given them no advice at all beyond describing how to let the water in the carrying bag reach the same temperature as the water in the bowl.

The care of fish is first and foremost care of the aquarium, so it is not surprising that fish keepers are also referred to as aquarists. The successful aquarist provides fish with:

- good water quality
- sufficient water surface
- correct water temperature
- a balance of light and darkness
- appropriate habitat
- proper diet

In the wild, water is constantly evaporating and being replenished by rain and melting snow and ice; animal waste products and decaying matter such as dead plants and animals do not have a chance to accumulate. But an aquarium, no matter how large, is a tiny, closed system compared to nature, and only regular human intervention can maintain *good water quality.*

Water quality is the single most important key to a successful aquarium, and it depends on establishing and maintaining the nitrogen cycle, sometimes referred to as the life cycle: the presence of useful bacteria that convert fish waste products into nitrates and nitrites which in turn must be regularly removed from the aquarium. The most common cause of fish disease and mortality is buildup of pollutants in the water. Fish depend on their owners to clean and replenish their water with a filtration system and regular partial water changes.

Fish need oxygen to breathe. Oxygen is absorbed into the water where water meets the air; the greater the *water surface*, the more oxygen in the water. Fish deprived of oxygen will suffocate.

Fish are cold-blooded; their body temperature is governed by their environment, so *water temperature* must be suited to the species. If the water is too hot or too cold, fish can die.

Fish need darkness to rest or sleep, or they can become stressed and easily get sick. Light is necessary for illumination, normal fish activity, and plant growth. A *balance of light and darkness* is needed in the aquarium, which can be provided by artificial or natural light.

Fish have adapted to their total environment, not only to the water. To create an *appropriate habitat*, owners decorate the tank to suit the fish as well as their own aesthetics. Some fish need rocks or a "cave" made from wood or a small clay flowerpot, and others need plants to hide in.

Fish are either carnivorous, vegetarian, or omnivorous, and a *proper diet* varies accordingly. Fish have different feeding habits as well as different nutritional needs, and fish anatomy has developed to reflect whether the fish is a top, midwater, or bottom feeder. Commercial foods are designed to meet these adaptations: pellets and flakes that float on the surface for top feeders, sink to the bottom quickly for bottom feeders, or sink slowly for midwater feeders. Experts recommend that dry commercial foods be supplemented with frozen and live food.

One expert working in an aquarium shop described how the same family returned, week after week, to replace fish that died. "The little girl, about six years old, would take a handful of fish flakes and throw it into the water. I could not convince the parents to put a stop to it. All they had to do was hide the food. Finally, I refused to sell them any more fish. Maybe it wasn't any of my business, but I thought it wasn't good for the little girl to be allowed to keep killing things, and I do care about fish."

Overfeeding is a common mistake made by beginners. Fish eat very little, and excess food promptly decays in the aquarium, polluting the water. Fish should be fed no more often than twice a day, and only as much as they consume in a minute.

CHILDREN AND FISH. *"Every night at bedtime,"* recounts David, father of two boys, *"we go and feed the fish together. We watch them and talk about them. I got interested in fish when I was about nine or ten years old, and I'm still interested. I do a lot of the maintenance work on the aquarium, but the boys, who are eight and ten, help me and really enjoy watching the fish."*

Fish are wonderful pets for children of all ages, and some children become very attached to them. Seven-year-old Michael described how his fish, Blackie, would swim to the surface whenever Michael came near the aquarium. Other children give similar accounts.

Watching fish is fun and relaxing; studies confirm that it has a calming effect and lowers blood pressure. Children are thrilled to learn that fish have individual personalities and that they play, hide, and communicate; some lurk, some glide, some dart; some are slow swimmers and others very fast; some school and others are loners.

An aquarium especially appeals to children who like to observe and who are curious about science and biology. Many are fascinated by an aquarium once they understand that it is a miniature world, and they love to decorate it with plants, rocks, and accessories. Advanced aquarist Maurizio DiPietro says that this is the part of fish keeping that he enjoys the most: creating a beautiful, functional environment that he calls "living art." Another aquarist commented, "Adults tend to like the natural look in an aquarium, while kids go for everything from neon skulls to tiny dinosaur skeletons. As long as it's bought in an aquarium shop and is fish safe, why not?"

Almost all children, regardless of age, need help setting up a tank. Children need to learn not to overfeed, not to tap on the aquarium glass, and not to put their hands or other objects in the tank.

Experienced fish keepers caution that this hobby is often one of trial and error, especially for beginners. It is almost unavoidable for one or more fish to die an untimely death, often for reasons unknown. Some fish, predictably or unpredictably, become aggressive: They harass, attack, kill, and even eat other fish alive. These deaths and predatory behaviors can frighten children.

Another issue is the proximity of water and electrical equipment. A child who does aquarium maintenance chores must be old enough to understand and observe safety precautions.

COMMITMENT. The biggest commitment of time and money comes during the initial setup stage. Thereafter, the daily or weekly commitment is not time-consuming. Life span varies with the species and aquarium conditions.

What You Need to Know About Freshwater Fish *Before* You Get Some

SIZE. Species vary in length from one inch to twelve inches. Whether fish grow to full size depends on factors such as genetics, water quality, diet, and general health.

LONGEVITY. The average life span for most goldfish in a well-maintained aquarium is five to ten years. Depending on the species and quality of care, tropical fish live from two to ten years.

LEGAL RESTRICTIONS. Check your rental agreement and your rental or home insurance. A lease may limit the amount of weight that can be placed on the floor, and some insurance policies may not cover water damage from leaking or broken aquariums.

COSTS. Most costs occur at the outset; expect initial costs to be $150–$250. Expenses vary depending on the number and type of fish and the size of the aquarium, which in turn determines the size and cost of other necessary equipment.

It is difficult to estimate the cost of maintaining an aquarium because its longevity usually doesn't depend on the life span of a single fish. Rather, some fish will die while others live, new ones will be added, and some may give birth. An aquarium can last as long as you like; for many people, this literally is a lifelong hobby.

Food costs about $15 to $25 annually for half a dozen fish. This includes a combination of commercial dried, frozen, and live food. Water test kits and conditioners cost $20–$30 a year. Your *electric bill* will increase slightly as you operate electrical equipment. Unless you have an extremely large tank, the impact on your *water bill* should be negligible.

Do not scrimp on the equipment. It is better to buy a more powerful filtration system or more accurate thermometer than live with the consequences. You may be able to save money by waiting for sales or buying used equipment.

Fish vary in price from $1.50 to $50 each and even more. Fish need not be expensive to be pretty and interesting.

Although fish get sick, few veterinarians specialize in fish medicine. As usual, the best medicine is preventive. According to Dr. Gregory Lewbart, a nationally recognized practitioner and professor of fish medicine, "Ninety percent of all fish disease is due to poor environmental management. There is no substitute for good water quality, but many owners want someone to give them a magic bullet instead. If you isolate the sick fish, keep it rested, give it a good environment and nutrition, it usually will recover. Medicine won't help if the fish is in water that is dirty, has chlorine, is too hot or too cold, or has too little oxygen."

Basic equipment for a freshwater aquarium includes:

• comprehensive book(s) about fish keeping	$10–20
• medium-size aquarium (20–30 gallons) setup including: tank, electric air pump, hose, air stone, filtration system, hood with lights, gravel	$100–150
• tank stand (optional)	$50–80
• grounded timer for lights (optional)	$15–20
• power strip	$10–15
• algae scraper or sponge	$2–8
• net	$2–5
• siphon with gravel cleaner	$5–10
• bucket	$5–10
• scrub brush	$3
• thermometer	$3–5
• underwater plants (real or artificial)	$2–15
• rocks and/or wood, slate	$3–15
• decorations (optional)	$3–30
• heater and thermostat (for tropical tank only)	$15–40

If these measures don't work, try to locate a qualified veterinarian by asking at your aquarium store or the nearest school of veterinary medicine.

EQUIPMENT. Buy the biggest aquarium that you can afford and have room for. Most fish keepers prefer glass over acrylic tanks because acrylic tends to scratch and turn yellow over time. A hood that fits securely prevents splashing, keeps cats' paws and other undesirable items out of the tank, and keeps in fish that might leap out. A hood often is sold with the tank; it should open easily and may be equipped with lights.

An electric pump circulates water through one or more air stones (porous rocks available in various decorative forms), creating a slight current, and an air hose connects the pump to the air stone. The pump also helps maintain a constant temperature throughout the tank. The type of pump you use may depend on the type of filtration system, which is essential for removing waste material. Tropical fish tanks need a heater with a thermostat that automatically adjusts to respond to changes in water temperature. All tanks need a thermometer, either external or internal. A power strip allows you to collect electrical cords from your equipment in one place and helps ensure a dependable electrical flow.

Gravel on the bottom of the tank makes it more attractive, nourishes bacteria, and provides a bed for aquaplants (both real and artificial) to stand in. Gravel is available in aquarium shops in different sizes, colors, and compositions; some types will work well for the fish you want to keep, and others may be harmful. Stones, rocks, wood, imitation wood or slate, also from an aquarium shop, create a habitat for fish and an attractive setting. Underwater plants, real or artificial, add beauty and interest. For some fish, they are an important part of the habitat. Get expert advice and choose hardy plants that like the same water as your fish. If you begin with artificial plants, you can substitute real plants later.

An algae scraper or sponge is used to remove algae that inevitably collects on the panes of the aquarium. If not removed, it can grow to such proportions that it threatens water quality and obscures the view of your fish. A siphon and gravel cleaner remove waste material, and a net is used to remove fish. At least one five-gallon bucket is needed for water changes, and so is a new scrub brush (that has not been used in detergent) to clean the tank and equipment before use. Always use sponges purchased in an aquarium shop (not the supermarket).

SPACE. Many shops offer ten-gallon "beginner" tanks, but you are well advised to buy a twenty- or thirty-gallon tank if you can. The larger the aquarium, the easier it is to maintain water quality and keep your fish alive. You can wait longer intervals between water changes, and a larger aquarium usually is more interesting to kids because it houses more fish, plants, and decorations.

Aquariums are made in various shapes. Select one with the maximum bottom area, or footprint: a long or wide aquarium, rather than a tall, narrow one. Seek to maximize water surface: the larger the footprint, the greater the water surface. Water surface, rather than water volume, determines the number of fish you can keep.

Before you buy an aquarium, discuss with your family where you will put it. It is extremely difficult to move an aquarium once it is set up, because you cannot move it without first emptying the water. Consider a number of factors:

- An aquarium is heavy. A rectangular, thirty-gallon glass aquarium weighs 40 pounds *empty*. The addition of gravel (30 pounds) and water (250 pounds) brings the total weight to more than 300 pounds.
- It must rest on a sturdy piece of furniture or stand. If you have toddlers or young children, be particularly careful to use furniture that is wide and stable and won't easily be tipped over. The surface must be level and at least as large as the footprint.
- It should be near electrical outlets for plugging in equipment and, if possible, near a shelf or cupboard where you can keep food and supplies.
- It should not rest on a windowsill or in direct sunlight. Sunlight encourages too much algae growth and affects water temperature unevenly. Do not put an

aquarium on top of a television or other appliance that emits heat, or near radiators, air conditioners, or heating vents, all of which adversely affect water temperature.

- It should be in a location where your family will see and enjoy it often, in a family, recreation, or living room. Try to place it at a convenient height for children. If it is too high, a child will not be able to see or take care of the fish. Since most people don't spend a lot of time standing in front of an aquarium, put it within view of a comfortable chair or couch.

Ted Coletti, Ph.D., sums up his advice this way in *Aquarium Fish* magazine: "Location, location, location! The three rules for buying real estate also apply to the aquarium hobby. . . . An aquarium is not enjoyed if it's not experienced. I always recommend placing a tank near regularly used furniture. A nice easy chair next to your tank can be the making of a very relaxing evening ritual. And your whole family can be there too. . . . Spend quality time with your tank . . . keep your tanks at eye level whenever possible. With aquariums, it's often 'out of sight, out of mind.' "

TIME REQUIREMENT. Fish keeping involves two stages: aquarium setup and ongoing maintenance.

Setting up an aquarium is time-consuming. The most important step is research, before you buy anything, because you need to have some idea of the type of fish you want before you buy equipment. Find an aquarium shop that will serve as a source of information and advice, as well as equipment and fish. Ask aquarists and local aquarium clubs for suggestions and visit several shops. Choose one where the staff is knowledgeable and willing to take time to answer questions. As you set up your aquarium, include your child in the decisions and explain the need for each piece of equipment and each stage of the process. An understanding of how an aquarium works can help keep children involved. In general, your steps will be:

1. Find out the kind of water that you can most easily provide by checking with your water supplier or aquarium shop about the properties of the local water. Your life as a fish keeper will be easier if you choose fish that can survive in the pH level and relative hardness of your water.

   Chlorine and chloramine found in tap water are harmful to fish. You can remove chlorine from water by letting it stand for twenty-four hours or treating it chemically. Chloramine can be removed only by using a commercial preparation.

2. Decide whether you want a cold- or warm-water tank. Goldfish are cold-water fish that can withstand a range of temperatures. There are more than 120 varieties of goldfish, in exotic colors and shapes and with many differences in size and habits. Tropical fish need to live in heated water with a constant, specific temperature. Do not mix cold- and warm-water fish in the same tank.

3. Decide whether you want a species of community tank. A species tank contains a single species of fish. Usually, the most interesting choice is a schooling variety, fish that live in a group. It is fun for kids to observe the structure and behaviors of this little society.

   A community tank contains several different species that get along with each other, usually a top, midlevel, and bottom-dwelling species. If you choose a community tank, select fish that like the same temperature and type of water and are "socially compatible." A mismatch could lead to one species or individual dominating the tank, and harassing or killing other fish.

4. Decide on the species of fish you want. Begin with fish that are hardy and easy to care for. Selecting a fish for its beauty alone may be tempting, but its beauty will be wasted if you cannot keep it alive. Exotic species with exotic needs can wait for the time when you and your children have more experience. Goldfish are the best cold-water fish for beginners. Guppies, zebra danios, and neon tetras are recommended for tropical tanks.

5. Decide what size tank you can afford and have room for. (See ''Place and Space'' below.) Plan to buy the largest aquarium possible.

6. Calculate the surface area of your tank in inches by multiplying width times length. (Kids who like math get a kick out of this part.) Allow twenty-four to thirty square inches of water surface for one adult inch of goldfish (not counting the tail) and twelve square inches for adult tropical fish, even if you are buying young fish. Now you can figure out how many fish you can keep. S. Lynne Hudson, in ''First the Fish, then the Tank,'' warns: ''The number one problem for a fishkeeper is overstocking an aquarium. An overstocked tank is simply trouble waiting to happen. Too many fish make it difficult, or even impossible, to maintain good water quality, and good water quality is what fishkeeping is really all about. It may take some time, but the effects of chronically poor water quality will eventually take their toll. Clean water is to fish what fresh air is to you. . . . Your fish won't thrive, or even survive, if the water quality is poor.''

7. Once your decisions are made, buy your equipment (but not the fish). Follow setup directions meticulously. A slipup at this stage, such as using detergent in your tank and leaving a residue behind, can doom your fish. Setting up the tank will take several hours.

8. Once the aquarium is set up and filled with water, give it several days to stabilize. This may be the hardest time of all for your child: watching an empty tank.

9. After a few days, introduce two fish, preferably the hardiest of all the fish that you eventually want. Follow directions carefully about how to add fish to the tank. It is a stressful proposition for them to be netted at the aquarium store, put in a bag, carried around, and then be dumped into a new home. Following the correct procedure will reduce stress for the fish and help keep them alive. Add fish gradually, one or two at a time, every few weeks until you have reached the number that your aquarium can support.

Once your tank is set up and populated, a child or parent should perform **ongoing maintenance**.

Fish should be *fed* once or, at most, twice a day. It takes a few seconds to scatter flakes or pellets. Providing frozen or live food is also a brief chore.

Turn *lights* on in the morning and off at night, unless you have an automatic timer to do this. Quickly *check* the water temperature and equipment each day and *watch* the fish for a while to see if they seem healthy. This takes just a few moments.

Make a *partial water change*—simply remove some of the water in the tank and replace it with clean dechlorinated water—at regular intervals. This may take fifteen to thirty minutes. Frequency depends on the size of the aquarium (the smaller the tank, the more frequent the change), filtration, and number and type of fish. A rough rule of thumb is one change a week, but the key is regularity.

Along with the water change, *rinse* the filter media, *clean* the gravel with a siphon and gravel cleaner, and *scrape* algae off the inside panes of the tank. Wipe dirt and condensation off of the hood, *trim* live plants and *remove* or *replace* dead or dying ones. These tasks take five or ten minutes.

Your equipment, especially the filtration system, needs *regular maintenance*. A piece of equipment may appear to be working, but if it is clogged or dirty it may not be doing what it is supposed to do. Follow the advice of experts and manufacturers about cleaning and replacement of equipment.

SMELLS? Fish in water do not smell. An aquarium that is not cared for regularly will smell eventually.

CHARACTERISTICS AFFECTING CHILDREN. Fish are restful to watch. Only a few species kept in captivity are dangerous, and they are not recommended for children.

PERSONALITY TRAITS. Behavior varies with the species and individual. Some fish are communal and others are loners. Some are aggressive, others timid. Many aquarists, including children, testify that individual fish have unique personalities.

NEED FOR PARENTAL SUPERVISION. Children need help setting up a tank and may need help making partial water changes. Parents should ensure that children follow safety precautions.

Child's Age and Care of Fish

Children often enjoy learning to care for fish. With parental supervision:

Children **age three to five** can drop pre-measured food into the tank, help an adult choose decorations and fish.

Children **age five to seven** also can turn lights on and off, help an adult with setup by rinsing gravel, stones, decorations.

Children **age seven to ten** also can check water temperature, rinse filter medium, clean hood, and help an adult with water changes, gravel cleaning, and algae removal.

Children **age ten to twelve** also can feed fish, rinse decorations, vacuum or siphon gravel, help an adult test water quality.

Children **age twelve and up** also can test water, make partial water changes, trim and fertilize plants, help an adult with annual equipment maintenance.

Your Family's Pet Resources

Inventory your resources to see if they enable your family to keep a fish aquarium.

TIME. Which family members will set up the aquarium? Who will feed and check on the fish daily? Who will test water and make partial water changes every one to three weeks, including cleaning gravel, scraping algae, and rinsing the filter? Who will maintain the equipment?

COST. Can you afford $150–$250 in setup expenditures and $20–$50 a year for food, test kits, chemicals? Can you pay for a veterinary emergency?

ABILITY. Are your children old enough to help with setup or maintenance chores?

PLACE AND SPACE. Do you have room for at least a twenty-gallon aquarium, away from direct sunlight, heat, and drafts? Will the floor and stand support its weight? Is the location near an electrical outlet? Is it in an area where family members can comfortably view it? Does your insurance cover damage from a spilled or broken tank? Does your apartment building permit a tank of this size?

HEALTH. An aquarium has both water and electrical equipment, a potentially dangerous combination. Are your children old enough to follow safety guidelines?

TRAVEL. If you will be away from home for more than a week or two, who will care for your fish?

HOUSEKEEPING. Will spilled water from the aquarium bother you?

SPECIAL ISSUES. Will your children be too upset by the actions of predatory fish?

*   *   *

Mike Wickham, in *Aquarium Fish* magazine, is encouraging: "In the end, your success will largely depend on how much research you've done beforehand. Don't let this intimidate you. Fishkeeping is easy. If you follow some basic rules, you will be successful."

Where to Get Fish

You can get fish from a friend, an aquarist's club, or even an animal shelter, but it is most likely that you will buy your fish from a shop. Choose one where the aquariums are clean and well kept. The water should be clear, the plants healthy, the fish active and alert. The staff should be knowledgeable and willing to take time to help you. Shops specializing in fish are much more likely to have well-informed staff and healthy fish than chain or variety stores.

I have found it helpful and interesting to ask employees whether they keep fish themselves (those who do are the true hobbyists) and then ask what kind, why, how they got started, and what fish they recommend for beginners and children. People who are not fish keepers but sell equipment are not always well informed, such as the young woman in one store who assured me that a bag of sand labeled "marine sand" would be all right to use in a fresh-water aquarium, which is not true.

Of course you want to choose healthy fish, but for a novice, this is easier said than done. Advice from a trust-worthy supplier is obviously helpful, and here are a few guidelines:

- Choose fish from a tank where the fish seem healthy and active and the water clear. Do not take a fish from a tank where there are dead or sickly fish, or cloudy water.
- Choose fish that have fins and tails that are intact, not ragged or torn.
- Choose fish with bright, clear eyes.
- Choose fish with normal-looking skin that does not have white spots or fungus growth.
- Choose a fish that has spent at least a few weeks in a tank in the aquarium shop, not one that has just arrived.
- Do not choose a fish that is swimming on its side, or in a small, tight circle, or with it fins flat against its sides.
- Do not choose a fish that is scraping itself against objects.

As you and your children get to know fish, and spend some time watching them, you will learn how to tell a ro-bust, healthy fish and how to spot signs of illness.

Questions That Parents Ask

We are looking for a pet for our shy daughter, who suffers from asthma and a number of allergies. We don't seem to have many options. We know that fish aren't much work, but will she get any fun out of a tank full of fish? This depends on your daughter's personality and interests and, to some extent, on yours as well. Your daughter can't cuddle a fish or take it for a walk. But for children who like to observe, who like nature and science, an aquarium offers hours of fascination. Many children become very fond of their fish.

An aquarium is a tiny, complex piece of nature to care for and enjoy. If you feel some of this wonder, it may be transmitted to your daughter. Her interest could be bolstered by a magazine subscription, joining the junior branch of a fish hobbyists' club, or chatting on the Internet with fellow fish enthusiasts.

Our twelve-year-old son has been saving money for an aquarium and fish. We've urged him not to go overboard in case he loses interest, but what if he's determined to blow all his savings? Actually, your son is on the right track. With aquariums, bigger *is* better. It is not possible to add equipment gradually—you need it all to get started. Not only will a large aquarium make your son's hobby more interesting, but he will have a better chance of success.

We live in an apartment, and my husband and I work full time. We think that fish would be an interesting hobby for our boys, age ten and twelve, yet not require a lot of time as we all lead hectic lives. Aren't fish the easiest pets to care for? Setting up an aquarium takes a lot of time. If that is properly done, daily care is not time-consuming. There are, however, some weekly chores that need to be taken care of, such as partial water changes.

We are somewhat strapped for cash but would like to get a pet for our children. Wouldn't fish be the cheapest, as well as the easiest pets? Fish and commercial fish food are both inexpensive. Startup costs, however, are fairly high. A bowl is not a good home for a fish, and it won't hold a child's interest for long, and a small aquarium is harder to maintain than a large one because it becomes polluted more quickly. By starting small in order to save money, you may end up with dead fish and disappointed children. One option is to buy used equipment advertised for sale in newspaper classifieds and in aquarium shops.

Our daughter is clamoring for fish. Why not start her out with a goldfish in a bowl, to see if she's interested and can keep it alive? A goldfish in a bowl, almost by definition, is not interesting, especially when you think of how beautiful, complex, and fascinating a community of fish in a proper aquarium can be. As experienced aquarist Gregory Skomal writes in *Setting Up a Freshwater Aquarium*, "A brief mention of the fish bowl will hopefully prevent the beginner from buying one. The confined, inhumane fish bowl is not a proper environment for a fish, whether it's a goldfish or any other freshwater fish. Water in a fish bowl is unfiltered, not properly aerated and very poorly maintained. A fish bowl is no more an aquarium than a closet is a house."

Why do so many children have goldfish? Why not introduce them to more interesting fish? Goldfish are hardy, adaptable, and easier to keep alive than more exotic species. They can survive and even flourish in cool water, eliminating the need to heat and control water temperature.

Goldfish are far from boring. Their many varieties are characterized by a range of body shapes and differences in tails, fins, size, and color. Some are slow swimmers, some moderate, and others extremely fast. A good goldfish tank includes aquascaping—gravel, rocks, plants, wood—that both children and fish enjoy.

Is there any reason not to let our son set up an aquarium in his bedroom? No, except that the rest of the family may not get much exposure to or pleasure from it.

How long can we leave our aquarium untended when we go on vacation? Usually for up to two weeks, but the answer depends in part on your equipment and your fish. If you have a small or crowded tank, you may have to ask someone to make a partial water change after a week.

You can buy long-term feeding tablets—for three days up to two weeks—to feed your fish while you are gone. Be certain that your equipment is in good working order, and make a partial water change before you leave. If you will be away for several weeks, ask an experienced fish keeper to check on your fish and equipment and do a partial water change while you are away.

Resources

CLUBS AND SOCIETIES

American Cichlid Association
Dept. GAM
PO Box 5351
Naperville, IL 60567-5351

Federation of American
Aquarists Society
4816 East 64th Street
Indianapolis, IN 46220-4828

Goldfish Society of America
9107 West 154th Street
Prior Lake, MN 55372-2119

International Aquarium
Society
PO Box 373
Maine, NY 13802

Aquarium and fish-keeping clubs for people of all ages, some devoted to specific species, exist in every state. Ask a local aquarium shop for information about local clubs and check in magazines such as *Aquarium Fish* and *Freshwater and Marine Aquarium* for information about clubs, meetings, and shows.

BOOKS FOR ADULTS

Andrews, Dr. Chris, and Dr. Ulrich Baensch. *Tropical Aquarium Fish.* Blacksburg, VA: Tetra Press, 1993.

Barrie, Anmarie. *Goldfish As A New Pet.* Neptune, NJ: T.F.H. Publications, 1995.

Carrington, Dr. Neville. *The Healthy Aquarium: A Fishkeeper's Guide.* Blacksburg, VA: Tetra Press, 1996.

DeVito, Carlo, with Gregory Skomal. *The Goldfish: An Owner's Guide To a Happy, Healthy Pet.* New York: Howell Book House, 1996.

Levine, Joseph S. *The Complete Fishkeeper: Everything Aquarium Fishes Need To Stay Happy, Healthy, and Alive.* New York: William Morrow, 1991.

Mertlich, Robert. *Goldfish: A Complete Introduction.* Neptune City, NJ: T.F.H. Publications, 1995.

Mills, Dick. *You and Your Aquarium: A Complete Guide to Collecting and Keeping Aquarium Fishes*. New York: Knopf, 1997.

Randolph, Elizabeth. *The Basic Book of Fishkeeping: A Comprehensive Reference for the Home Aquarium Owner*. New York: Fawcett Crest, 1990.

Skomal, Gregory. *Setting Up a Freshwater Aquarium: An Owner's Guide To a Happy, Healthy Pet*. New York: Howell Book House, 1997.

NONFICTION FOR CHILDREN

Arnosky, Jim. *Crinkleroot's 25 Fish Every Child Should Know*. New York: Bradbury Press, 1993.

Evans, Mark. *ASPCA Pet Care Guides for Kids: Fish*. New York: Dorling Kindersley, 1993.

Morley, Christine, and Carole Orbell. *Me and My Pet Fish*. Chicago: World Book, 1997.

Piers, Helen. *Taking Care of Your Goldfish: A Young Pet Owner's Guide*. Hauppauge, NY: Barron's, 1993.

Stadelmann, Peter. *Adventure Aquarium: Observing and Understanding Aquatic Life*. Hauppauge, NY: Barron's, 1997.

Wu, Norbert. *Fish Faces*. New York: Henry Holt, 1993.

FICTION FOR CHILDREN

Leonni, Leo. *Swimmy*. New York: Pantheon, 1963.

PART FIVE

Unusual, Wild, and Exotic Pets

SEVENTEEN

Unusual and Exotic Pets

"I was at one point desperately convinced that we had to have a sloth as a pet. My mother . . . was less than wildly enthusiastic. My father convinced me to put together a detailed scientific and literary notebook about sloths. He suggested that . . . I also . . . design a habitat for them that would work within our current home, and make detailed observations of their behavior at the zoo . . .

"What they both knew, I am sure, was that I was simply in love with the idea of a strange idea, and that given some other way of expressing my enthusiasms, I would be quite content. They were right, of course, and this was only further driven home by actually watching the sloths at the National Zoo. If there is anything more boring than watching a sloth—other than watching cricket, perhaps, or the House Appropriations Committee meetings on C-SPAN—I have yet to come across it. I had never been so grateful to return to the prosaic world of my dog, who, by comparison, seemed Newtonian in her complexity."

They are called exotics, alternative pets, fad pets, non-traditional, and specialty pets. In her inimitable style, Kay Redfield Jamison captured in *An Unquiet Mind* the impulse behind her wish, shared by many children, for a strange animal.

Children are attracted to what is odd or bizarre: Owning an unusual pet is cool. Especially for teenagers, owning a peculiar animal can be perceived as defining oneself or conferring celebrity. Some exotic pets promise a macho image.

An unusual pet may gain sudden popularity because of a rock star, television program, or movie. Children clamored for pet turtles during the Teenage Mutant Ninja Turtle craze, and iguanas shot to the top of the charts after the movie *Jurassic Park*.

But, according to a recent article in *Petlife* magazine, "Most people who wind up owning an alternative pet shouldn't. They may be influenced by impulse, peer pressure or the idea of owning something different, but invariably the demands of upkeep prove too grueling or the novelty simply wears off. Most owners wind up forsaking their animals somewhere along the way."

It is especially important for parents to do their homework before they buy or adopt an alternative pet. Some of these pets are dangerous, some transmit disease, and their care is often complex and difficult to provide. Says Jim Monsma, a humane society employee who gives foster care to cast-off exotic animals, "Sellers don't always level with people about how much work it is, and how expensive and time-consuming caring for these animals can be. If they did, I'm convinced that most people would get a dog, a cat, or a bird instead." Adds Debbie Ducommon, author of several pet books, "Just because an animal is for sale in a pet shop doesn't mean it's a pet."

ORIGINS. With the exception of fish and birds, traditional pets are mammals. Alternative pets are mammals, reptiles, arthropods, amphibians. "Specialty" mammals run the gamut from the diminutive hedgehog, wallaby, degu, chinchilla, and sugar glider to the not-so-tiny potbellied pig. Reptiles include snakes, lizards, crocodilians, and chelonians (turtles, tortoises, and terrapins). Amphibians live part or all of their life cycle in water and include toads and frogs (known as anurans, or amphibians without tails), newts, and salamanders. Arthropods are invertebrates (they have no backbone) with an external skeleton, and include spiders and crustaceans such as hermit crabs.

Alternative pets originate on every continent except Antarctica. (I have yet to hear of pet penguins.) Many are imported. This is true of the green iguana, currently the most popular exotic pet. While some are now raised on "farms," many of the 750,000 sent to the United States from Central and South America annually are collected from the wild; in some exporting countries they have nearly disappeared because of overcollection and habitat loss. Many baby iguanas, packed into shipping crates for transport, die in route. The remainder arrive badly stressed, often dehydrated and infested with diseases and parasites. A similar, sad journey is made by tens of thousands of snakes, amphibians, and mammals imported from Africa as well as South America. The continued existence of some animals indigenous to North America, such as the leopard frog and box turtle, is imperiled in the wild due to habitat loss and overcollecting for sale to domestic and foreign markets.

A growing number of legal restrictions in America and other countries, designed to protect threatened species, has encouraged the captive breeding of some of them. Although this practice may help to protect some species from extinction in the wild, it does not transform a wild animal into a pet. Richard Farinato and Rachel A. Lamb of the Humane Society of the United States caution that, "With few exceptions, fad species are difficult to care for under the best of circumstances. At the worst, they are impossible to maintain humanely as pets. They are always dangerous and unpredictable. Just because a wild animal is born in a cage to a captive mother does not mean he/she is domesticated. Such an animal is genetically programmed to behave as a wild animal and will do so."

NEEDS. *As I waited in the lobby of Angell Memorial Hospital in Boston, my eyes were drawn to a young woman standing alone in a corner, holding an animal wrapped in* *a gaudily colored orange and yellow towel. I could not see the animal. Two young men in jeans and leather jackets passed by her, then stopped.*

"Wow!" cried one of them. "Look at that! This is a big one. What is it?"

"A green iguana," the woman answered. "This is actually a little one." More questions followed, rapid-fire. Later, the woman—Siri was her name—and I talked. She invited me into the examination room to meet Wiley, one of her six adopted iguanas.

Wiley had lived in a pet shop for most of his first year, where, Siri said, "He seemed to do okay." After he was purchased, without the nutrition or full-spectrum lighting his metabolism required, he began to degenerate. Siri had agreed to take care of him after his owners gave him up and a veterinarian at Angell Memorial called her. Somehow, along with the vets, Siri brought Wiley back from the brink of death.

His body never recovered. His hind legs were permanently paralyzed, his spine twisted into an L shape. At one foot long, he was less than half the size of a healthy four-year-old iguana.

Wiley suffered from metabolic bone disease, or MBD. According to Dr. Douglas Mader, a leading national practitioner of reptile medicine, MBD is common in captive reptiles. This insidious disease stems primarily from improper nutrition and improper light.

The results of deficient care are not evident overnight. Part of the problem, Dr. Mader notes, is that most owners don't know what a healthy iguana looks like and don't realize when it is sick, a problem with exotic pets of all kinds. Also common are health problems stemming from inappropriate diet or environment or both.

The needs of exotic pets vary, of course, with every species. With a few exceptions, what you can be sure of is that the needs of exotic pets are . . . well, exotic. While some of them may survive in your home, they won't necessarily thrive. It has been estimated that only about two out of ten of iguanas purchased as pets live more than a year. Like other reptiles, they have specific nutritional and habitat needs that are not easily met. Dr. Connie Orcutt of Angell Memorial explains the challenge this way: "With reptiles, you have to try to artificially re-create their natural environment. This is a *lot* of work."

Before you try to approximate a natural habitat, you must know what it is. Zoologists, biologists, and herpetologists are still studying how some of these animals live in the wild. Often, no one really knows how to care for a new fad pet that has never lived in captivity outside a zoo. Information about diet, temperature, habitat, and lighting requirements is new and untested, and much of what is known to a few experts is not known by those who sell and buy these animals. Even veterinarians are ill prepared; few are trained to provide medical care to reptiles, amphibians, or unusual mammals.

Mammals are warm-blooded, or exothermic—their bodies generate warmth. Most specialty mammals, although they need a special habitat, can live indoors in temperatures that people find comfortable. Because reptiles and amphibians are cold-blooded, or endothermic—their bodies absorb warmth and take on the temperature around them—they need to live in a specific temperature range which, for most reptiles, is tropical. Reptiles need exposure to direct outdoor sunlight or artificial full-spectrum lighting in order to metabolize nutrients. Amphibians also have specific heating, lighting, humidity, and dietary requirements.

Dietary needs of exotic pets are harder to meet, and sometimes harder to identify, than those of other pets. A wild sugar glider (a tiny, furry marsupial) eats nectar, pollen, flowers, buds, fruit, sap, and insects—not an easy diet to duplicate. Snakes are carnivorous and must eat "whole food"—an entire small mammal. Contrary to popular belief, they do not need to eat live animals. In fact, most herpetologists recommend against feeding live prey. Feeder rodents do, quite rightly, fight for their lives, can inflict damage, and may carry parasites or diseases that then infest the snake that eats them. Pre-killed mice and rats can be bought and kept frozen, which destroys potentially harmful parasites.

Some amphibians eat insects, others are vegetarians, some eat worms, and others eat small mammals. Specialty companies will mail-order live mealworms, crickets, fly larvae, and other delicacies to your home, or they can be purchased at some pet stores. Shopping is not always easy, explains Jim Monsma:

> *Feeding crickets sounds easy, but I've been there and let me tell you about it. If you're not mail-ordering, you drive to the pet store once a week to buy live crickets. The first store doesn't have any, so you drive to the next store. They have a few, but not enough, so you go on to the next store. It's pouring rain, no doubt.*
>
> *Some people decide to raise the crickets themselves. They need "gut-loading" to be nutritious. So now you're taking care of your crickets and you're taking care of your reptile, and the crickets in the basement smell awful!*

Psychological needs of exotic pets are not well understood. It is common for nontraditional mammals, although apparently social creatures, to be sold singly. Without substantial attention, a single sugar glider or degu may become depressed, aggressive, and ill. While some "herpers" report that their pets relate to them, most experts seem to agree with herpetologist Caroline Seitz, who says that reptiles and amphibians do not require the social contact and mental stimulation that most mammals do. Most snakes and lizards seem to prefer being left alone; they tolerate but do not particularly enjoy being handled. Amphibians as a rule should be handled as little as possible. Their extremely delicate skin is part of their respiratory system. The warmth and sweat of human hands can damage their skin and cause health problems, and overhandling can be fatal. Some amphibs secrete toxic substances through their skin that can irritate human skin.

Many reptiles seek security, which they can find in a burrow, nest, or hide box. Wildlife rehabilitator Brian Kristal has come across snake owners who refuse to provide a hide box because it "interferes with viewing the animal," even when it is the type of animal that needs privacy. Weighing the fact that owners generally watch their reptile pets for only a small portion of the day against the animal's strong need to hide leads quickly to the conclusion that responsible ownership calls for a hide box. Snakes that cannot get privacy may refuse food and even starve themselves to death.

Millions of exotic animals are sold each year, most of them reptiles, the fastest growing portion of the U.S. pet population. Dr. Michael Riegger, who has adopted, written about, taught, and practiced veterinary medicine on exotic and traditional pets, comments on the trend: "After twenty-five years of owning and working with animals, I have concluded that exotic animals are not happy in the human environment. For the most part reptiles are loners that want to be left alone. They don't really appreciate human companionship. Even the humble turtle wants to be free. In my back yard our family has created a large enclosure for turtles that people give up or abandon; the turtles keep trying to escape." No wonder: In the wild, the American box turtle's territory is about the size of a football field. Even the tiny hedgehog can walk a mile a day in its natural environment.

CHILDREN AND EXOTIC PETS. Some exotic pets are downright dangerous; unless Mom or Dad has extensive experience with the species, these animals should not even be considered as pets for children. Any wild animal that is aggressive or fierce, can inflict a serious bite, deliver poison, or squeeze a child to death should not be a family pet. Remember that a wild animal is unpredictable. Says Jim Monsma, "I never tell a potential adopter, 'This reptile won't bite.' I can only say that he hasn't bitten me yet!''

The Tokay gecko, green tree python, emerald boa, monkeys, skunks, and snapping turtles are some of the serious biters to stay away from. Rule out poisonous snakes. The ''small'' anaconda or python for sale in the pet shop can grow very quickly and end up weighing two hundred pounds, measuring twenty feet and possessed of prodigious strength. Monitor lizards, crocodiles, caimans, and tegus can inflict real injury. Bears and large cats are not pets.

Avoid species that pose difficult or insurmountable challenges for children. Animals such as hedgehogs and snakes need careful, consistent, gentle handling or they will resist any handling at all. Amphibians should be handled very little. These dos and don'ts can be difficult for children to comprehend and observe. Will your son, who is fascinated by salamanders, be content to ''look, not touch''? Will your daughter, who is begging for a hedgehog, be able to quietly, consistently, repeatedly give it gentle handling?

Some exotic pets raise human health concerns. Salmonellosis is a disease that humans can contract from reptiles. It causes fever and diarrhea and can lead to sepsis, meningitis, and even death. Infants, children under the age of five, the elderly, pregnant women, and people with compromised immune systems are at increased risk for infection or complications from salmonellosis. People in these groups should not have contact with reptiles.

Salmonella bacteria are common in reptiles. One study in Canada revealed that nearly three-fourths of all pet store turtle tanks tested positive for salmonella. In 1975, responding to public alarm over salmonellosis, the U.S. Food and Drug Administration prohibited the sale of turtles with shells less than four inches long. At the time, small red-eared slider turtles were popular pets for children. The ban, which is still in effect, does not extend to other reptiles, which carry the same bacteria.

Salmonella can be present in native, imported, and captive-bred reptiles, and it is common in iguanas and water turtles. Testing can detect whether a reptile carries the bacteria but cannot definitely prove that the animal does *not*. If you decide to get a reptile, it is important to obtain (from your state or local health department, veterinarian, or pediatrician) and follow recommended precautions to guard against transmittal of the disease.

Perhaps the most important lesson that a child can learn about an exotic animal is that it should not be a pet at all. Parents can help a child learn about an animal's life in the wild, can help a child empathize with an animal that needs to be free or left alone, can teach respect for nature and the tragedy of endangered species. Educating a child about why an animal for sale in a pet store should not be a pet is an exercise in critical judgment: Simply putting a label on an animal doesn't change its nature.

Luckily, there are extraordinary opportunities available for children to learn about, observe, and enjoy wild animals: books, videos, classes, the Internet, zoos and nature centers, educational zoologists and herpetologists who give child-oriented presentations. In fact, more Americans visit zoos than attend all sporting and cultural events combined. If you call your local zoo, herpetological society, or nature center, you should be able to find an activity for an interested child.

COMMITMENT. The phenomenon of the "pet du jour" races on, fueled by media coverage of celebrities draped in snakes or cuddling monkeys. Only a small percentage of owners are able to provide humane living conditions to nontraditional pets; indeed, many experts believe that it is inhumane even to try to keep these animals as pets.

As the number of alternative pets sold continues to grow, so does the number discarded. Every day, owners of reptiles, amphibians, and mammals call nature centers, zoos, and even pet shops looking for a home for a pet they no longer want. Zoos and nature centers rarely accept these animals. Nontraditional pets of all kinds have been left, literally, on the doorsteps of veterinary clinics and deposited with humane societies, which may have no choice but to euthanize them. Lizards, snakes, monkeys, and other animals have been turned loose in freezing conditions that kill them.

Owners who fill out ''give up sheets'' at animal shelters write: ''We can't take care of it.'' ''It's biting me.'' ''We can't handle it.'' ''I'm afraid of it.'' ''It looks sick.'' ''We didn't know it would get this big.'' Before you choose one of these pets, be certain that you understand its limits, nature, eventual size, and housing and dietary requirements and that you have access to expert advice about how to care for it.

The commitment to care for a nontraditional mammal throughout its life is not short: four to seven years for a hedgehog, eight to twelve years for a prairie dog or wallaby, ten to fourteen years for a sugar glider, eight to fifteen years for a chinchilla. Potbellied pigs can live to be twenty, and some monkeys have a life expectancy of thirty to forty years.

The commitment for some reptiles and amphibians can be considerably longer than for traditional pets. Some frogs live to thirty years, some snakes to twenty. The red-eared slider turtle can live for more than thirty years, box turtles for fifty, and other turtles for fifty and even eighty years.

What You Need to Know About an Exotic Pet *Before* You Get One

SIZE. This varies with the species, care, and sometimes sex. Many exotic pets, such as monitor lizards, iguanas, and potbellied pigs, grow surprisingly large. A four-inch-long baby female slider turtle can grow to a foot in length.

LONGEVITY. This varies with the species and level of care. Some chelonians are so long-lived that they will outlive not only you but may also outlive your children.

LEGAL RESTRICTIONS. State and local governments place numerous restrictions on the sale and keeping of exotic animals. Restrictions vary from one jurisdiction to another. Some jurisdictions forbid some mammals, such as monkeys and potbellied pigs, from being kept in residential areas. Some prohibit ownership of certain amphibians and reptiles, or "wild" or "dangerous" animals, usually interpreted to include many types of snakes and lizards. International treaties and federal laws also regulate and restrict capture, sale, import, export, or ownership of some animals marketed as exotic pets.

Before buying or adopting a nontraditional pet, make certain it is legal to own it where you live. You can check with your local SPCA, animal shelter, or animal control agency; the state or local wildlife control agency; the state Department of Agriculture or Natural Resources; state or local public health agencies; or your local zoning authority.

Check your homeowner's or renter's insurance policy. Personal liability coverage frequently does not extend to harm done by exotic pets, and some companies may refuse coverage if you own an exotic animal.

COSTS AND EQUIPMENT. Overall costs vary greatly, depending on the species, type of equipment needed, prices in your region, your consumer choices, whether you buy equipment and supplies through a catalog or a pet shop, and whether you raise your own food, harvest insects or worms for free, or buy them from a pet shop. The information given here is necessarily general, intended to suggest issues to research to arrive at your own cost estimates.

The most important item every exotic-pet owner should have is a recently written, comprehensive book about the animal. Because the quality of such books is uneven, ask a veterinarian, herpetologist, zoologist, rescue worker, or wildlife rehabilitator to recommend one. This can be supplemented by specialty magazine articles, videos, Internet Web sites (which vary in quality), and establishing a relationship with a knowledgeable veterinarian or other expert who can provide ongoing advice. Unfortunately, many people who give advice, including pet shop personnel, are not always equipped to do so.

Ongoing costs will include *food*. A prairie dog needs a mix of rodent lab blocks, seeds, nuts, vegetables, and fruit. Commercial foods are available for chinchillas and should be supplemented with fruit and vegetables. Pelletized diets are available for potbellied pigs.

Some amphibians eat insects, worms, and small rodents. Aquatic species eat aquatic vegetation. Snakes eat pre-killed mice, rats, guinea pits, rabbits, and chickens. Herbivorous lizards need vegetables; omnivorous lizards need animal sources of protein as well. Box turtles eat mealworms, snails, slugs, earthworms, fruit, berries, and vegetables. Commercial foods are available for some types of turtles. Many exotic pets, particularly amphibians, lizards, and chelonians, need mineral and vitamin supplements added to their food.

Another ongoing cost is *substrate*, which varies from shavings to sand, indoor-outdoor carpeting, moss, sterile potting soil, newspaper, or plain packing paper, depending on the animal.

Veterinary costs for exotic pets are substantially higher than for traditional pets. Any animal that you buy or adopt should receive a checkup. Some nontraditional pets, such as potbellied pigs, require regular vaccinations and should be spayed or neutered. Finding a veterinarian qualified to treat an exotic animal is often difficult and in some areas impossible. One expert estimated that only about a dozen veterinarians in the United States are truly qualified to treat reptiles, yet any veterinarian can offer to do so because there is no formal professional certification for practitioners who treat nontraditional pets. To find a qualified veterinarian, ask for recommendations from other owners, zoos, nature centers, wildlife rehabilitators, and humane societies.

Basic equipment varies with the species. Chinchillas should be housed in a large two-, three-, or four-story cage with a dust bath, hide box, toys, hay rack, and large exercise wheel. Feeding implements—water bottle and food bowl—are similar to those used by traditional small mammal pets. Chinchillas prefer a cool temperature and low humidity. The costs of properly housing a chinchilla will be $150–$200.

It is no small undertaking to set up an appropriate habitat for a reptile or amphibian. It is expensive: $200 is probably the least you can spend, unless you have turtles, the right climate, and a backyard to comfortably house them. Amphibians are usually housed in an aquarium (also referred to as a vivarium or terrarium) with a secure mesh lid. The larger the enclosure the better: Toads and frogs need room to exercise and jump. Various species have different habitat needs: desert, woodland, rain forest, or semiaquatic environment.

Depending on size, an aquarium and lid may cost $30–$50, or substantially more for wood or plastic enclosures with Plexiglas sliding doors ($100–$200). A swimming bowl, cave, basking ledge, water filter, and dechlorinating chemicals can add up to $25–$75.

Reptiles are housed in cages or vivariums, which must be secure and escapeproof. Snakes need enough room to stretch out and move around; their enclosure should be as long as they are, plus one-half. Arboreal reptiles need tall enclosures. Some turtles need both water and a dry surface. If you have a yard and live in a temperate or warm climate, a secure outdoor enclosure is recommended for chelonians, at least during the months when temperatures are safe for them.

I have rarely seen a pet reptile kept in a large enough enclosure. One exception is Madonna, an iguana belonging to my neighbor Hannah and her parents. As Madonna grew, so did her habitat, until today she lives in a vivarium six feet high and four feet wide that seems to fill an entire corner of Hannah's bedroom. Large enclosures for iguanas and other reptiles cost $400–$800.

It is critical to provide appropriate lighting, heat, and humidity to amphibians and reptiles. Carefully research the temperature range—for both day and night—for the animal you are interested in. The heat source should be outside the vivarium or cage; "hot rocks," though sold everywhere, should not be used. The size and shape of the enclosure and needs of the animal determine the type and number of heating units. A heat lamp ($20–$50 for fixture and bulb) provides a heat source above the tank; a heating pad ($15–$100) or heating tape (about $2.50 per foot) can be placed under the tank. An infrared heat bulb and ceramic heat element ($30–$40) provide nighttime heat. The enclosure must have a range of temperatures, warmer at one end, for basking, than at the other. This temperature gradient is more difficult to achieve in small enclosures. A thermometer ($5–$30) is essential for monitoring, as is a thermostat for controlling temperature ($30–$100); humidity gauges also are available ($10–$20).

Size and type of lighting depend on the animal and size of the enclosure. Many reptiles and amphibians need ultraviolet light to metabolize their food, obtained indoors through use of full-spectrum fluorescent bulbs, which are expensive ($20–$40 each). Lighting fixtures are usually contained in a hood that fits on top of the aquarium or cage ($100–$250), or in strips ($25–$100).

Appropriate driftwood, branches, rocks, logs, hanging ropes, or shelves should be provided to lizards and snakes, and a water container large enough for a snake to soak in or lizard to drink from ($2–$30). A hide box or log can be bought ($4–$15) or made and is important for snakes and some chelonians. One expert noted that making a habitat interesting and attractive—with plants, a background, rocks, and such—is not only important for the inhabitant, it's important for the caretaker as well. "I realized that when I fixed a terrarium up to replicate nature, I wanted to look at it more; I paid more attention to the snake or lizard inside, too," said Brian Kristal.

It can be difficult to find the right equipment for exotic pets, and the assortment is limited. Speciality mail-order catalogs offer equipment for reptiles and amphibians. Equipment made for traditional pets sometimes can be used for exotic mammal pets, but sometimes equipment must be custom-made.

Unless you adopt an exotic pet, your *acquisition costs* will usually be higher than for a traditional pet. A flying squirrel costs about $100; a sugar glider, $200–$500; a wallaby is more than $1,000. Some lizards, chelonians, and small amphibians can be bought for $5 to $50. The less expensive snakes and large lizards (excluding iguanas) cost from $20 to $100, and many other species cost $200 to $500 and more.

SPACE. Caged mammals deserve as much space as possible. Some of them, such as the sugar glider, need an enclosure that is tall as well as wide and deep. A potbellied pig is a large animal that can take up indoor space and also needs outdoor exercise.

Give chelonians as much room as possible, ideally in an outside enclosure or pond if the climate permits. Many lizards, including iguanas and monitors, grow large quickly; they need large enclosures that may take up twenty square feet of floor space or be very tall. Snakes also grow large quickly, and some snakes need a six-foot-long enclosure. Smaller reptiles and amphibians can usually be accommodated in smaller terrariums.

Herpetologist Melissa Kaplan notes that, ''One of the most common mistakes is that people buy enclosures that are too small. While the enclosure may fit the animal at time of purchase, reptiles grow, often reaching adult size within a year or two. It is cruel and inhumane to house an animal in an enclosure that is too small. It not only causes severe stress which leads to illness and behavioral problems—it also makes taming and working with territorial species that much more difficult.''

TIME. Setup can be time-consuming as well as expensive for reptiles and amphibians. Daily or weekly care varies with the species. Animals that are fed daily usually eliminate daily, and the enclosure may need to be spot cleaned every day. These are tasks that, together with providing fresh water, may take ten to twenty minutes a day. Again depending on the circumstances, enclosures need a thorough cleaning weekly or monthly, a process that may take about thirty minutes.

Some snakes eat once or twice a week and eliminate at about the same rate. (Keep in mind that when dealing with a very large reptile, you are also dealing with a large amount of waste.) Daily care, other than providing fresh, clean water and checking on equipment, is minimal. Some amphibians and reptiles should be misted at least once a day. Weekly partial water changes are necessary for aquatic or semiaquatic animals.

Specialty mammal pets kept in cages need food and fresh water daily, and cages need to be spot cleaned daily. A thorough cage scrubbing is needed once a week. Exotic small mammals require consistent and sometimes intensive attention to help them become and remain tame, and many have exercise requirements that cannot be met inside a cage.

SMELLS? Some habitats require frequent cleaning, or an unpleasant odor results.

CHARACTERISTICS AFFECTING CHILDREN. Each species has its own characteristics. Because exotic pets are wild animals, many of them have characteristics that pose problems for families with children.

NEED FOR PARENTAL SUPERVISION. Parents should closely supervise children if the animals are likely to cause injury or transmit disease. Children must learn and follow safety precautions.

Your Family's Pet Resources

TIME. Which family member will research how to care for this pet, find a qualified veterinarian, and find appropriate equipment and supplies? Who will provide fresh water, feed it, if necessary raise, order, or buy fresh food, or chop fresh fruits and vegetables? Who will clean the enclosure, either daily or weekly, and make water changes in aquatic habitats? Who will check heating and lighting?

COSTS. Can you afford $200 or more in setup costs, and the $100 or more purchase price that is common for exotic pets? The cost of food? Can you afford veterinary care?

ABILITY. Are your children old enough to help with chores? Are they old enough to follow safety precautions?

PLACE AND SPACE. Is it legal to own this pet? Do you have room for its habitat when it grows to full size?

HEALTH. Are you certain that the pet you are considering will not harm your child? Are your children more than five years old and able to follow precautions to avoid salmonellosis? Do seniors visit or live in your house, or are you planning on having or adopting more children? (Seniors, pregnant women, and infants should avoid contact with reptiles.)

TRAVEL. Who will care for this pet when the family travels? If necessary, can you find, and can you afford, a place to board it, or someone to care for it?

HOUSEKEEPING. Will spillage or odors from a cage or terrarium bother you?

SPECIAL ISSUES. How do you feel about feeding live mammals, crickets, worms, or other insects to another animal? How do you feel about having frozen rats or mice in your freezer? Will you keep this pet when it grows large? Will you take it with you if you move? Will friends, relatives, babysitters, or housekeepers be afraid to set foot in your home because of a scary pet?

If You *Really* Want an Unusual or Exotic Pet

Some children are truly fascinated with reptiles or amphibians. Many of the herpetologists I spoke with became interested in these animals and learned to care for them at a young age. Yet they felt that, in the words of Caroline Seitz, "Most reptiles don't make good pets for most people."

Most herpers felt that leopard geckos, box turtles, ball pythons, and some of the hardier varieties of frogs and toads could make appropriate pets for families with children. There was less unanimity about king, rat, corn, and milk snakes, although some experts suggested these snakes for beginners. Hermit crabs (arthropods, not reptiles) make interesting, entertaining pets. All of these animals require understanding and daily attention. With all of these, the key to being a responsible owner is finding and using good information about their care.

If you or your children want a mammal as a pet, I strongly recommend that you choose among the traditional pets.

Where to Get an Exotic Pet

To locate a herp or arthropod pet, call your local animal shelter or humane society, your local nature center or zoo, veterinarians in your area, or local herpetological societies or clubs. One or more of these organizations may have available, or may be able to direct you to, responsible owners or foster caregivers who have healthy animals for adoption.

Check in specialty magazines for listings of herp breeders, clubs, shows, and expos. Attending these shows is a good way to learn about these animals and meet breeders. Buy from breeders who seem genuinely interested in the animal's welfare and your ability to care for it. Before you buy an animal, read about it or talk to experts to get guidance in how to select a healthy one.

Resources

CLUBS AND SERVICES

American Federation of
Herpetoculturists (club)
PO Box 300067
Escondido, CA 92030-0067

Association of Reptile and
Amphibian Veterinarians
PO Box 605
1 Smith Bridge Road
Chester Heights, PA 19017

Society for the Study of
Amphibians and Reptiles
Department of Zoology
Miami University
Oxford, OH 45056

T.E.A.M. (Tortoise Education
and Adoption Media)
3245 Military Avenue
Los Angeles, CA 90034

Herp societies and clubs for people of all ages exist in many cities and states. Ask local zoos or nature centers for information and check in magazines such as *Reptiles* for information about clubs, meetings, and expos.

BOOKS FOR ADULTS

Alderton, David. *The Exotic Pet Survival Manual*. Hauppauge, NY: Barron's, 1997.

Bartlett, R. D., and Patricia P. Bartlett. *Turtles and Tortoises: A Complete Pet Owner's Manual*. Hauppauge, NY: Barron's, 1996.

Coborn, John. *Frogs and Toads As a New Pet*. Neptune City, NJ: T.F.H. Publications, 1996.

David, Al. *Turtles as a New Pet*. Neptune City, NJ: T.F.H. Publications, 1990.

Jes, Harald. *Lizards in the Terrarium*. Hauppauge, NY: Barron's, 1987.

Mattison, Chris. *The Care of Reptiles and Amphibians in Captivity*. London: Blandford, 1992.

————. *Lizards of the World*. New York: Facts on File, 1989.

Marke, Ronald G., and R. D. Bartlett. *Kingsnakes and Milksnakes*. Hauppauge, NY: Barron's 1995.

Palika, Liz. *The Consumer's Guide to Feeding Reptiles*. New York: Howell Book House, 1997.

Pronek, Neal. *Hermit Crabs*. Neptune City, NJ: T.F.H. Publications, 1982.

Siino, Betsy Sikora. *You Want a WHAT for a Pet?!* New York: Howell Book House, 1996.

Walls, Jerry G. *Rat Snakes*. Neptune City, NJ: T.F.H. Publications, 1994.

Wilke, Harmut. *Turtles: A Complete Pet Owner's Manual*. Hauppauge, NY: Barron's, 1983.

————. *Turtles: How to Take Care of Them and Understand Them*. Hauppauge, NY: Barron's, 1991.

Zug, George R. *Snakes in Question: The Smithsonian Answer Book*. Washington, DC: Smithsonian Institution Press, 1996.

NONFICTION FOR CHILDREN
Ballard, Lois. *Reptiles*. Chicago: Childrens Press, 1957.

Butterfield, Moira. *1,000 Facts About Wild Animals*. New York: Kingfisher Books, 1992.

Burns, Diane L. *Frogs, Toads and Turtles*. Minocqua, WI: NorthWord Press, 1997.

Demuth, Patricia. *Snakes*. New York: Grosset & Dunlap, 1993.

Elliott, Leslie. *Really Radical Reptiles & Amphibians*. New York: Sterling Publishing, 1994.

Fichter, George S. *Snakes and Lizards*. New York: Golden Books, 1993.

————. *Turtles, Toads and Frogs*. New York: Golden Books, 1993.

Lacey, Elizabeth A. *The Complete Frog*. New York: Lothrop, Lee & Shepard, 1989.

Maynard, Christopher. *Incredible Little Monsters*. New York: Covent Garden Books, 1994.

Parsons, Alexandra. *Amazing Snakes*. New York: Alfred A. Knopf, 1990.

Resnick, Jane P. *Eyes on Nature: Spiders*. Chicago: Kidsbooks, 1996.

Retan, Walter. *101 Wacky Facts About Snakes & Reptiles*. New York: Parachute Press, 1991.

Robbins, Robin. *Frogs are Fantastic*. Wilton, CT: Reader's Digest Young Families, 1995.

Stoops, Erik D., and Annettte T. Wright. *Snakes*. New York: Sterling Publishing, 1994.

FICTION FOR CHILDREN
Baker, Keith. *Who Is the Beast*? New York: Harcourt Brace Jovanovich, 1990.

Cannon, Janell. *Verdi*. New York: Harcourt Brace Jovanovich, 1997.

Grahame, Kenneth. *The Wind in the Willows*. New York: Aladdin, 1908.

Lobel, Arnold. *Frog and Toad All Year*. New York: HarperCollins, 1976.

————. *Frog and Toad Together*. New York: HarperCollins, 1971.

Mazer, Anne. *The Salamander Room*. New York: Alfred A. Knopf, 1991.

EIGHTEEN

Wildlife as Pets

Sooner or later, your child will probably stumble on a baby squirrel or bird, or find a raccoon with a broken leg. Wild animals are intriguing, often beautiful, and, especially when young, almost irresistible to children. But wild animals, no matter how cute, are not pets. A pen or cage is a prison for them. Some carry diseases communicable to humans. Others are or will grow into a danger to children and adults because, as wild animals, they instinctively bite or scratch when stressed, panicked, or fearful. The humane course of action is to rehabilitate injured or orphaned wildlife and return them to their natural habitat as quickly as possible.

If your child finds an injured or apparently orphaned animal in the woods, or if one wanders into your yard, do not try to treat it yourself. By law, only a licensed wildlife rehabilitator can do this. To find a "rehabber," contact your local shelter or animal control agency, or state department of wildlife, natural resources, or environmental conservation.

Resources

ORGANIZATIONS

Fund for Animals
200 West 57th Street
New York, NY 10019
Urban Wildlife Hotline:
(202) 393-1050

National Wildlife
Rehabilitators Association
14 North 7th Avenue
St. Cloud, MN 56303-4766
(320) 259-4086

National Wildlife Federation
1400 16th Street NW
Washington, DC 20009
(202) 797-6800

The last two national organizations can help you find a licensed wildlife rehabilitator or center in your area. Some also can be found on the Internet.

BOOKS

Carlson, Dale. *I Found a Baby Bird, What Do I Do?* Madison, CT: Bick Publishing, 1997.

————. *I Found a Baby Duck, What Do I Do?* Madison, CT: Bick Publishing, 1997.

————. *I Found a Baby Opossum, What Do I Do?* Madison, CT: Bick Publishing, 1997.

————. *I Found a Baby Rabbit, What Do I Do?* Madison, CT: Bick Publishing, 1997.

————. *I Found a Baby Raccoon, What Do I Do?* Madison, CT: Bick Publishing, 1997.

————. *I Found a Baby Squirrel, What Do I Do?* Madison, CT: Bick Publishing, 1997.

Humane Society of the United States. *Wild Neighbors: The Humane Approach to Living with Wildlife.* Golden, CO: Fulcrum Publishing, 1997.

PART SIX

Pets for Children with Special Needs

NINETEEN

Service and Therapy Pets

The little girl sat, sullenly, on the floor of the pediatric ward's day room. Her dark eyes were fixed on the tiles in front of her. Her hair, what was left, was all but hidden by white bandages. Her name was Kayla, and she was angry.

Only six years old, and this was her third visit to the hospital, her third operation. She blamed no one in particular but held everyone responsible, including her parents and the doctors. For weeks she had refused to speak. Her mother had not seen her smile in months. The adults in the room pressed their backs against the wall, not knowing how to reach or comfort her.

A tall, lean man hesitated in the doorway. "Would you like to meet a dog?" he asked.

Kayla raised her eyes.

"Sure," her mother said hopefully. A golden retriever/shepherd mix loped into the room at the end of a purple leash. She stopped in front of Kayla, looked at her inquiringly, sat, then lifted a paw.

The little girl's eyes lit up. She smiled.

"Her name is Sunshine," said the man.

"Sunshine!" breathed Kayla and reached to hug the dog. Her mother started to cry, and even a few doctors had tears in their eyes.

Animals of all kinds bring joy and healing to sick children. Dogs, cats, birds, bunnies, guinea pigs, fancy mice =and rats, and gerbils participate in **Animal Assisted Activities** in pediatric wards across the country. These are primarily social activities, where animals visit to "meet and greet" patients and help cheer them up. Sometimes, animals can reach a withdrawn or depressed child when people, even a parent, cannot. Bedridden or chronically ill children find comfort and companionship in pets of their own.

Other animals participate in **Animal Assisted Therapy**, also known as **Animal Facilitated Therapy.** These animals are part of a team that works with a child toward one or more specific goals, which may be physical, psychological, or cognitive—or all three. Learning to hold a cat or regularly groom a dog can help to develop motor skills and self-confidence in developmentally delayed or disabled children. Because the animal responds to the child's developing skills, the feedback is immediate and motivating.

Animals can serve as a bridge between a mental health worker and a patient, and can be a catalyst for sharing thoughts and feelings. In *The Latham Letter* Dr. Patricia Olson related how a group of tough teenage boys, most of whom had been victims of sexual abuse, opened up to her after she described how her therapy dog, Lucy, had been abused, homeless, and finally rescued; each of the boys connected the dog's history with his own and began to talk about himself. Forming a relationship with, and in some cases accepting responsibility to help care for, an animal has given children with mental disabilities and emotional problems opportunities to develop self-esteem and learn to trust. Some therapists bring dogs, cats, or birds to residential facilities where they work with teenagers and younger children who have been removed from abusive homes. Dr. Frances Ilg, the noted child psychologist, used gerbils in therapy with some emotionally disturbed children.

Many activity and therapy animals come from shelters and rescue leagues. Perhaps their history gives them a unique ability to bond with troubled or sad children; certainly, there are children who identify with them. Humane societies around the country use their facilities to sponsor programs for children in need of special attention. In Bellevue, Washington, at-risk teenagers are assigned the task of working with a homeless dog or cat to make it adoptable. Their responsibilities include grooming, training, socializing, and helping to place the animal. At Green Chimneys in Brewster, New York, about one hundred children who have been removed from chaotic or dangerous homes help care for 250 animals, some of whom need special care. Commented Green Chimneys director Sam Ross, "If a child helps heal a disabled animal and sees that it can survive, then he gets the feeling that he can survive too. They both [the animals and the children] get a second chance."

Another category of helping animals are **Service Animals**, including Seeing Eye or guide dogs and hearing dogs that alert hearing-impaired human companions to the sound of the telephone, alarm clock, doorbell, and smoke alarm. Service dogs work with children who are wheelchair-bound or reliant on crutches, helping to carry and to pick up dropped objects, open doors, turn lights off and on, and push elevator buttons. Seizure-alert dogs can detect symptoms of oncoming epileptic seizures even before a child is aware one is imminent; the dog will warn the child and if necessary bark for help and protect its owner during the episode.

Companion animals such as dogs, cats, birds, and rabbits also serve children with developmental disabilities or mental illness by giving companionship and love, and in some cases helping to calm children and bring them into contact with their peers and the world around them. In North Yarmouth, Maine, fifth grader Michael Harmon, who is autistic, is more confident and independent since acquiring his golden retriever, Cranston, from Canine Companions for Independence.

Cranston is Maine's first social dog for the disabled, and he has made a believer out of Michael's special education teacher, who was at first skeptical about Cranston. "Michael smiles a lot more now when he's walking with Cranston and almost has this little dance. He's real proud that he's in charge and he's the boss," she said.

Many service dogs, like therapy dogs, come from humane societies and rescue leagues. These dogs need not be purebred or have been born into or raised in a special environment. They do go through special training (not all candidates graduate) and must have appropriate temperaments.

Resources

ORGANIZATIONS

American Humane
Association Hearing Dog
Program
9725 East Hampden Avenue
Denver, CO 80231
(303) 695-0811

Canine Companions For
Independence
4350 Occidental Road
PO Box 446
Santa Rosa, CA 95402-0446
(800) 767-BARK

Dogs for the Deaf
13260 Highway 238
Jacksonville, OR 97530
(503) 899-7177

Foundation for Pet-Provided
Therapy
3809 Plaza Drive #107-309
Oceanside, CA 92056

Great Plains Assistance Dogs
Foundation
PO Box 513
Jud, ND 58454
(701) 685-2242

Guide Dog Foundation
371 East Jericho Turnpike
Smithtown, NY 11787
(212) 263-4885

Guide Dogs for the Blind, Inc.
PO Box 1200
San Rafael, CA 94915
(415) 479-4000

Guiding Eyes for the Blind
611 Granite Springs Road
Yorktown Heights, NY 10598

Handi-Dogs
Alamo Reaves
PO Box 12563
Tucson, AZ 85732
(602) 326-3412

Hearing Dogs of the South
998 Sousa Drive
Largo, FL 33541

Latham Foundation
Latham Plaza Building
Clemen & Schiller Streets
Alameda, CA 94501
(510) 521-0920

National Education Assistance
Dog Services Inc.
PO Box 213
West Boylston, MA 01538
(508) 422-9064

Pet Partners
Delta Society
PO Box 1080
Renton, WA 98057-1080
(206) 226-7357

Support Dogs for the
Handicapped
4419 Butler Hill Road
St. Louis, MO 63128
(314) 487-2004

Therapy Dog International
6 Hilltop Road
Mendham, NJ 07945

This list is necessarily incomplete. There are dozens of regional organizations that train and/or provide information about service or therapy pets. Check your local phone directory or contact a national organization.

PART SEVEN

Children, Pets, and Safety

TWENTY

Protecting Children And Pets

Below are some simple rules that apply to all children and all pets that will help protect both children and pets from harm.

A pet that feels threatened is the pet most likely to bite or scratch. This is as true for a hamster or rabbit as it is for a dog or cat. Teach your child how to handle an animal with kindness, how to understand it, and how to read its body language. These lessons are as important for your child as they are for the pet.

PARENTS SHOULD:

- Supervise infants, toddlers, and young children when they are with animals, including animals in tanks, aquariums, or cages.
- Not allow children to play roughly with a pet.
- Make certain that your children have current tetanus shots before you bring a pet home.
- Keep your pet's inoculations, especially against rabies, up-to-date.
- Check your child, dog, or cat for ticks after they have been outside, and remove ticks immediately. Consult a doctor if a red "bull's-eye" rash develops at the

site of a tick bite or elsewhere on a child's body, or a veterinarian if it appears on a pet.

- Use a different sponge when cleaning your pet's dishes, tank, cage, or equipment, and save it for that purpose. Clean your sink or tub thoroughly after using it to bathe an animal, empty aquarium water, or wash tanks, cages or other equipment.
- Keep veterinary medications, pet shampoos, and dips away from children.
- Never give a pet any medication, shampoo or dip not prescribed or recommended by a veterinarian. Never use a veterinary medication, shampoo, or dip on a child.

PARENTS SHOULD TEACH CHILDREN:

- To wash their hands after playing with or feeding a pet, putting their hands in an aquarium, or cleaning cages or other pet equipment.
- To unplug electrical equipment before performing cleaning or maintenance chores on or in an aquarium; not to touch plugs or switches with wet hands.
- Not to poke, grab, or startle a sleeping animal.
- Not to interfere with an animal when it is eating or chewing on a toy.
- Not to pull an animal's tail or ears, or try to lift it by the tail or ears.
- Not to frighten an animal by yelling at it, chasing it, shaking or throwing something at it.
- Not to ever throw, kick, or hit an animal.
- Not to put a pet inside a container and close it (lunch box, dryer, jar).
- Not to take fish out of an aquarium, and not to drop anything in an aquarium.
- Not to poke fingers or objects into a pet's cage or enclosure.
- Not to try to sit or lie down on an animal.
- Not to pat, hug, kiss or try to pick up another person's

pet until you have asked for, and received permission from the owner; *then ask the owner for advice about* how to approach and handle the pet.

- If a strange animal approaches you and you are afraid of it, or if it chases you: don't run, yell, or scream. Stand still, with your arms at your sides. Don't make noise and don't stare at the animal. If you have time, crouch down and curl into a ball, with your face toward the ground, and your hands covering your neck. Don't move until the animal goes away.

The classic bestseller that began James Herriot's extraordinary series...

All Creatures Great and Small

JAMES HERRIOT

Let the world's most beloved animal doctor take you along on his wonderful adventures through the Yorkshire dales as he tends to its unforgettable inhabitants—four-legged and otherwise.

"This warm, joyous and often hilarious first-person chronicle of a young animal doctor...shines with love of life."

—*The New York Times Book Review*